The Poetry of Brecht

UNC | COLLEGE OF ARTS AND SCIENCES
Germanic and Slavic Languages and Literatures

From 1949 to 2004, UNC Press and the UNC Department of Germanic & Slavic Languages and Literatures published the UNC Studies in the Germanic Languages and Literatures series. Monographs, anthologies, and critical editions in the series covered an array of topics including medieval and modern literature, theater, linguistics, philology, onomastics, and the history of ideas. Through the generous support of the National Endowment for the Humanities and the Andrew W. Mellon Foundation, books in the series have been reissued in new paperback and open access digital editions. For a complete list of books visit www.uncpress.org.

The Poetry of Brecht
Seven Studies

PHILIP THOMSON

UNC Studies in the Germanic Languages and Literatures
Number 107

Copyright © 1989

This work is licensed under a Creative Commons CC BY-NC-ND license. To view a copy of the license, visit http://creativecommons.org/licenses.

Suggested citation: Thomson, Philip. *The Poetry of Brecht: Seven Studies*. Chapel Hill: University of North Carolina Press, 1989. DOI: https://doi.org/10.5149/9781469656854_Thomson

Library of Congress Cataloging-in-Publication Data
Names: Thomson, Philip.
Title: The poetry of Brecht : Seven studies / by Philip Thomson.
Other titles: University of North Carolina Studies in the Germanic Languages and Literatures ; no. 107.
Description: Chapel Hill : University of North Carolina Press, [1989] Series: University of North Carolina Studies in the Germanic Languages and Literatures. | Includes bibliographical references and index.
Identifiers: LCCN 88014834 | ISBN 978-1-4696-5684-7 (pbk: alk. paper) | ISBN 978-1-4696-5685-4 (ebook)
Subjects: Brecht, Bertolt, 1898-1956 — Criticism and interpretation.
Classification: LCC PT2603.R397 Z889535 1989 | DCC 831/ .912

Chapter 7 of this book is a slightly modified version of "'Exegi momentum': The Fame of Bertolt Brecht," originally printed in *The German Quarterly* Vol. 53, No. 3, 1980.

The author is grateful for permission to reproduce poems from Bertolt Brecht, *Die Gedichte* © Surhkamp Verlag Frankfurt am Main 1981. All rights reserved by and controlled through Suhrkamp Verlag Berlin.

Contents

Acknowledgments	ix
Introduction: Rereading Brecht's Poetry	1
1. Author and Reader: The Dialectic of Response	25
2. Nihilism, Anarchism, and Role-Playing: The Young Man from Augsburg	45
3. Autobiography and Poetry: Conquering the Big Bad City	75
4. The Poet in Dark Times: Messages from Exile	96
5. Poetry, Conscience, and False Consciousness: The *Buckower Elegien*	120
6. Problems with His Readership: Brecht's Bad Poetry	158
7. *Exegi monumentum*: The Poet's Fame	181
Notes	193
Bibliography	199
Index	209

Acknowledgments

Thanks are due to a number of my colleagues in the Department of German at Monash University in Melbourne, particularly Professor Leslie Bodi and Dr. David Roberts, for valuable criticism and suggestions.

This book is published with the generous assistance of the Monash University Publications Committee.

The Poetry of Brecht

Introduction:
Rereading Brecht's Poetry

Meine Lyrik hat mehr privaten Charakter.
—Brecht to Bernard Guillemin

This book is a series of studies of different kinds of poetry by Bertolt Brecht, from all periods of his life. Each chapter addresses a different problem or question. Two underlying concerns, however, are continually present, guiding my inquiry and my interpretation. One is the question of the poet's relationship in his poetry to the reader. The other is the interplay of self-revelation and self-concealment which is a central feature of Brecht's poetry from the time he sets out on his own path as a writer around 1918 to his death in 1956. These two concerns are related, since it is in his relationship to his reader that Brecht reveals or conceals himself. We sometimes see a poet referred to as a "poet's poet," suggesting that the writer in question enjoys a greater appreciation among his fellows than with the public at large, or that the way he writes reflects an orientation to an audience conceived of as consisting of his fellow poets. We might call Brecht a "reader's poet" to emphasize the poet Brecht's very marked and close relationship with his reader. This relationship is highly visible, first of all in the simple statistical sense that the thousand pages of his poetry contain a high percentage of poems that address the reader or that feature an *I*, thus foregrounding the presence of the poet in his poem and his activity as a speaker of utterances directed at the reader. The poet-reader relationship also claims our attention in Brecht's work, however, because of its scope and its complexity. There are several *I*'s in this poetry, ranging from the "tough and cool" anarcho-nihilist of the Augsburg period to the "kind-hearted sage" of the later work. And the verse where the poet speaks directly to his reader includes many of Brecht's major and best-known poems: the great autobiographical poems *Vom armen B. B.* and *An die Nachgeborenen*, the enigmatic reminiscence *Erinnerung an die Marie A.*, key poems of the exile years such as *Schlechte Zeit für Lyrik*, and responses to the crisis of 1953 like *Böser Morgen*.

Even poems that contain no obvious poet-reader relationship must of course be understood as communications from a sender (the writer) to a receiver (an audience). This audience may be conceived of very vaguely, and not much importance may be attached by the poet to establishing and maintaining a relationship with his reader. The poet may even deny, like Gottfried Benn in "Probleme der Lyrik," that he has any such intentions. Nevertheless, the mere act of writing something, even "for the bottom drawer," constitutes a communicative act. Every text has a reader, even the text left, unread, in a vault. This reader is implicit in the text itself, present in it by conscious or unconscious design of the author. In the case of Brecht, all this seems on first reflection to present no problem. He is a poet one immediately thinks of as being very present in his poems, striking up an instant rapport with his reader. It is the argument of this book, however, that this very visible or keenly sensed presence of Brecht in his poetry creates major problems of interpretation and of judgment. Specifically, it will be argued that the openness of the poet Brecht frequently conceals ironies and even a kind of wide-eyed deviousness reminiscent of his character Herr Keuner; that this openness is usually part of a rhetorical strategy, the grasping of which is the precondition of an adequate critical understanding of Brecht's poetry; and that, whereas much of the characteristic brilliance of Brecht's poetry has its origins in a cleverly managed rapport with the reader, in those cases where he is uncertain about the addressee of his poetry, he writes badly. To put this in a different way: Brecht was from the outset a brilliant creator of roles and masks, not just in his plays but also in his poetry, where they are at once self-revelatory and self-concealing. Unless both sides of this process are understood, we will mistake the relationship between Brecht's life and his poetry, and misread them both. Finally, where Brecht's self-understanding becomes uncertain, his first-person poetry, and the poetry where an open communication with the reader is set up, is correspondingly unsure and tends to be forced and strident.

The above comments will perhaps engender the suspicion that this book sees itself as demystifying Brecht, even "deconstructing" him. There is some truth in this. Ironically, the German writer who saw his work over the last thirty years of his life as primarily one of demystification is himself in need of that hard-nosed scrutiny that he loved to recommend. Especially in Germany over the last twenty years, the literature on Brecht has tended to regard its object as privileged, in the sense that his works have acquired a taken-for-granted aspect and become the subject not of criticism but of exegesis. Of this, more later. It is important to stress here that, whereas my general approach is questioning and critical and some of my judgments are unflattering, I write out of the conviction that Brecht is a great poet. Such criticism is not an act of iconoclasm but an act of understanding and in this way a kind of tribute. Nevertheless, it is to be anticipated that a certain hostility may be created, the more so since this book carries a certain corrective intent, directed against what we might call the current establishment in Brecht studies. This resides for the most part in West Germany and has been responsible for the canonization of Brecht mentioned above.

In questioning some of the assumptions of this establishment—though this is by no means the primary aim of the book—I am conscious of my own position as a foreign Germanist, that is, a non-German specialist in German literature and culture working in a non-German environment. There is much to be said about the advantages and disadvantages of such an ambiguous situation, and about the implications for the role of the foreign Germanist. He can be a kind of pipeline for the culture(s) of the German-speaking countries into his own native culture, transmitting and informing. He can, on the other hand, be a sort of Germanist in exile, tuned into the culture of his profession and participating in its intellectual discourse as a member of an international specialist group. And third, he can, in a continuous two-way process, use his ambiguous situation, his feet in two camps, to illuminate and subvert his native culture and intellectual discourse by means of the foreign culture of his expertise—and vice versa. In most cases foreign Germanists do all three things, and indeed it is difficult to imagine them doing the first two without implicitly or explicitly doing the third. The present book attempts to fulfill this third function by using its author's standpoint outside Germany as a vantage point from which to appraise critically the work of a major poet, resisting where necessary certain confining and distorting influences within German literature and intellectual life. The following comments on that literary and intellectual life, and on the place of Brecht in it, are intended to form a background to my specific project of rereading Brecht's poetry.

Brecht is an outsider, a maverick, where German poetry is concerned. His reputation and influence should not be allowed to obscure the fact that, in the history of German literature, the kind of poetry he wrote and attempted to promote occupies a minority position. Brechtian poetry—I use the term to include the poets who in one way or another followed in Brecht's path from the 1950s on—has little to do with the two great German lyrical models, the *Erlebnislyrik* of Goethe and the *Stimmungslyrik* of the Romantics. These kinds of poetry (the two merge at many points in the history of German literature) are rejected by Brecht. This rejection is to be found not so much in theoretical statements—although comments such as those in the short essays "Lyrik und Logik," "Logik der Lyrik," and "Der Lyriker braucht die Vernunft nicht zu fürchten"[1] clearly demonstrate Brecht's position—as in the actual poetry he wrote, from the beginning of his career to the end of his life. In virtually all the types of poetry for which Brecht became famous, and in almost all the stylistic and technical features we now associate with his poetry, there is an implicit denial of that central German tradition identified with the name of Goethe on the one hand and Hölderlin and the Romantics on the other. Sometimes this denial is overt, as when the young Brecht parodies Goethe's *Wandrers Nachtlied II* in *Das Lied vom Hauch*. But simply by writing ballads and Moritaten, by borrowing folk forms and adapting them—so differently from Goethe and the Romantics in their mock naive "folk-poetry"—Brecht was attempting to undermine German literary tradition. *His* ballads were modeled on the vagabond outsider Villon's earthy verse, and what he took from the Moritaten was their directness and their closeness to the common people, not their conventional moralizing.

The language of Brecht's poetry was similarly designed in sharp contrast to the language of mainstream German poetry. Averse from his early days to all sentimentality, effeteness, and excessive displays of emotion, Brecht had developed as early as 1918 a remarkably spare and matter-of-fact style. Using often no more than basic German and a syntax very close to that of the normal spoken language, he was nevertheless able to achieve subtle and powerful effects. Brecht had discovered the value of understatement and of underplaying (a lesson later adapted to his theater practice). Using this spare style, to which he added elements of Luther's Bible language and South German speech forms, he developed a poetry that could be powerfully lyrical, but in a new sense: while retaining the verbal concentration, the rhythms, and often the traditional subgenres and forms of poetry, he replaced what he saw as the self-indulgence, bombast, and metaphysical obscurities of mainstream lyrical poetry with an apparently simple and direct but highly artistic and subtle kind of verse that was completely new.

Brecht's impatience with poetry written in the mainstream German tradition emerged most notoriously in 1927 when he acted as judge in a poetry competition organized by the journal *Die literarische Welt*. Of the four hundred aspiring poets who submitted entries, Brecht could not find one worthy of a prize. They were all guilty of "Sentimentalität, Unechtheit und Weltfremdheit," which was not surprising since, maintained Brecht, they were all modeling themselves on Rilke, George, and Werfel. These three, representatives of precisely that central line going back to Goethe and the Romantics, were anathema to Brecht. Contemptuously he brushed aside all four hundred poets too: "Da sind ja wieder diese stillen, feinen, verträumten Menschen, empfindsamer Teil einer verbrauchten Bourgeoisie, mit der ich nichts zu tun haben will!"[2] One might in turn brush Brecht's remarks aside as the unqualified criticism of a young man who himself was still learning the poet's craft were it not for the fact that in this same year, 1927, Brecht's *Hauspostille* appeared. These poems for the most part date back even earlier to the period from 1918 to 1921 and represent, by any standards, artistically and historically the most significant first collection by any German poet of this century.

For all his importance and fame as a poet, however, Brecht's work remains the countertradition to the central development of German poetry. The gulf between the two is even more apparent if we compare Brecht not just with Rilke, George, and Werfel but with that contingent of slightly later German poets identified by Hugo Friedrich as truly "modern." Friedrich's book *Die Struktur der modernen Lyrik*, which first appeared in 1956, has fundamentally influenced the way modern poetry has been defined and judged. For Friedrich the key German figures for the development of truly "modern" poetry are Gottfried Benn and Georg Trakl. The pairing is significant. These two writers represent, for Friedrich, one large aspect of modernism—the irrational, the obsessive, the febrile imagination. Benn also incorporates the other principal "modernist" characteristic: the idea of the *constructed* work of art, the poet as a mixture of technician and magician. Both poets display in their work, moreover, the central features enumerated by Friedrich as constituting modern poetry: its hermetic and monologic qualities, its radically subjective nature (the imagination unfettered), and its urge to deconstruct language and reality. Nothing could be further from the poetry of Brecht, and accordingly Friedrich is unable to fit him into his array of "modern" poets. His book, influential as it was and still perhaps is, has been rightly attacked for its narrowness of focus and its elevation of one kind of poetry over others. Helmut Kreuzer, for example, has criticized Friedrich's inability to come to grips with Brecht's poetry as a defect that places in doubt Friedrich's whole notion of what constitutes "modernity" in poetry.[3] Friedrich is quite correct in identifying the line that runs from Baudelaire, Rimbaud, and Mallarmé to Benn and Trakl, Eliot and Pound, and Ungaretti and Montale, and on into the second half of the twentieth century, as the modernist line, given his definition of *modern*. But problems arise when one is confronted with a completely different kind of poetry—Brecht's, for example—that has equal claims both to excellence and historical importance as innovation.

The question of whether Brecht is "modern" or not, and in what sense, is by itself unproductive. More is illuminated if we examine what Brecht's differentiation from the modernist movement and tradition has meant for the understanding of his poetry. One of the features of modernist literature and art generally, but most importantly of poetry, is its emphatic rejection of the notion encapsulated in the German term *Erlebnisdichtung*. Modernism in Germany as elsewhere broke with the idea of a direct, easily traceable connection between a writer's experience and his art. Again and again the manifestos of modernism and the statements of modernist writers emphasize the nonexperiential nature of art and the overwhelming influence of compositional needs and considerations, denying the possibility of establishing any but indirect and arbitrary connections between a writer's life experience and his work. The belief in a straightforward and immediate relationship between an author's experience and his art had been deeply entrenched in German literary studies ever since the young Goethe had rejuvenated German literature with "spontaneous" poetry directly expressing, as it was thought, his immediate feelings and experiences. This belief is broken with in modernism, most famously, as far as German literature is concerned, in Gottfried Benn's "Probleme der Lyrik"—an essay written in 1951 towards the end of his life but expressing ideas that had guided his writing from the beginning.

This development in the line of poetry *not* Brecht's would be of no interest to us here if it were not for a curious logical short circuit that seems to have taken place in the minds of most readers and critics of Brecht. Since modernism had so explicitly distanced itself from the idea of art as *Erlebnis*, the thinking seems to go, and since Brecht is the antithesis to modernism, Brecht's kind of writing must be the kind that directly feeds from, and expresses, experience. His poetry in particular, as that genre most devoted to the expression of life experience—as confession, as self-analysis, as recall and contemplation—must represent the innermost intimate thoughts and feelings of the man Brecht. In this way the rather simplistic belief in literature as lived experience appears to have crept in the back door, so to speak, where Brecht studies are concerned.

My speculation in the above paragraph aside, Brecht positively invites, at first glance, this belief in the straightforward and direct nature of his communications to his readers. He is the very model of the poet who engages his reader in conversation, in verse that, far from being a monologic or one-way communication, establishes a role for the reader as well as an image of the poet. Again and again Brecht builds into his poetry a "reading attitude" (*Lesehaltung* or *Leserrolle*, in the terminology of Wolfgang Iser) that directs the way the reader is to see the poet, the responses the reader implicitly makes to the communication or the message (to speak semiotically) sent to him by the poet. Thus a kind of implicit dialogue ensues in which the role of the reader is important, indeed crucial, to the poem.

These comments should serve to make clear a major aim of this book. The way I have been describing of looking at literary texts is central to reader-response theory, or *Rezeptionsästhetik* in German terminology. Chapter 1 will deal in some detail with this area of literary theory and the interpretive methods connected with it, but some general remarks on the appropriateness of reader-response theory for the analysis and interpretation of *poetry* are necessary here. This body of theory, including the German *Rezeptionsästhetik*, has been developed with reference to prose fiction, and virtually all work done on the basis of this approach has likewise confined itself to prose. This may be partly chance, but there are good reasons for concentration on prose narrative. Drama eliminates itself because of the absence of an authorial "voice." Insofar as a dramatist speaks to us in his work he does so through his characters, and this immediately removes the dramatic genre from the target area of reader response analysis. (I leave aside the problematical status of stage directions of the kind indulged in by Pirandello, in which the possibility of the kind of reader address we are concerned with seems to be present.) In the case of poetry we enter difficult terrain. The nature of the lyrical *I* and its relationship to the reader have been the subject of a great deal of debate over the years, and it has to be said that little agreement or even clarity exists about the precise processes—verbal, semiotic, psychological—involved in a poem viewed as an act of communication. Radical views like the hard-line New Critical one whereby the *I* in a poem was always, as a matter of principle, *not* to be identified with the poet proved to be oversimplified and untenable, just as had the earlier simplistic assumption of that identity. Current thinking on the subject seems to boil down to an acceptance that, in general terms, the *I* in a lyrical poem is and is at the same time not the poet. This is not helpful, but in fairness it should be said that it reflects the impossibility of covering theoretically the considerable range of relationships between the poet or the *I* and the reader.

Because of its frequently monologic and hermetic qualities, modernist poetry seems on the face of it to be the least open to reader response interpretation. I am not convinced that this is in fact true, but in any case it is not with such poetry that we are concerned here. On the contrary, the kind of poetry that Brecht is famous for and that is associated above all with his name is the open, engaging sort that tends towards the overt address or, even when it does not, implicitly reckons with a response and is conscious always of the light its author is appearing in. Precisely this kind of poetry is well suited to reader response criticism. The questions that underlie this line of interpretation—who is speaking, and in what function or capacity? To whom is the poem addressed, and what does it seek to persuade him of?—are questions that appear natural in the case of poetry that creates such an immediate sense of the poet's presence, such a strong awareness of the authorial personality.

In directing our attention to the poet Brecht's relationship to his reader and to the account of himself given in his poetry, we need to proceed with a certain amount of caution and skepticism. Brecht was assiduous in propagating images of himself from his earliest days; and we do well to bear in mind the fictional nature of art, its status as construct, as well as the notorious pitfalls involved in the examination of autobiographical art. German literary criticism has traditionally been vulnerable in this regard, all too ready to accept literary utterance as life expression and take at face value the self-definition of the poet. The critic anchored in an Anglo-Saxon tradition fundamentally influenced by the strictures of the so-called New Criticism regarding the identity of the poetic *I* will not so easily be misled by first-person pronouncements in poems. I make this point because, though the term is no longer used, the old German notion of *Erlebnislyrik* or experiential poetry seems to be alive and well in Brecht studies. The same critic to whom it would never occur to look for direct transpositions from life experience in Brecht's plays—they are, of course, demonstrations of sociopolitical relations—reverts, where the poetry is concerned, to the long-established belief that *Ich-Lyrik* is the expression of the author's basic beliefs and life experiences.

In a well-known article of 1967, René Wellek traced the history of the *Erlebnis* concept in German aesthetics and literary criticism, demonstrating its centrality as a key notion whose influence has been powerful and virtually uninterrupted since the latter part of the eighteenth century. Wellek makes the point that "lived experience, intense, private experience became precisely the central value criterion in German lyrical (and not only lyrical) theory. 'Erlebnis' became the term around which they crystallize."[4] An eagle's eye view—or better, a view through a long-range telescope located outside Germany—of the German literary critical scene over the past two hundred years reveals the tenacity of the view that poetry is experiential, explicitly reflecting the writer's life experience, which therefore exists in some pure and untrammeled way in his work, despite the *theoretical* concession that a literary text necessarily structures, transforms, and alters its basic material.

Wellek was attacking in particular the criticism and theoretical writing of Emil Staiger and his followers, and those theorists such as Käte Hamburger who accord lyric poetry a special status as a mode of "utterance" (*Aussage*) that directly expresses life experience. But it is doubtful whether he would need to change his appraisal today. Though the terminology and style of the Staigerians has become impossible and though the term *Erlebnislyrik* is avoided these days because of its association with past literary critical fashions now despised or smiled at for being hopelessly unprofessional, the habit of mind is still widespread by which, *in practice*, literary texts and especially lyrical texts are seen as the direct if heightened expression of the author's experience and psyche. My emphasis on the practice of literary criticism in German studies is intended to highlight the disparity between theory and practice—frequently to be found on the same page of a critical work—that allows a theoretical statement about the strictly artistic, fictive, and constructed nature of literary texts to exist side by side with text analyses that assume the identity of author and text-statement. Two examples of such disparity are given later in this introduction.

This practical attitude, for which the title of Wilhelm Dilthey's famous book *Das Erlebnis und die Dichtung* might serve as a shorthand, has survived even despite assertions by poets themselves denying the experiential basis of their work and emphasizing the constructed nature of their art, its status as verbal calculation. Well-argued statements by major poets such as Gottfried Benn, whose essay "Probleme der Lyrik" (1951) was widely discussed in the 1950s and early 1960s, tend to have a brief and temporary impact. In the case of Benn's essay, mere lip service was paid to the notion of literature as verbal calculation or, more frequently, a neat division was maintained between the formal qualities of the poem (in which area Benn's remarks were taken seriously) and its status as the expression of the poet's inner life (where the old paradigm continued unaffected). Benn's description of poetry and its creation is an interesting mixture of the ultrarational (poetry as artifact) and the mystical (poetry as word-magic). Significantly, it was the latter aspect that was seized upon by German literary critics.

The resistance of German literary criticism to the fictionality of poetry can be gauged from the uncertain status of the term *lyrisches Ich*. Since its introduction by Margarete Susman and Oskar Walzel early this century, the term has been widely used by all kinds of critics to denote the *I* in a poem who both is and is not the author. Perusal of Kaspar H. Spinner's *Zur Struktur des lyrischen Ich* and Karl Pestalozzi's *Die Entstehung des lyrischen Ich* reveals the uncertainties that exist about the term and its usage. Spinner attempts admirably to keep the two balls of fictionality and real author constantly in the air, but it is hard work:

> In der Lyrik ist weder eine fiktive noch eine tatsächliche Kommunikationssituation . . . faßbar. . . . In der Lyrik aber ist keine fiktive Person vorhanden, auf die das Ich verweisen könnte,— deshalb spricht K. Hamburger davon, daß im Gedicht das Aussagesubjekt als ein reales vorgefunden werde. Doch diese Realität des Aussagesubjekts täuscht. . . . Die Lyrik teilt also mit der dichterischen Prosa die Loslösung vom Bezugsfeld des Autors, aber die Konstituierung eines fiktiven Bezugsfelds im Hinblick auf die Personendeixis will nicht eindeutig gelingen. Der "aktuelle Bezug", den (mit dem Linguisten E. Benveniste zu sprechen) das Wort 'ich' jeweils besitzt, weist bei der Lyrik ins Leere, weil das Gedicht im Augenblick des Verstehens den Bezug zum Augenblick der Entstehung verloren haben und trotzdem adäquat verstanden werden kann.[5]

The twisting and turning here reflect the awkward position of the term *lyrisches Ich* within the German critical context. As a theoretical concept it is messy and vague, and as a practical tool therefore useless.

A further indication that the *lyrisches Ich* is not a term that sits very easily in German literary criticism is the relatively small number of publications, even in article form, dealing with it. By comparison, the English term *persona* has received an enormous amount of attention. The two concepts are not synonymous, of course, and in any case I have chosen to avoid both. *Persona* is too narrowly associated with rigid New Criticism. The term is used in this book only to denote those roles in poems that are clearly distinct from the author (in other words, in the sense of the German *Rolle*). As for *lyrisches Ich*, I am of Walter Killy's opinion that the term, as it has been used, is better not employed, "weil seine Nützlichkeit für die Mehrzahl der

Zeiten und Gegenstände bezweifelt werden darf."[6] What cripples the term is its disharmonious mixture of theoretical insight into the fictional-communicative nature of poetry with a deeply entrenched belief in poetry as *Erlebnis*. The two balls juggled by Spinner are not compatible, and to understand their relationship a more sophisticated theory and procedure are needed. Above all, the belief in poetry as the direct expression of "lived experience" must be dispensed with.

Since the 1960s, though much has changed in German literary studies, this traditional and powerful belief has *not* changed. Current German theories that attempt to break with the *Erlebnis* view of literature in favor of a communication or reader approach, such as the *Rezeptionsästhetik* practiced by the Constance group and others, tend to be foreign imports or else originate from non-Germanist literary critics. In the case of *Rezeptionsästhetik*, it is significant that its main proponents in Germany are specialists in English and American studies, influenced by theoretical developments in the English-speaking world, especially North America. There the dominant legacy of the New Criticism has ensured a preoccupation with the text as above all a rhetorical structure or set of structures. The narrowly exclusive approach of New Criticism proper has, since the 1950s, been broadened so that, whereas the focus on text structures and strategies remains of fundamental importance, the original dogmatic rejection of "intentionalist" and "affective" considerations has largely been abandoned in favor of a more comprehensive examination of texts as communications in a network that includes not only author and reader but also the various contexts in which every text is embedded.

There are of course exceptions to this generalization about the Anglo-Saxon scene. Particularly in England the legacy of F. R. Leavis remains strong, and this has meant an emphasis in English criticism on the "quality of experience" as embodied in the work of art. But even in the Leavis tradition, with its insistence on fineness and "integrity" of experience in art, the Anglo-Saxon habit of looking hard at the text *as text* has ensured an approach relatively free of the metaphysical obscurities and the hushed tones of reverence that, well into the 1960s, characterized much German criticism. A comparison between a Leavis appraisal of a poem in *Scrutiny*, the journal most associated with his name, and a discussion by Staiger of, say, a Goethe text[7] makes the difference clear.

The hushed tones of reverence have since become passé, and few will regret their passing. But the attitude to the literary text as a direct expression of its author's life, privileged in a way that prevents skeptical questions from being asked, goes on largely unchanged in German literary studies. There would be little point in taking Staiger and his disciples to task if they represented merely one more fashion, now dead and buried, in the history of literary criticism. The roots of Staigerism, however, went deep to a powerful German tradition, whose influence today is still strong. As the recent examples I cite in this book indicate, beneath the changing surface of literary studies in *Germanistik*, the old assumptions regarding a literary text's status as direct expression of the author's psychic and experiential life continue intact, for the most part even unchallenged. Ironically, the main factor ensuring this continuity in recent years has been the swing towards Marxist approaches and methods from the late 1960s on. This swing seemed to represent an almost total opposition to the assumptions and practices of German *Literaturwissenschaft*, especially to the Staigerian mode, and a determination to put literary studies on a more sophisticated theoretical footing and to direct attention to the sociological, political, and historical dimensions of literature. One deeply entrenched assumption not jettisoned during this large-scale overhaul, however, was precisely what I have referred to as the belief in *Erlebnis und Dichtung* or "poetry as lived experience." Shorn of its metaphysical woolliness and its reverence for the sacredness of *Dichtung* it might have been; but this approach, to poetry in particular, remained basically intact after 1968, even if it was not articulated or spelled out as part of a system of theory.

The reasons for this are not confined to the continued strength of the traditional and deep-seeted attitudes outlined above. Marxist-oriented literary studies do not cope well with the fictionality of literary texts. The proposition that this fictionality is primary and that, for example, the presentation of an author's life in his writings is fundamentally influenced by the need to structure the text and the desire to set up a certain kind of communication with the reader is apt to produce the charge of "formalism." This is not the place to enter into a discussion of this knee-jerk reaction, or of the misunderstandings which give rise to it. Suffice to say that the overall tendency in Marxist or Marxist-influenced approaches to literature is to play down the rhetorical nature of the literary text and thereby run the risk, when it comes to first-person texts, of making too simple and undifferentiated a connection between text-statement and author's life and views.

In the case of Brecht another factor enters the picture. If Goethe's works had assumed the status of holy relics for the Staigerians, those reverential custodians of *Dichtung*, the same process can be seen taking place from the late 1960s on with Brecht's work and the Marxists. As perhaps the most important Marxist creative writer, Brecht became a key figure for the new wave of German literary critics produced by the radical changes in German universities and intellectual life. He fitted the bill in several ways. He was a major author, a German, a Marxist, and—like the new literary critics after 1968—a tireless attacker of intellectual establishments. He was also an important theoretician, and theory was definitely "in" after 1968. The thousand-odd pages of theoretical writings by Brecht, and the further nine hundred on literature, aesthetics, and politics, represented a treasure trove for the new breed. Brecht quickly came to enjoy the classical status that he had accorded to Marx, Engels, and Lenin and that—half coyly, half boldly—he had sought in turn for himself. As "classics" his writings are privileged, whether consciously or not, for those critics who identify in some way with Marxism. Though parts of Brecht's work remain deeply problematic for those states where "actual socialism" (*der real existierende Sozialismus*) holds sway, and though there is much in his work that is also uncomfortable for Western Marxists of various hues, this does not significantly detract from the master's sacrosanct status, in the Federal Republic as well as in the Democratic Republic, and for that matter among Anglo-Saxon critics who took their cue from the new would-be orthodoxy in Germany. When Max Frisch remarked in his 1964 speech "Der Autor und das Theater" that Brecht, eight years after his death, had achieved "die durchschlagende Wirkungslosigkeit eines Klassikers,"[8] he incurred the undying animosity of the new Brecht critics, who were determined to rescue Brecht from the anesthetizing clutches of the bourgeoisie. Ironically, in defining and privileging a new Brecht, these critics, quickly imitated by their colleagues in North America, built merely a different "classic," one who looked, not surprisingly, very much like them: radical, iconoclastic, austerely intellectual, and theory obsessed.

This has had two serious effects on Brecht criticism, one general and one specific. The general effect is to place Brecht, his utterances, and his works beyond the reach of real criticism. Criticism is replaced by exegesis, which can have various purposes but does not involve questioning the value of the sacred texts. Martin Esslin has described Brecht research as a "geradezu unwahrscheinlich gut erhaltenes Überbleibsel mittelalterlicher Scholastik"[9] and claims that Brecht's works have become in this way "der heilige Text, auf dem sich die ersten Kommentare aufbauten, die dann von immer neuen Generationen von Kommentaren über Kommentare neu kommentiert wurde, so daß man sich jetzt nur noch mit Kommentaren über Kommentare über Kommentare abgibt."[10] These remarks are made in the context of a rather polemical review, but there is no denying the validity of Esslin's points. One has only to survey the vast amount of literature devoted since the late 1960s to various aspects of Brecht's *theories*—everything from his understanding of dialectics to all conceivable aspects of his theater theory—to be made aware of the exegetical nature of Brecht research. In this the most typical development was the veritable cult of the *Lehrstück* that blossomed in the wake of Reiner Steinweg's book.[11] Membership of this virtually fetishistic cult was dependent on the conviction that the major plays of the exile years, from *Der gute Mensch* to *Galilei*, are flawed compromises, and only the *Lehrstücke* represent purity. The fixation on the didactic plays is a chapter for itself. In all the writing on didactic play theory, the question that was scarcely raised, let alone answered, was, Does the theory work?—just as in a more general way the same crucial question about Brecht's overall theater theory was never put. I quote Martin Esslin again:

> Wäre es nicht nützlich und erkenntnisfördernd zu erforschen, inwieweit die Verfremdung, die dialektische Methode Brechts, es erlaubt, die realen Widersprüche in der Gesellschaft seiner Zeit aufzudecken? Zum Beispiel: Stimmt die Darstellung des Mechanismus einer durch Börsenspekulation hervogerufenen Wirtschaftskrise in der *Heiligen Johanna der Schlachthöfe*? Ist die Darstellung des aufhaltsamen Aufstiegs des Arturo Ui eine der Realität entsprechende dialektische Verfremdung von Hitlers Aufstieg zur Macht? Trifft die Analyse des Verhältnisses von Faschismus, Rassismus und Kapitalismus in den *Rundköpfen und den Spitzköpfen* zu?[12]

These questions are asked by a well-known and influential member of what one might call the liberal right. It is to the discredit of Marxist critics (and ultimately to their disadvantage) that *they* have not asked them.

The second, more specific result of Brecht's canonization is the inability or unwillingness on the part of critics to see his poetry as containing anything but straightforward statements of truth. The various pictures of himself that Brecht gives us, the remarks he makes to us, tend—unless they are blatantly ironic—to be taken as gospel. There is a feeling perhaps that not to do so would constitute an attack on the great man's status. In this way, the old belief in poetry as lived experience, the Marxist disinclination to view literature in ways that, however mistakenly, were associated with "formalism," and the new classical status of Brecht, have combined to remove Brecht's work from searching critical enquiry, however much exegesis goes on. This has meant a reluctance or inability to read Brecht against the grain, to make critical distinctions between explicit and implicit statements or even between autobiographical statements in a poem and verifiable facts. The aim in making such distinctions is not to expose the poetry as distortions of fact, but to make it clear that one cannot move from the poetry to the biography and vice versa in a simple way, without considering the structures and stratagems necessarily involved in the transposition of experience into literature.

It is not only critics oriented toward Marxism who slip into the dangerous identification of the poem's statement with the experience or views of its author. There is in fact a general tendency in Brecht studies to practice this identification. Peter Paul Schwarz, for example, whose *Brechts frühe Lyrik, 1914–1922* remains one of the few book-length studies of Brecht's poetry, repeatedly operates on the unspoken assumption that what is in the early poetry is simply the young Bertolt Brecht. In his review of Schwarz's book, Jürgen Bay points out that Schwarz

> schließt . . . , obwohl er nur Werkzusammenhänge beschreiben will, deduktiv von den verschiedenen Ausprägungen des Nihilismus in den Gedichten auf entsprechende weltanschauliche Positionen des jungen Brecht. Ist schon die Behauptung eines persönlichen Erfahrungscharakters von Lyrik bedenklich, so ist der von Schwarz unreflektiert gezogene Schluß von der Lyrik auf den Lyriker erst recht fragwürdig. Brecht selbst mahnt an einer Stelle: "Wer immer es ist, den ihr sucht: ich bin es nicht." Auch Hans Mayer, der Brecht gut kannte, hat davor gewarnt, das lyrische Subjekt in Brechts Gedichten mit dem realen Brecht gleichzusetzen.[13]

But it is perhaps an indication of how resilient the old attitude to poetry as "lived experience" (*Erlebnis*) is in Germany that Bay, having clearly discerned and described the trap, then insists on walking into it himself:

> Dennoch ist angesichts der Stringenz der nihilistischen Thematik die Identifizierung des lyrischen Subjekts mit dem Lyriker Brecht nicht ganz abwegig. Ja, im Hinblick auf Brechts Selbst-

kommentare und die Zeugnisse seiner Freunde Hans Otto Münsterer und Peter Suhrkamp, dessen prononcierter Hinweis auf den "zynischen Nihilismus" des jungen Brecht Schwarz übrigens entgangen zu sein scheint, ist das zumindest generelle "argumentum ex carmine ad poetam" wohl nicht nur erlaubt, sondern sogar geboten.[14]

On the basis of the "stringency" of the nihilism in the early poetry, and of statements by old friends of Brecht about his nihilism, the warning about equating poetry with real experience and real views is withdrawn and the "doubtful" nature of this procedure waved aside. It does not take much persuasion to tempt Bay to abandon his theoretical principles. As if intensity of expression is a guarantee of the "authenticity" of the experience, in the naive understanding of that term as the convergence of actual experience and artistic expression. And as if Brecht's later comments on his early work, or the opinions of his friends, no matter how certain or honest in intention, can have the status of evidence.

I shall take issue with Schwarz's (and Bay's) reading of the young Brecht's "nihilism" and "anarchism" in chapter 2. The point here has been to illustrate the continuing potency in German literary criticism of the experiential view of poetry, that entrenched set of assumptions about the relationship between poetic text and author's life that underlies the interpretation of poetry, either in an unreflecting way (as in the example of Schwarz above) or based on argument that will not stand up to scrutiny (as in the example of Bay). These assumptions perhaps have a special function within, but are by no means restricted to, Marxist criticism. My comments about the effects on Brecht studies since 1968 of a strong orientation to Marxism should not be taken as a wholesale rejection of Marxist viewpoints. It is merely that the most clearly profiled and rapidly expanding branch of Brecht criticism has been Marxist, and that by an irony of history this has produced a continuity in the traditional German view of literature as the direct expression of experience. Moreover, the new Brecht critics have constructed a Brecht who is to be like a monument: fenced off, unchanging, and impervious to questions.

There are very few exceptions to this. Genuinely critical and questioning approaches to Brecht's work, where they exist, do not achieve prominence. Hans-Dieter Zimmermann's "Fünf Thesen" (five theses) on Brecht, which are severely critical and raise basic questions about Brecht's theories and praxis as a dramatist, were delivered at the 1978 Brecht Symposium in Frankfurt. They seem to have had scarcely an echo in the profuse professional literature on Brecht, and as far as I am aware were not published until 1983, in the *Brecht Jahrbuch,* which is essentially an Anglo-American enterprise.[15]

Even challenging and unorthodox attempts by German scholars to view Brecht's work from a fresh perspective suffer from their imprisonment in the traditional attitude described above. Carl Pietzcker's book *Die Lyrik des jungen Brecht: Vom anarchischen Nihilismus zum Marxismus* uses Freudian categories to analyze Brecht's poetry. But this attempt is crippled from the outset by Pietzcker's failure to clarify the relationship between the *I* of a literary text and the author. He refers to "jenes dichtende Subjekt . . . , das hier verkürzend das 'dichtende Ich' genannt wird, das 'dichtende Ich', in dem der Austrag des Konflikts zwischen Es, Über-Ich und Realität als Dichtung seinen Niederschlag findet."[16] From here on confusion sets in:

> Vom "dichtenden Ich", in dem der Phantasievorgang greifbar wird, ist das "dichtende Individuum" zu scheiden, d.h. das Individuum im Zustand des Dichtens; sein Es und sein Über-Ich lassen sich nur erkennen, soweit sie das "dichtende Ich" bestimmen. Das "dichtende Ich" ist von dem "Ich des Autors", dessen nur vorübergehender Zustand es ist, ebenso zu scheiden, wie das "dichtende Individuum" vom "Autor". Von ihnen allen ist wiederum das "sprechende Ich" zu unterscheiden, d.h. das Ich, welches das Gedicht in einer bestimmten Rolle spricht. Das "sprechende Ich" kann selbst hervortreten, dann wird es "explizites Ich" genannt.[17]

It is difficult to see how this can be of use in analyzing and interpreting literary texts. In any case, whatever this means as theory, Pietzcker's practice leaves no doubt as to the critical tradition to which he is bonded. Just two pages after his labored attempt to sort out literary creation from authorial psychology, Pietzcker embarks on a psychoanalytic commentary on *Apfelböck oder Die Lilie auf dem Felde* which begins with the statement: "Brechts Phantasie vom Elternmord holt, wie die der Expressionisten auch, ihre Energie aus dem infantilen Wunsch, den Vater zu töten, einem Wunsch, der sich nach Freud bei jedem männlichen Mitglied unserer Gesellschaft findet."[18] All distinctions made, however confusedly, on the theoretical level between Brecht and the "dichtendes Ich" of his poetry are promptly forgotten once the actual interpretation of a text is undertaken, and the old unexamined assumption reasserts itself: that if a young writer writes about parents being murdered, no matter what the context, known biographical facts or *textimmanent* indications themselves, then he must somehow be expressing a personal desire to murder his own parents.

The above remarks on the German literary critical tradition, and my insistence on the clear distinction between the life experience of writers and the expression of this experience in literary texts, should not be misunderstood as a plea for a return to the radical *divorce* of life and literature that characterizes formalism in its extreme guises. Nothing could be further from the intention of this book than to banish considerations relating to Brecht's life and career from the interpretation of his work. A reading of any one of the seven chapters will make this clear. Indeed, it is precisely the relationship between life and career on the one hand and creative writing on the other that again and again is moved into the foreground of these studies. It is not the case, moreover, that this relationship is conceived of as necessarily an antithetical one, with life and art facing each other in an opposing fashion. The art-life model being proposed here is a dialectical one involving the constant interpenetration of life and work and the continual modification of each by the other—a process that has to be seen, however, within the context of the peculiar modes and structures of artistic expression. The distinction between the two realms of life and art is necessary in order to be able to appraise adequately the *fusion* of the two in the life work of the author. It is here that the author's life in its social and political context on the one hand, and the *I* that speaks in the poetry on the other, merge to create the overall picture of a writer. My insistence on the peculiar circumstances accompanying the creation and communication of the poetic *I* is intended to direct attention to the pitfalls of unreflected and simplistic assumptions about the transposition of life experience into literature. Once again: not the *divorce* of life and literature should be our aim but an adequate *distinction*, which can then be the basis for a dialectical understanding of the relationship between the two. The fundamental assumption underpinning my analysis of Brecht's poetry—and it is especially relevant to the first-person poetry—is that all artistic expression is at once self-revealing and self-masking, and that it is crucially determined by the nature of the relationship of the author to his reader. The implications of this are spelled out in chapter 1.

This book differs from other studies of Brecht's poetry in two respects. It differs from books such as those by Klaus Schuhmann[19] and Peter Paul Schwarz[20] in that it assumes, as these earlier accounts could not, that the general contours of Brecht's poetry, its range and its main concerns, are reasonably familiar to the student of German literature. The studies by Schuhmann and Schwarz were in many ways pioneering works, and offer either a first orientation (Schuhmann) or deal with a manageable chronological segment of Brecht's poetry (Schwarz, although his study of Brecht's poetry up to 1922 also has a thematic focus, expressed in its subtitle *Nihilismus als Werkzusammenhang der frühen Lyrik Brechts*). Later studies have attempted to uncover governing structures and underlying principles and to demonstrate the development of Brecht's poetry—again for the most part limited to one era—and its various motors. Here the book by Carl Pietzcker is a good example,[21] a marrying of Marx with Freud (the latter being the dominant partner) in an ambitious attempt to give substance and detail to the view that the young Brecht was assailed by psychic pressures and problems, to which his anarcho-nihilism was the response. This is an updated and apparently sophisticated version of Martin Esslin's earlier and too schematic characterization of the young Brecht as a vulnerable rootless and restless type seeking a hold in life and eventually finding it in Marxism—a view in its turn hotly contested by most Marxist critics, for whom these are presumably not the correct reasons for embracing Marxism.

The present study differs from all these books, and from Schwarz's later contribution,[22] in that it does not confine itself to any one period. In the seven chapters all the major phases of Brecht's work are represented. However, the book does not attempt to trace the development of Brecht's poetry from Augsburg to Buckow. Rather, the focus is on themes and topics, examined in conjunction with lyrical *modi operandi*. Sometimes, of course, a theme belongs inextricably to a certain period (exile, for example), and sometimes key problems or questions for the poet Brecht make themselves felt at watershed moments in his career (for example, the problem of what kind of poet to be when he moves to Berlin in the 1920s). But my central preoccupation remains the relationship between Brecht and his reader. In particular, in highlighting Brecht's concern with the way he is seen by his audience and public, I am drawing attention to a specific aspect— a very important one—of this relationship. Always highly conscious of his image, and always disposed towards the address to the reader, whether direct or oblique, Brecht offers us the very model of a *personal* poet, entering into intimate, but also intricate, dealings with his reader.

The focus on the poet Brecht's relationship with his reader gives this book a constancy of purpose that is necessarily lacking in Franz Norbert Mennemeier's *Bertolt Brechts Lyrik: Aspekte, Tendenzen*.[23] Mennemeier's work is a heterogeneous collection of pieces on Brecht's poetry that does not claim to produce any overriding theory or view. Though this would be a tall order, the lack of any cohesion in such studies tends to create the impression of randomness and fragmentariness.[24] Two other book-length studies do attempt an overview of Brecht's lyrical production. Jan Knopf's *Brecht Handbuch: Lyrik, Prosa, Schriften* is a valuable contribution to Brecht studies, combining an impressive mastery of detail with a fine critical sense. While one might argue with some of Knopf's assertive declarations, his book does not shirk the task of confronting the numerous received truths, the unsatisfactory interpretive procedures and the comfortable omissions that have marred writing on Brecht. Peter Whitaker's *Brecht's Poetry: A Critical Study* presents a coverage of the major periods and concerns of Brecht's verse. Though it is clear that a single book cannot hope to be completely inclusive, some of Whitaker's choices regarding what to omit from mention and what to dwell on are puzzling. A more serious problem is that, despite the claim of the subtitle, very little genuine criticism goes on. The book thus accomplishes neither a survey on the one hand nor a critical appraisal on the other.

My approach has been to seek a certain unifying perspective without denying the sheer range of the poet Brecht and without committing the other common sin of imprisoning his work in a narrowly conceived theory that acts as a straitjacket. Thus within the framework of the poet Brecht's relationship with his reader, the seven studies that make up the book focus on various matters. These may be themes that recur in his work or problems that preoccupy him at specific stages of his life and career. At the same time, the seven chapters deal with somewhat different theoretical and critical problems—all, however, connected in some way with the poet-reader relationship. In this way it is hoped that although no attempt is made to offer a systematic coverage of Brecht's large poetic output, a considerable breadth of poetry can be critically discussed, while the fundamental theoretical problems that the book addresses are kept continuously in view.

In chapter 1 just two poems are examined. Both are from the *Hauspostille* and represent two key poem types in Brecht's work, the reminiscence (*Erinnerung an die Marie A.*) and the ballad of social accusation (*Von der Kindesmörderin Marie Farrar*). In this initial chapter there is an exposition of the critical theory that underpins much of the book's approach, reader-response theory. Chapter 1 demonstrates that this branch of literary theory is especially productive when brought to bear on the kind of poetry that features an address to a reader or establishes an explicit communication between poet and reader. Reader-response theory can prevent misreadings of a poem (the case of *Marie Farrar*), or help in the interpretation of difficult poems (*Erinnerung an die Marie A.*).

Chapter 2 is concerned with Brecht's early poetry from the Augsburg years and the nihilist and anarchist attitudes that characterize it. The argument here is twofold: first, that such attitudes are adopted, put on like a mask, rather than representing intensely held beliefs; second, that the primary purpose of these masks is not to conceal the true self or ward off threats to the psyche, but to experiment with possibilities and roles. This second chapter aims to show that Brecht is far more detached in his early poetry than is generally acknowledged. Attempts to see in the poems of the *Hauspostille* evidence of a seriously threatened and vulnerable psyche, of existential doubt and nihilism, take such poems too seriously in the sense that they fail to take into account the role-playing needs of the young poet, who runs through a range of guises, trying out different modes, styles, and authorial possibilities. It is not until the move from Augsburg to Berlin that life becomes very serious for Brecht.

Chapter 3 takes this move and its accompanying trauma as its subject matter. Here the thesis is put forward that this was a crucially determining experience for the young writer, so painfully intense that only from a later, more secure vantage point could he give expression to it. In this chapter two very different kinds of big city poetry, involving different relationships with the reader, serve to illustrate the difference between the poetry of experience and the experience proper. It is in this chapter in particular that the *indirect* nature of the relationship between life and art is demonstrated. The city poetry of the 1920s is a classic example of how writing must be made to serve the psychological needs of the author, and of how the transposition of experience into art is characterized by indirectness and delay.

Chapter 4 looks at the large theme of exile in Brecht's poetry from the 1930s and 1940s, when some of his most famous work was written. Well-known poems from this period are examined for the image projected by the poet in exile and for the subtle and complex addresses to the reader that take place. Here the central question about whom these poems are written for and with what intention leads us into the crucial area of Brecht's self-understanding as a writer and intellectual. For the poet in exile, the issue of his identity and function as a "practical writer" becomes critical, and the frequency of major poems attempting to define this identity increases.

When the exile ended and Brecht returned to a socialist Germany, this problem of identity seems to have ceased. But as chapter 5 argues, another problem takes its place. The citizen of the German Democratic Republic has *other* identity troubles. These suddenly and painfully emerge during the great political and personal crisis of the summer of 1953. The collection of poems resulting directly from this crisis, the *Buckower Elegien*, is the record of Brecht's attempts now to confront, now to evade, the questions raised by the events of June 1953, including questions about his own identity. Though the poet's relationship to his reader seems less immediate in these poems, it is precisely through this relationship that we can observe Brecht caught between honesty and false consciousness as he attempts to respond to the implications of the 1953 uprising.

One of the problems that arises in the *Buckower Elegien* is brought into the foreground in chapter 6. It is the problem, scarcely addressed in criticism on Brecht, of his bad poetry. Chapter 6 is an attempt to demonstrate a direct link between Brecht's poor quality verse and his problems after 1948 in identifying whom he is addressing in his poetry. In contrast to those poems of the 1930s in which communism is eulogized, the GDR poetry praising the achievements of the new German state is characterized by a falseness of tone that betrays the man not happy in his work. It is not the relative plausibility of these accounts of communism that is the issue. Rather, the point is Brecht's conviction or lack of it. No matter how crass, idealistic, or one-eyed we may find, say, the pro-Soviet poems of the thirties, they are written with unmistakable conviction, a certain élan and buoyancy. The equivalent poems about the GDR, by contrast, limp and stumble; they are flat, forced, and strident. A large part of Brecht's difficulty can be traced to his inability to relate to his new public—the populace of the GDR—and to establish a new kind of poetic profile for himself.

Finally chapter 7, though not a conclusion, draws together many of the aspects of Brecht's relationship to his public. The poet's self-image is looked at here through the considerable number of poems that deal with the way Brecht is viewed as a writer, and will be viewed by future generations: in other words, with his status and historical place as a writer. This last chapter emphasizes the rhetorical nature of all such self-assessment and self-projection in literature and demonstrates once again that statements in Brecht's first-person poetry can rarely be taken at face value.

Brecht's presentation of himself, his image of himself as a man and a writer, and the various issues connected with this, such as his historical status and his relationship to his public, are not the concerns solely of his poetry. The stories about his alter ego Herr Keuner, as well as *Me-ti*, to name perhaps the most obvious, offer important insights into the way Brecht projected himself to his public and the image(s) of himself he hoped would remain. I have chosen not to sacrifice the unity of genre by including these and other suitable texts in my examination of the concerns and problems sketched above. To do so would have been to introduce, perforce, other questions and other areas of investigation that lead away from my chosen target. In addition, it is in the poetry that one can see most plainly the writer Brecht at work conveying images of himself, establishing modes of communication with his reader, and defining and redefining himself and his relationship to this reader. Brecht's much-quoted comment to Bernard Guillemin of *Die literarische Welt* in 1926— "Meine Lyrik hat mehr privaten Charakter"—should be read two ways. Compared to his play writing the poetry is indeed more personal, more "private" where the theater work is public. But in another sense Brecht is stating, as so often in his remarks about himself and his work, only half the case. Brecht's poetry is not private in the sense of being hermetic or designed for himself or an inner circle alone, inaccessible to the uninitiated. On the contrary, it is precisely in his first-person poetry—the term I shall use to equate to the German *Ich-Lyrik*—that Brecht is constantly seeking to establish a communication and a relationship with his readers. It is in the poetry that the voice of Brecht emerges most *engagingly*, most clearly— though not necessarily most directly.

Somewhat varied methods are applied to the seven chapters with their diverse subject matter. Although reader-response theory informs a good deal of my analysis and interpretation, it is not enough if one is to deal satisfactorily with the range of issues, themes, and problems in Brecht's poetry. Close attention to a poem's rhetorical strategies may not give us, by itself, an adequate understanding of that poem's place and function within the life and career of its author. Therefore, although there is a fairly constant attention to the rhetorical and communicative structures—understood in that broad sense outlined above—that direct the way we read a poem, other methods of analysis and appraisal are used where the subject matter and the critical problem suggest or demand them. This book is unashamedly and consciously eclectic in its methodology. It reflects its author's belief in the value of a controlled eclecticism, and the concomitant rejection of a single embracing theory of literature or methodology of critical practice. Connoisseurs of horse racing have a saying, "Horses for courses," meaning that certain horses are a good bet on certain courses though not on others. It is a view that literary critics might profitably take over. Far from reflecting an indiscriminate pluralism, such an approach means that decisions about methods to be employed—horses to be backed—are made with an eye to their likely productiveness. This does not necessarily mean adhering to well-tried practices that in the past have seemed to be effective. These may in fact be in need of revision, and their continued use may be closing rather than opening up the object of study. Under these circumstances new practices, a procedure against the grain, may be appropriate. In the case of Brecht, I have argued that the well-tried practices have tended to accept too much and question too little and that it is time to open up Brecht's work with some judiciously applied levers. One does not need to go along with the more ludic and ultimately self-indulgent prestidigitations of some deconstructionists to perceive the positive value in an against-the-grain attitude to literary texts, particularly those in danger of becoming rock-hard monuments. In the process of "deconstructing" Brecht a little, pieces may fall off the monument, it may become unstable, and the writer we are left with may look different. But it is time we took a hard look at Brecht. We need to subject his work to a genuinely critical gaze in order to ensure that its genuinely great achievements are not compromised by our unwillingness to admit its faults.

1. Author and Reader: The Dialectic of Response

I am conscious that some of my remarks in the introduction regarding the ipso facto rhetorical status of literary texts may be contentious and give rise to misunderstanding. Contentiousness is no bad thing, but some clarification may be necessary if misunderstanding is to be avoided. In using the terms *rhetorical* and *fictive* to characterize statements made within a literary text, I am making a distinction, not a value judgment—and certainly not a moral judgment. A statement made or a self-image presented by a writer in his work may coincide exactly with the factual (as far as it can be determined), or not coincide at all. Neither case, a priori, merits our praise, or even our attention, ahead of the other. It is only in the larger context of an author's life and work that we may wish to inquire into the reasons and the justification for "bending the facts" and perhaps censure him. In that case, however, we do not criticize the author because of the *fact* that he has employed devices, strategies, and structures that transform experience into art and in the process "distort" them—all art does this—but because we take issue with his motives.

This condemnation on ideological or moral grounds is not the point for the time being. In drawing attention to the fictionality of literary texts, my purpose was to emphasize their communicative and persuasive nature. It is not only to first-person poems that these remarks apply. All poetry sets up communication between a voice and a reader and thus contains rhetorical structures and stratagems that direct our reception of the text. First-person poetry merely draws attention to the problem. The same goes for poems that address the reader in some fairly direct way. Here Brecht immediately springs to mind. He is one of the first poets one thinks of when direct communication with the reader is in question. From Rimbaud and especially Villon he had learned very early the possibilities inherent in the address to the reader. There are many obvious examples, but my point might be made if we examine a relatively early poem, justly famous, where the address to the reader may at first sight seem minimal and in any case unproblematic:

VON DER KINDESMÖRDERIN MARIE FARRAR

Marie Farrar, geboren im April
Unmündig, merkmallos, rachitisch, Waise
Bislang angeblich unbescholten, will
Ein Kind ermordet haben in der Weise:
Sie sagt, sie habe schon im zweiten Monat
Bei einer Frau in einem Kellerhaus
Versucht, es abzutreiben mit zwei Spritzen
Angeblich schmerzhaft, doch ging's nicht heraus.
    Doch ihr, ich bitte euch, wollt nicht in Zorn verfallen
    Denn alle Kreatur braucht Hilf von allen.

Sie habe dennoch, sagt sie, gleich bezahlt
Was ausgemacht war, sich fortan geschnürt
Auch Sprit getrunken, Pfeffer drin vermahlt
Doch habe sie das nur stark abgeführt.
Ihr Leib sei zusehends geschwollen, habe
Auch stark geschmerzt, beim Tellerwaschen oft.
Sie selbst sei, sagt sie, damals noch gewachsen.
Sie habe zu Marie gebetet, viel erhofft.
    Auch ihr, ich bitte euch, wollt nicht in Zorn verfallen
    Denn alle Kreatur braucht Hilf von allen.

Doch die Gebete hätten, scheinbar, nichts genützt.
Es war auch viel verlangt. Als sie dann dicker war
Hab ihr in Frühmetten geschwindelt. Oft hab sie geschwitzt
Auch Angstschweiß, häufig unter dem Altar.
Doch hab den Zustand sie geheimgehalten
Bis die Geburt sie nachher überfiel.
Es sei gegangen, da wohl niemand glaubte
Daß sie, sehr reizlos, in Versuchung fiel.
    Und ihr, ich bitte euch, wollt nicht in Zorn verfallen
    Denn alle Kreatur braucht Hilf von allen.

An diesem Tag, sagt sie, in aller Früh
Ist ihr beim Stiegenwischen so, als krallten
Ihr Nägel in den Bauch. Es schüttelt sie.
Jedoch gelingt es ihr, den Schmerz geheimzuhalten.
Den ganzen Tag, es ist beim Wäschehängen
Zerbricht sie sich den Kopf; dann kommt sie drauf
Daß sie gebären sollte, und es wird ihr
Gleich schwer ums Herz. Erst spät geht sie hinauf.

Doch ihr, ich bitte euch, wollt nicht in Zorn verfallen
Denn alle Kreatur braucht Hilf von allen.

Man holte sie noch einmal, als sie lag:
Schnee war gefallen, und sie mußte kehren.
Das ging bis elf. Es war ein langer Tag.
Erst in der Nacht konnt sie in Ruhe gebären.
Und sie gebar, so sagt sie, einen Sohn.
Der Sohn war ebenso wie andere Söhne.
Doch sie war nicht, wie andre Mütter sind, obschon—
Es liegt kein Grund vor, daß ich sie verhöhne.
   Auch ihr, ich bitte euch, wollt nicht in Zorn verfallen
   Denn alle Kreatur braucht Hilf von allen.

So laßt sie also weiter denn erzählen
Wie es mit diesem Sohn geworden ist
(Sie wolle davon, sagt sie, nichts verhehlen)
Damit man sieht, wie ich bin und du bist.
Sie sagt, sie sei, nur kurz im Bett, von Übel-
keit stark befallen worden, und allein
Hab sie, nicht wissend, was geschehen sollte
Mit Mühe sich bezwungen, nicht zu schrein.
   Und ihr, ich bitte euch, wollt nicht in Zorn verfallen
   Denn alle Kreatur braucht Hilf von allen.

Mit letzter Kraft hab sie, so sagt sie, dann
Da ihre Kammer auch eiskalt gewesen
Sich zum Abort geschleppt und dort auch (wann
Weiß sie nicht mehr) geborn ohn Federlesen
So gegen Morgen zu. Sie sei, sagt sie
Jetzt ganz verwirrt gewesen, habe dann
Halb schon erstarrt, das Kind kaum halten können
Weil es in den Gesindabort hereinschnein kann.
   Und ihr, ich bitte euch, wollt nicht in Zorn verfallen
   Denn alle Kreatur braucht Hilf von allen.

Dann zwischen Kammer und Abort—vorher, sagt sie
Sei noch gar nichts gewesen—fing das Kind
Zu schreien an, das hab sie so verdrossen, sagt sie
Daß sie's mit beiden Fäusten, ohne Aufhörn, blind
So lang geschlagen habe, bis es still war, sagt sie.
Hierauf hab sie das Tote noch durchaus
Zu sich ins Bett genommen für den Rest der Nacht
Und es versteckt am Morgen in dem Wäschehaus.

> Doch ihr, ich bitte euch, wollt nicht in Zorn verfallen
> Denn alle Kreatur braucht Hilf vor allem.
>
> Marie Farrar, geboren im April
> Gestorben im Gefängnishaus zu Meißen
> Ledige Kindesmutter, abgeurteilt, will
> Euch die Gebrechen aller Kreatur erweisen
> Ihr, die ihr gut gebärt in saubern Wochenbetten
> Und nennt "gesegnet" euren schwangeren Schoß
> Wollt nicht verdammen die verworfnen Schwachen
> Denn ihre Sünd war schwer, doch ihr Leid groß.
> > Darum, ich bitte euch, wollt nicht in Zorn verfallen
> > Denn alle Kreatur braucht Hilf von allen.
>
> (GW, 4:176–79)

With the refrain at the end of the first stanza direct contact is made between author and reader:

> Doch ihr, ich bitte euch, wollt nicht in Zorn verfallen
> Denn alle Kreatur braucht Hilf von allen.

But this refrain, repeated at the end of all stanzas, is addressed to a *fictive* reader, a created audience—created by the preaching Moritat style, though compassionate here rather than condemnatory as in a real Moritat. This stylized mode of address establishes a stylized audience: the people listening to the Moritat in the marketplace or fairground. We as readers perceive this and react accordingly; it is not we who are being addressed—we are the observers of a fictive act of communication. We are confirmed in this by the fact that the voice of the refrain is clearly distinct from the voice of the narrative, which is characterized by a bureaucratic factualness. To the question, Which of these voices is the real voice of Brecht? the answer of course is neither. Both are constructed, fictive voices. The refrain, appearing in italics, is almost a kind of quotation. Indeed many readers might well reach for their Villon at this point. There is in fact no clear source in Villon's work for these lines, but their tenor and style are clearly imitative of similar refrains in the *ballades*.

In the rest of the poem—narrated in the style of the court report of the facts of the case—we react as someone who is indirectly addressed, and respond with sympathy, horror, or anger, depending on the text. Paradoxically, it is at those points of the poem where a reader is *directly* addressed that we perceive this reader to be not us, but a fictive reader. At such points we temporarily stand outside the poem, looking on. Apart from the refrain, it is only in stanza 6 and in the final stanza that the intrusions into the courtroom narrative by the Moritat speaker addressing a fictive audience occur:

So laßt sie also weiter denn erzählen
Wie es mit diesem Sohn geworden ist
(Sie wolle davon, sagt sie, nichts verhehlen)
Damit man sieht, wie ich bin und du bist.

At this point there is a kind of fusion between the court narrator ("Sie wolle davon, sagt sie, nichts verhehlen") and the moralizing, sententious but at least compassionate Moritat speaker ("Damit man sieht, wie ich bin und du bist").

In the final stanza, similarly, the "factual" narrative and the naive Moritat plea for understanding come together:

Marie Farrar, geboren im April
Gestorben im Gefängnishaus zu Meißen
Ledige Kindesmutter, abgeurteilt, will
Euch die Gebrechen aller Kreatur erweisen.
Ihr, die ihr gut gebärt in saubern Wochenbetten
Und nennt "gesegnet" euren schwangeren Schoß
Wollt nicht verdammen die verworfnen Schwachen
Denn ihre Sünd war schwer, doch ihr Leid groß.

We do *not* primarily identify with those directly addressed here—"Ihr, die ihr gut gebärt in saubern Wochenbetten," etc.—but perceive the people addressed as part of the poem's text-world. Carl Pietzcker, in an otherwise accurate and thorough analysis of *Marie Farrar*, is quite wrong in positing as the reader of the poem "Bürger bzw. Bürgerinnen, die im Gegensatz zu Marie 'in saubern Wochenbetten' gebären, Bürger, zu deren Bewußtseinsgut die christliche Tradition wenigstens noch so weit gehört, daß sie sich von ihr ansprechen lassen, potentielle Käufer der *Hauspostille* in der Weimarer Republik."[1] Not that there might not be, or have been, actual people of this kind who read the poem. That is scarcely demonstrable, nor is it the point. What matters for an adequate understanding of the poem is how we as readers are being asked to react; and the answer to this is that we are invited to be critical, even contemptuous, of those *other* complacent and self-righteous bourgeois addressed by the poem.

Pietzcker commits the common error of confusing three kinds of reader. The easiest of these to envisage, the *actual* reader of a text, is properly the object of empirical sociological or historical study. Then there is what I have so far called the *fictive* reader, a character created by the text. Finally, and most difficult to define and describe, there is the *ideal* reader, created likewise by the text in the sense that the text implicitly envisages a reader whose role as addressee the text creates. The distinctions between these three readers may, paradoxically, be clearer if we observe Pietzcker confusing them. "Das Gedicht ist also auf die Aktivität des Lesers angewiesen, es konstituiert sich im Bezug auf ihn und muß von hierher verstanden werden," he rightly says (this is true of all literary texts, of course), but he then demonstrates the confusion encountered so frequently in German critics: "Das bringt der Interpretation Schwierigkeiten, denn die Aktivität des Lesers ist nicht objektiv zu erfassen, nicht alle Leser verhalten sich gleich. Dennoch läßt sich die von der Ballade angebotene Leserrolle rekonstruieren."[2] Here the first "Leser" referred to is, properly speaking, the ideal or implied reader; it is *his* "Leserrolle" that must be reconstructed (actually, constructed). The "Leser" in "alle Leser" on the other hand clearly means the *actual* readers, who have nothing to do with Pietzcker's argument. This is confusion enough, but Pietzcker goes on to introduce a further mixup, equating the "Leserrolle" with the "Bürgerinnen, die im Gegensatz zu Marie 'in saubern Wochenbetten gebären,'" thus confusing implied reader with fictive reader. The real appeal in stanza 9 is not to the well-to-do bourgeois ladies—they are the characterized readers, and appeals to these are never genuine—but to the implied reader for whom these women are part of the poem. Our reaction to them is, if anything, hostile. For one thing the poem imputes to them at least the likelihood of condemnation of Marie (otherwise why the plea to them?) and sets up a contrast between the appalling circumstances of the servant girl and the comfortable ease of the middle class who sleep and give birth "in saubern Betten." In particular, once the poem makes clear the class relationships between these two in stanza 4 and especially stanza 5 ("Man holte sie noch einmal, als sie lag: / Schnee war gefallen, und sie mußte kehren / Das ging bis elf. Es war ein langer Tag.") and spells out the girl's human and social status in stanza 7 with the single line "Weil es in den Gesindabort hereinschnein kann," we are committed to a response of antagonism to such ladies and their class in the measure that our sympathy goes out to the wretched Marie.

Let us be clear: it is quite possible that among the actual readers of this poem there have been, or are, women of the kind addressed in the final stanza. They may respond to this text in a variety of ways, ranging from sympathy for Marie, and perhaps shame for their own comfort, to indignant rejection of a slut who got what she deserved. Only a properly conducted investigation by means of interviews, questionnaires, and the like would determine this with any degree of certainty. Carl Pietzcker's assertion that "Die Ballade sucht das gesicherte Selbstverständnis 'des Lesers' [his quotation marks] zu erschüttern" is valid if one identifies, as Pietzcker does, the characterized reader (the women addressed in stanza 9) with the actual reader.[3] But the rhetorical force of the poem is to win the support of the implied reader against the characterized reader.

My comments on the three kinds of reader in *Von der Kindesmörderin Marie Farrar* are based on reader-response theory, which is directed to the way literary texts demand from the reader a certain reading behavior. Analyzing the act of communication from author to reader in this way is not meant to establish facts or set up theories about the behavior of real readers or reading publics. That is a branch of the sociology of literature and as such other methods and theories—sociological, historical, and statistical—are appropriate to it. Reader-response criticism is rather concerned with the relationship embodied in the text between an author and an implicit reader, with the aesthetic and rhetorical means employed by an author to elicit certain responses from or initiate certain relationships with a posited *ideal, intended, fictive,* or *implied* reader. All these terms have been used, some of them not very clearly, to mean the same thing, namely the *receiver* for whom the message in the text is intended. This receiver, for whom I prefer the term *implied reader*, is a *construct* used in analysis and interpretation, in the same way that Wayne Booth's *implied author* (*The Rhetoric of Fiction*) is a construct that enables us to talk about the nature of the authorial *voice* or *role*. Booth's critical procedure and the terminology associated with it allowed us to look at the authorial presence in a more sophisticated and differentiated way than the comparatively crude New Critical distinction between *author* and *persona* had permitted. Basing themselves partly on Booth's insights, recent critics in Germany and North America have built up a body of theory aimed at elucidating how literary texts (though not only these) suggest to the reader, indeed force upon him, a certain reading behavior, a response to the text that includes a response to a consciously or unconsciously perceived authorial presence; and *mutatis mutandis* how the author's picture of the reader he aims at helps to shape and structure what he writes.

Unfortunately, this body of theory is marked by some terminological confusion and by basic disagreements (not always realized) between German and North American writing on the subject. The North American Germanist W. Daniel Wilson has done an excellent job of sorting out these confusions and disagreements, and in the process makes his own forceful contribution to reader-response theory.[4] I shall quote him at some length in what follows.

Though the distinction between actual author and implied author is clear enough (between, say, the citizen and Gerichtsrat E. T. A. Hoffmann and the author in *Der Goldene Topf*), the same kind of distinction between different sorts of readers is not so readily grasped, though it is crucial. Whereas we can say "Hoffmann" in an interpretation of *Der Goldene Topf* and be understood to mean not the person but the author as he appears to us, speaks to us, is present for us in that tale, we should not say "the reader" without making it clear which of three readers we mean. The actual reader, like the actual author, can be left aside from our discussion: he is the subject of sociological or historical study. Of properly interpretive interest is what the Germans call the *fiktiver Leser* and English-language criticism calls *fictive* or *characterized* reader. Wilson illustrates what is meant by this term by quoting a classic passage from *Tristram Shandy*: "—How could you, Madam, be so inattentive in reading the last chapter? I told you in it, *That my mother was not a papist*.—Papist! You told me no such thing, Sir.—Madam, I beg leave to repeat it over again, That I told you as plain, at least, as words, by direct inference, could tell you such a thing.—Then, Sir, I must have missed a page" (47–48). Wilson comments:

> Even when readers do not speak up, they belong to the same basic type as long as they are characterized in some way in the text. Even such a comparatively innocent address as to "the gentle reader" serves to characterize a reader, to fix a sociological status for him or her. We shall also see that the reader need not be referred to directly in order to be characterized. That this figure is a fictional creation of the author (much as the characters are) rather than a real reader is obvious enough.[5]

Since *fictive* is rather too broad a term, Wilson proposes *characterized* reader to denote this kind of reader who exists as a character in the text.

A more difficult reader to describe is the abstract reader associated with the *Leserrolle* or reader's role and called by Wolfgang Iser, the leading German reader-response theorist, the *implied reader* in analogy to Booth's *implied author*. Wilson defines this construct as "the behavior, attitudes, and background—presupposed or defined, usually indirectly, in the text itself—necessary for a proper understanding of the text. This idealized reader may be consciously or unconsciously conceived by the author, but he or she exists in every work, since almost every 'message' presupposes a certain kind of recipient and implicitly defines him or her to some extent."[6] In texts where an *I* overtly addresses a reader, we must beware of accepting this reader too readily as the implied reader and the message to him as the intended message to *us*. German reader-response criticism has tended to confuse the fictive or characterized reader and the implied reader (or *intended reader*, as some critics, for example Erwin Wolff, call him).[7] Yet it is vital that they be kept apart. This is relatively simple with those direct addresses to a reader who has the status effectively of a character in the text. At least, one would think it is a simple matter. Wolff, however, discussing the passage from *Tristram Shandy* quoted before, refers to "Madam" as the *intended* reader, that is, the reader for whom the novel, or this bit of it, is intended. This is plainly not so. Madam, directly addressed here by the author, is not the same as the *implicit* reader here. The intended or implied reader is not at all addressed by the author's remonstrations; he is rather an amused onlooker who is likely to regard Madam as a rather dim-witted character. This reader is the recipient of the author's *message*; he has entered into a familiar relationship with the author. It is for him that the author writes. To imagine, as Wolff does, that he writes for a readership represented by "Madam" is to fundamentally mistake what Sterne is doing.

Wilson also demonstrates, taking Wolfgang Iser to task, how careful we ought to be about identifying the "reader" overtly addressed in the text with the implied reader, the reader the author wants for his work. Iser and his German colleagues, and Wilson in his discussion of them, use examples from the English novel, but here is a typical passage from E. T. A. Hoffmann. After the three letters that constitute the first part of *Der Sandmann*, we are confronted with the following:

> Seltsamer und wunderlicher kann nichts erfunden werden, als dasjenige ist, was sich mit meinem armen Freunde, dem jungen Studenten Nathanael, zugetragen, und was ich dir, günstiger Leser, zu erzählen unternommen. Hast du, Geneigtester! wohl jemals etwas erlebt, das deine Brust, Sinn und Gedanken ganz und gar erfüllte, alles andere daraus verdrängend? Es gärte und kochte in dir, zur siedenden Glut entzündet, sprang das Blut durch die Adern und färbte höher deine Wangen. Dein Blick war so seltsam, als wolle er Gestalten, keinem andern Auge sichtbar, im leeren Raum erfassen, und die Rede zerfloß in dunkle Seufzer. Da frugen dich die Freunde: "Wie ist Ihnen, Verehrter?—

Was haben Sie, Teurer?" Und nun wolltest du das innere Gebilde mit allen glühenden Farben und Schatten und Lichtern aussprechen und mühtest dich ab, Worte zu finden, um nur anzufangen. Aber es war dir, als müßtest du nun gleich im ersten Wort alles Wunderbare, Herrliche, Entsetzliche, Lustige, Grauenhafte, das sich zugetragen, recht zusammengreifen, so daß es wie ein elektrischer Schlag alle treffe. Doch jedes Wort, alles, was Rede vermag, schien dir farblos und frostig und tot? . . .

Mich hat, wie ich es dir, geneigter Leser! gestehen muß, eigentlich niemand nach der Geschichte des jungen Nathanael gefragt; du weißt ja aber wohl, daß ich zu dem wunderlichen Geschlechte der Autoren gehöre, denen, tragen sie etwas so in sich, wie ich es vorhin beschrieben, so zumute wird, als frage jeder, der in ihre Nähe kommt, und nebenher auch wohl noch die ganze Welt: "Was ist es denn? Erzählen Sie, Liebster!"—So trieb es mich denn gar gewaltig, von Nathanaels verhängnisvollem Leben zu dir zu sprechen. Das Wunderbare, Seltsame davon erfüllte meine ganze Seele, aber eben deshalb und weil ich dich, o mein Leser, gleich geneigt machen mußte, Wunderliches zu ertragen, welches nichts Geringes ist, quälte ich mich ab, Nathanaels Geschichte, bedeutend—originell, ergreifend, anzufangen: "Es war einmal!"—der schönste Anfang jeder Erzählung, zu nüchtern!—"In der kleinen Provinzialstadt S. lebte"—etwas besser, wenigstens ausholend zum Klimax.—Oder gleich medias in res: " 'Scher er sich zum Teufel', rief, Wut und Entsetzen im wilden Blick, der Student Nathanael, als der Wetterglashändler Giuseppe Coppola"—Das hatte ich in der Tat schon aufgeschrieben, als ich in dem wilden Blick des Studenten Nathanael etwas Possierliches zu verspüren glaubte; die Geschichte ist aber gar nicht spaßhaft. Mit kam keine Rede in den Sinn, die nur im mindesten etwas von dem Farbenglanz des inneren Bildes abzuspiegeln schien. Ich beschloß, gar nicht anzufangen. Nimm, geneigter Leser! die drei Briefe, welche Freund Lothar mir gütigst mitteilte, für den Umriß des Gebildes, in das ich nun erzählend immer mehr und mehr Farbe hineinzutragen mich bemühen werde.

(Der Sandmann, 343–44)

Do we feel ourselves to be directly addressed by the author here, identifying with the "günstiger Leser" of the text? I suggest that on the whole we do not. Standing aside and watching with amusement Hoffmann's game with what we perceive as a characterized reader (who is in this case, as in most, being appealed to by the author), we react rather with a knowing smile to a transparent though clever piece of Romantic irony. We (the implied readers) are not fooled: we see the author's game; we are moreover aware that we are *expected* to see it, and we delight in the inventiveness and playfulness of a fine writer.

Three further points need to be made about the implied reader. First, for all practical purposes, my perception of the role this reader is urged by the text to take up, of the reading behavior the text attempts to elicit from him, is part of *my* interpretation, *my* understanding of the text. (Wilson: "We must not claim that our interpretation of the implied reader is anything more than our interpretation.")[8] The implied reader is not an objective presence in the text but merely a construct, a device to aid interpretation. He is nothing but the interpreter's understanding of the reading role urged upon him by the text. This statement is apt to produce bewilderment or impatience in *my* reader. What has perhaps been taken as an objectively present element in the text now turns out to be just another kind of interpretive method, leading to a result that is no more than the subjective understanding of the interpreter. But then this is true of any reading of a text, no matter how solidly it is based on sound method and coherent and consistent principles. The latter merely act as constraints on interpretation, providing a certain guarantee against undisciplined or willful (mis)reading. All that is being claimed for reader-response theory is that, at a fairly early stage in the process of interpretation, it is a very useful tool, and sometimes an indispensable one. It allows or compels the interpreter to bring into focus the communication pattern and communication relationships in a text, to ask who is talking to whom and to distinguish between overt and covert communication and between ostensible and actual messages. And though I have been talking here principally of the way a text suggests or demands a certain reading behavior from its implied reader, it is important to bear in mind the corollary that the author's notion or vision of his implied reader helps to fashion his text.

Further, the implied reader has little or no bearing on reading behavior understood as part of *Rezeptionsgeschichte* or of the sociology of literature in general. As Wilson says, "True *Rezeptionsgeschichte* is concerned with real, historical readers, not primarily with fictive readers. The fictive reader is a tool for interpreting a work, not—except very indirectly and unreliably—for sketching historical reading habits."[9] The only real, historical reader that the implied reader in any given text has anything to do with is the interpreter of that text, whoever he may be at any given moment.

Finally, whether or not I *accept* the reader role that I perceive is demanded of me by a text depends on many factors, some of them aesthetic, some to do with ideological or moral views. I will not accept a reading stance that involves acquiescence in views and actions repugnant to me, no matter how "artistically" this acquiescence is sought. To posit an extreme example: in the case of a text that describes the mass murder of members of an ethnic group in a way that urges my approval, I will perceive the role assigned to me but not accept it. Similarly, a piece of kitsch that demands of me trivially sentimental reactions will fail to convince me that I *should* react this way. My refusal to acquiesce in the demands of the text then constitutes a critical rejection.

Though these hypothetical cases are obvious, the question of conforming to the reader role demanded by the text is a complex one. In general we must not see this role as binding or in any way normative. The implied reader is determined through analysis of the text, in particular the analysis of its communicative and rhetorical strategies. After that, it is up to the interpreter to accept or reject, or partially accept for that matter, the reader role called for. One such rejection occurs in chapter 5 of this book in connection with a famous poem from the *Buckower Elegien*. The dangers inherent in a normative attitude to the reader's role can be gauged from Lowrie Nelson's reading of Goethe's *Werther*. Nelson insists on the "duty of the reader to learn and fictively embrace the code of feeling in any work of any age by the contractual exercise of his historical imagination."[10] Quite apart from ignoring the sound principles of literary hermeneutics, the normative idea of reader role implied in this demand leads Nelson to direct us to identify with the "reader" addressed by the fictive editor of *Werther* in his prefatory remarks: "Und du gute Seele, die du eben den Drang fühlst wie er [Werther], schöpfe Trost aus seinem Leiden, und laß das Büchlein deinen Freund sein, wenn du aus Geschick oder eigener Schuld keinen nähern finden kannst"(p. 7). But the "gute Seele" is precisely a *characterized reader*, and we no more identify with him/her than we do with Hoffmann's *geneigter Leser*. The fictive editor may direct this characterized reader to identify with Werther, but numerous passages in the novel proper implicitly direct *us* to dissociate ourselves from Werther, at least to the extent of being able to see his extravagant and sometimes even ridiculous aspects. Had Nelson—and this case can stand for many similar misreadings—allowed the *text* to determine his perception of the reader addressed in the passage above, he would have seen that this reader is a characterized reader and that the reader role (for the implied reader) involves some distancing from him.

Reader-response criticism takes seriously the fact that literature is communication. Even the most monologic of writers, even those who claim not to write for anyone but themselves (they often claim this in published essays or interviews about their published work), write what they write as communication. Even writers who break all the rules of communication, making it impossible to understand them, are communicating something—the arbitrariness of communication rules, or the impossibility of really communicating, for example. This does not mean that the aspect of texts as communication is primary, or is to be privileged in some way within literary studies. As I emphasized in the Introduction, the only reason reader-response theory is used so extensively in these studies of Brecht's poetry is that it is suggested as appropriate by the subject matter itself: poems addressing a reader or written in the first person in a way that immediately establishes purposive communication with the reader. Nor does my use of reader-response approaches imply their exclusivity. Many methods, many critical principles, are appropriate to Brecht's writings, and several of them are used in this book. The emphasis on poetry as communication is only one emphasis.

In the case of Brecht, this view of literature as communication scarcely seems to need defending. He is always presenting and representing himself very openly, in an obvious attempt to influence his audience in various ways. He is the very model of the poet openly seeking dialogue. And yet this very openness contains pitfalls for the critic. There is a danger that, beguiled by his frankness, we may become blind to structures in the text that create ambiguities, extra dimensions and ironies that make nonsense of the frankness. Precisely in the case of those poems written in the first person or otherwise establishing contact directly or indirectly with a reader, we do well to exercise both caution and skepticism. We should not of course be over eager to declare every statement in such poetry as fiction and only fiction. The degree of overlap in a first-person poem between poem statement and fact may range from a hundred percent (though this is rare) to nil (complete fantasy). It is not important, however, to establish the exact degree of agreement. What is the point of knowing that the account of a poet's life offered in poem X accords 75 percent with the "facts"? What is important is the interplay between a writer's experience, physical and mental, and his art. Even the complete fantasy tells us something about the writer, something about how he renders thoughts and feelings into words and sentences.

Likewise, it would be absurd to assume that every address to a reader in a literary text is a ploy or gambit masking some ulterior motive. All we must insist on is the rhetorical nature of all such communication and the *possibility* of its being a strategy involving more than one kind of message and more than one kind of reader. In Brecht's work all the above possibilities are present, and it is one of the major tasks of the critic to sort these out. Sometimes the task is difficult. There are poems, some of them famous, where the nature of the communication with the reader is hard to pinpoint (harder than most Brecht criticism allows) and where the meaning is therefore elusive. These poems are not confined to Brecht's exile or later years, when the problem of his self-understanding is perhaps more visible. Even in his twenties he was writing poetry whose message, to speak semiotically, is difficult to decipher—not because of the obscurity of the content, but because the tone of the poet's voice, and the stance he adopts vis-à-vis the reader, are difficult to determine. The following, for example, may be Brecht's greatest love poem, or no love poem at all:

ERINNERUNG AN DIE MARIE A.

An jenem Tag im blauen Mond September
Still unter einem jungen Pflaumenbaum
Da hielt ich sie, die stille bleiche Liebe
In meinem Arm wie einen holden Traum.
Und über uns im schönen Sommerhimmel
War eine Wolke, die ich lange sah
Sie war sehr weiß und ungeheuer oben
Und als ich aufsah, war sie nimmer da.

Seit jenem Tag sind viele, viele Monde
Geschwommen still hinunter und vorbei.
Die Pflaumenbäume sind wohl abgehauen
Und fragst du mich, was mit der Liebe sei?
So sag ich dir: ich kann mich nicht erinnern
Und doch, gewiß, ich weiß schon, was du meinst.
Doch ihr Gesicht, das weiß ich wirklich nimmer
Ich weiß nur mehr: ich küßte es dereinst.

Und auch den Kuß, ich hätt ihn längst vergessen
Wenn nicht die Wolke dagewesen wär
Die weiß ich noch und werd ich immer wissen

Sie war sehr weiß und kam von oben her.
Die Pflaumenbäume blühn vielleicht noch immer
Und jene Frau hat jetzt vielleicht das siebte Kind
Doch jene Wolke blühte nur Minuten
Und als ich aufsah, schwand sie schon im Wind.

(GW, 4:232)

Unlike most of the later love poems associated principally with Margarete Steffin and Ruth Berlau, but also unlike the early, mostly playful poems to "Bi" Banholzer, which are generally written out of some immediate experience, this poem is an "Erinnerung," a remembering of a past love. The poem was written, according to Brecht's note beneath the manuscript in his notebook, on 21 February 1920 "abends 7h im Zug nach Berlin." But the composition may well predate this, or have begun earlier. This seems likely since the manuscript is complete and unamended.

The poem is a recollection of an earlier event. But it is a recollection that translates a possibly real occurrence with a possibly real girl into the fictive world of poetry. The standpoint taken up by the poet is that of an older man looking back to an occurrence long ago that, quite reasonably, he recalls only imperfectly. It matters little if, as seems highly likely, the "Marie A." of the title was Marie Rose Amann,[11] whom Brecht met and briefly pursued in Augsburg in 1916 when he was eighteen and she fifteen. The point is that a poet of at the most twenty-two years of age expands four or so years into "viele viele Monde," in the course of which "jene Frau hat jetzt vielleicht das siebte Kind."

But if the implied author is a man of considerable years musing on an event deep in his past, what role does the poem suggest to or demand of the reader? Brecht addresses us directly, in quite an unprepared fashion, at precisely that point of the poem—halfway through the second stanza—where the question is likely to suggest itself, What happened to the girl, how did the affair turn out? The poet anticipates the question only to disappoint the questioner with his reply. But a subtle shift has taken place here. The moment the poet spells out our half-formed question, we (the implied readers) retreat from it, dissociate ourselves from it, for we recognize that this question is taken out of the mouth of a *characterized reader*. We will perhaps dissociate ourselves from this reader all the more readily if we suspect that the poet's answer to the question is exposing it as naive, or sentimental. It may be that this "Und doch, gewiß, ich weiß schon, was du meinst" is an amused waving away by the poet of the standard response to such poems, that he is saying, "Yes, I know what you were expecting, but life and love and memory are not like that, are they?" But we cannot be sure of this. It is a legitimate question to want to ask, particularly since the structure of the poem is the familiar and conventional one, it would seem, of recollection of a past love, followed by a musing on how long ago it all was, followed by—we expect—disclosure of what became of the two youthful lovers. Brecht sets up this conventional structure, only to undercut it, transform it, and relativize it, as so often in the *Hauspostille* poems.

Sure that we have responded legitimately to the poem's structure and the set of expectations it raises, but made uncertain by the poet's short-circuiting of these expectations, we are compelled to occupy a wavering position of response, halfway between the conventional love poem and the ironic, even cynical undercutting of it. We are further compelled to adopt this wavering, ambiguous reading position by the poem's diction, tone, and images, which likewise suggest now the nostalgic poem of recall, now its send-up. After the first six lines the reader is already in the middle of this problem of how to respond to the poem. The title gives us a clear pointer to the familiar genre of lyrical recollection, and the first two lines of the poem bear out the expectations that this title engenders: a particular day is conjured up, a season, a tree. The language is entirely characteristic of Brecht's lyrical mode, richly suggestive yet simple ("Im blauen Mond September"). Though the experienced reader may think that this is a touch too idyllic for the young Brecht, the diction and images give no hint of parody. The "blue moon," the full late summer, Brecht's favored plum tree, are apparently straightforward elements of a poignant memory. The following two lines, however, clearly bear the stamp of parody. We now see that the "still" of line two was after all a signal of the tongue in the cheek (a word with altogether too many associations with that traditional verse favored by the sentimental *Bürger*). Certainly "stille bleiche Liebe" is too much, and any lingering doubts are dispelled by the "holden Traum" of line 4. *Hold* can only be used parodistically by Brecht: a word from the classic-romantic golden years of verse, since degenerated through epigonic overuse to the level of kitsch.

Were this poem wholly and solely a parody, however, we would now have a heightening of parodic effects, an extension of the range of target material, a general intensification of parody with its ridiculing and unmasking function. This does not happen. Instead, we are returned to a neutral, straightforward description, which is so plain as to be almost bare: "war eine Wolke," not *schwebte*, or some more "poetic" verb, and "die ich lange sah"—no more than basic German. This is continued in the final two lines of the stanza. The language is spare. Only "ungeheuer," with its connotations in Brecht's early work of freedom, expansiveness, and exhilaration, rises above a very basic diction made folksy and homely by the South German "nimmer."

There is thus a tension in this first stanza between what I have called Brecht's new lyricism and an obvious parody of outdated, cheapened forms and phrases. The main aim is not parody, as we have seen from the initial stanza; and the rest of the poem bears this out. The parody in any case might be self-deprecatory—Brecht sardonically, even embarrassedly, offsetting his genuine lyrical evocation with a couple of lines that show us the other side of lyrically poignant reminiscence: sentimental kitsch. This reading may be supported by the subtitle "Sentimentales Lied Nr. 1004" that appears on the manuscript, and especially by the crass quotation from *Faust* as a postscript: "Im Zustand der gefüllten Samenblase sieht der Mann in jedem Weib Aphrodite."

This unresolved mixture of the lyrically poignant and the parody of sentimentality is not carried on as such. But the uncertainty in the reader's response is maintained through to the end of the poem. The beginning of stanza 2 is characterized by a repetition of the moon image in an even more striking lyrical metaphor. This resumption of the lyrical mode coincides with the poem's movement to the second stage of the reminiscence structure, the musing on the passing of time and the changes this brings. It is, however, immediately followed by a line that undercuts and takes back some of this lyricism—not in the blatant manner of lines 3 and 4 of stanza 1, but unmistakably nonetheless, through the mundane nature of the speculation. Again the expectation of the reader is important at this point. After the first two lines of stanza 2 he expects, after "Die Pflaumenbäume" of line 3, something like "sind verdorrt" or even, unpoetically enough, "sind gestorben." This would be in tune with the theme of evanescence and time passing, and in keeping with the tone of the preceding two lines. But "abgehauen" is altogether too mundane and too crude.

This is the point then at which the anticipation of the reader's question, previously discussed, occurs. In a sense the admission of *non*recall is not surprising, given the foregoing with its multiple confounding of the reader's expectations. Nevertheless, in a poem with the title *Erinnerung an die Marie A.* the admission that the poet precisely *cannot* remember Marie A., but only the kiss—and even that only because of a memory association with a cloud—catches the reader off balance. (It is an example of that renewal through the breaking of expectation, the superseding of horizon, that Hans Robert Jauß associates with major literary works.) In these circumstances the reader wonders whether the abbreviation of Marie's last name is a sign not so much of the poet's delicacy as of his imperfect memory.

The admission of nonrecall itself happens gradually, in stages. After the statement "ich kann mich nicht erinnern" comes the qualification that, although the face is no longer recalled, the kiss is. That is, the experience of love is remembered, though its object is not. But this is then further qualified: the kiss is an incidental memory; it is really the cloud that occupies the central place, the cloud around which the memory congeals. The way is now open for the fairly obvious association of the white cloud with the transience of human experience, but before this is done there is a last bringing together of girl and cloud to produce a highly ambiguous tribute to the beauty of the moment. The poet takes back his speculation of the second stanza and now presumes the opposite: "Die Pflaumenbäume blühn vielleicht noch immer." In the second stanza the chopping down of the plum trees had been associated with the loss of love in the sense of time having passed on. But by the third stanza the poet, reconstructing the memory, reveals that it is the *cloud* upon which everything hinges ("Wenn nicht die Wolke dagewesen wär"). The plum trees, and the girl, can be presumed to have gone on existing; only that transitory experience of love has gone forever. This having been recognized, however, the plum trees and the girl—she now must be a woman—are uninteresting. What has happened to them is the subject of indifferent speculation ("vielleicht" as against the "wohl" of the earlier, mistakenly melancholic supposition) and a careless flippancy about "jene Frau" and her many children. The poet's interest, and his nostalgia, are completely transferred to the cloud; and our attention is transferred to it at the end also, leaving us with the final image of the delicate, short-lived cloud dissipated by the wind.

Brecht's "love poem" thus embodies two major retreats or withdrawals from the normal love poem. The first of these, the admission that it is only the experience of love, not the beloved, that the poet remembers ("Ich weiß nur mehr: ich küßte es dereinst") is relatively easy to accept. We can accommodate it by reference to other poems we know that concern the beauty not so much of the beloved as of love itself. The notion that poets and lovers are frequently infatuated with love and love poetry rather than, strictly speaking, with a beloved is familiar enough. But the second amendment to the conventional love poem of recollection is another matter—namely, the revelation that actually it is not even the experience of love that the poet feels urged to write about but the transience of this experience. The beauty he writes of is the beauty of evanescence. The recollection of love is so poignant and intense *because of* its fleeting nature. Conventional attempts to glorify the girl and pay her homage are rejected and mocked by Brecht as not genuine, as dishonest, as self-delusion. All such attempts result in is the inauthentic language of "stille bleiche Liebe" and "holden Traum." By contrast the genuine language of love's memory, though it may spell out unpalatable facts, is honest and simple: the cloud is described in utterly plain terms whose spareness is a guarantee of their seriousness.

Brecht's "sentimental song" is thus sentimental only in a limited sense. The poem certainly represents, in the context of the *Hauspostille*, a gentle exception, surrounded as it is by wild ballads telling of anarchic lifestyles and violent events. But its sentimentality is subtly controlled, undercut by the self-consciousness of the poet Brecht. The poem shifts frequently and subtly, from poignant lyricism to mocking parody, from apparent insensitivity to gentle delicacy of feeling. Above all, the poem's relationship to the reader is difficult to pinpoint, because the expectations he brings to the text through its title and its beginning are first thwarted, then transferred, and because he is not sure in what relationship he stands to the "du" addressed in the second stanza. Is this "du" being gently derided or genuinely appealed to? Perhaps both? This uncertainty on the reader's part—or, in the terminology of reader-response theory, in the role created for the (implied) reader by the poem—makes *Erinnerung an die Marie A.* an enigmatic text, simultaneously love poem and its deflation.

There are other examples of such ambiguity in the poetry of Brecht, texts where the reader's role is difficult to determine and the movement of the poem's rhetoric elusive. Far from detracting from the usefulness of reader-response theory, these difficult cases draw attention to the crucial part played in our reception and interpretation of a poem by the unique communication set up between author and reader—implied author, that is, because it is his "voice" that speaks to us, and implied reader, because it is his role that helps determine the text and its interpretation. It ought to be clear that the failure to distinguish among the three kinds of readers—characterized (*fiktiv*), implied (*implizit* or *intendiert*), and actual—leads to misunderstandings and misreadings of literary texts, since our apprehension of both the rhetorical structure and the function of a text depends largely on an accurate appraisal of the interrelationships between actual author, implied author, persona (*Rolle*), actual reader, characterized reader, and implied reader.

That these interrelationships can be complex and subtle to the point of ambiguity we have already seen and shall see again. Unfortunately, many critics who write on Brecht are prone to forget the rhetorical nature of all literary expression—no doubt because the poet Brecht seems so different from the usual kind of lyric poet whose writing we know we have to understand in terms of personae, voices, rhetorical figures and stratagems, and so on. German critics in particular are strongly aware of the gap between Brecht on the one hand and the exponents of the *lyrisches Ich* on the other. Brecht, spurning what he saw as the self-indulgent subjectivism, the soul-baring, the narcissistic self-exploration of most lyric poetry, appeared to offer a practical, down-to-earth alternative, a poetry where sophistication gave way to plain speaking and the intense obscurities of the *lyrisches Ich* were replaced by a clearly discernible *Gedichteschreiber* honestly addressing his readers. But if anything it is this kind of poetry that should alert us to the rhetorical structure of literary discourse. It is precisely with poems where the writer appears before us and lays his cards on the table that we need to pay close attention to what is taking place in the act of communication between authors and readers—*plural*, since there is more than one kind of each.

In making these remarks, I do not wish to deny the possibility of correspondence between these poem-utterances and reality, an identity between the actual Bert Brecht and the *I* of the poem; I merely insist on the distinction in principle between historical author and the rhetorical construct that constitutes the *I*. After that we can look at correspondences. The great bulk of writing on Brecht either blurs the distinction or avoids it and takes the correspondences for granted.

2. Nihilism, Anarchism, and Role-Playing: The Young Man from Augsburg

Ever since Martin Esslin's *Brecht: A Choice of Evils* appeared in 1959, it has been common, almost normal, to view Brecht's early period—the period of *Baal, Trommeln in der Nacht, Im Dickicht der Städte*, and the *Hauspostille*—as a time of nihilism and anarchism. This virtual unanimity about a writer whose life and work are the subject of frequently acrimonious debate is remarkable. The unanimity is perhaps due, however, less to the clearness of the case than to the disinclination of Brecht critics to subject this view to careful scrutiny. What we know of Brecht's early years in Augsburg, and the early work itself, will in my judgment not bear this interpretation, certainly not in the schematic and one-sided form in which it has been put forward.

The theory of the young anarchist and nihilist Brecht, shared by critics who otherwise agree on little, is fundamentally influenced by the need to explain Brecht's transition to Marxism in the late 1920s. Such events cry out for a demonstration of causes; and the causes, it is thought, are to be sought in the life and career of Brecht up to that point: here the seeds of later developments must lie. The young Brecht's anarchism, vitalism, and nihilism seem to offer the kind of basis from which his adoption of Marxism might satisfactorily be explained. Since these are negative, unproductive, and potentially self-destructive positions, the theory runs, the young Brecht was ripe for a worldview characterized by system, order, and logic. In addition, the intellectual challenge of Marxism was attractive to a mind like Brecht's.

At this point critical paths diverge. Very different emphases and values are given to this development in Brecht. These values are determined largely by political positions. Esslin reads Brecht's embracing of Marxism—his title indicates this at the outset—as a self-rescue operation, the grasping for an orderly worldview that will save him from despair and self-destruction: "For the anarchist Brecht, to whom the world had appeared without sense or purpose, and the individual so completely alone . . . the discovery of this great and simple pattern and purpose in history [the historical conception of Marxism] must have come as a tremendous relief."[1] Esslin also refers to

> the aesthetic roots of Brecht's furious negation of the existing order of things. He could not endure the ugliness and vulgarity of patriotic cant, the witlessness of respectable society, and the loathsome cynicism of the *nouveaux riches*. As it was clear that his sensitivity was not only aesthetic. He also was basically a puritan and idealist. When this moral sensitivity was shattered by the horrors of war and the post-war era, it turned into a violent denial of all values. But in the long run so purely destructive and negative an attitude was bound to lead to disaster. Brecht needed a new core of positive belief.
>
> Marxism, as Brecht understood it, provided such a framework: it allowed all these negative attitudes to crystallize into a positive pattern. And what was even more important to Brecht, it was aesthetically satisfying.[2]

It is above all the assertion that Brecht was attracted to Marxism for aesthetic reasons, and the suggestion of Brecht's desperation in embracing it, that has riled critics on the Left. Marxism as a security blanket is not an image calculated to please Marxist critics, and they have waged war on Esslin's views ever since. For them the truth is rather that Brecht, once he abandoned his futile asocial and nihilistic attitudes, adopted the only philosophy that offered a scientific and comprehensive explanation of man in society.[3] These two views, Esslin's and the Marxists', can be seen as the opposite points of a scale along which other positions, other variations, are located. But the points are in fact not so different from each other, and it is the common ground they share that this chapter will question.

This common ground is the insistence on the young Brecht's anarchism and nihilism either as a defense mechanism erected by an endangered personality or at any rate as a dead end from which Marxism provided the escape. It will be the argument of this and to some extent the following chapter that neither part of this can be sustained very strongly: that the Brecht of the Augsburg period led an existence characterized more by satisfaction than by frustration, and that Marxism is to be seen in connection not with the youth's supposedly unstable and self-destructive worldview but with the young man's later experiences in the metropolis of Berlin, beginning in the winter of 1921–22. It was in this intermediate stage of Brecht's life, the time between his initial encounter with Berlin at the beginning of the 1920s and his intense involvement with Marxism-Leninism in the latter years of the decade, that the young man from Augsburg was confronted by serious and immediate questions of a personal and social nature, to which ultimately his reading of the Marxist classics provided answers. This is the view presented twenty years ago by Klaus Schuhmann.[4] Since then, critical preoccupation with Brecht's conversion to Marxism in the later 1920s on the one hand, combined with the high profile of the Augsburg poetry on the other, has produced a lumping together of all Brecht's work prior to his Marxism, and an elision so to speak of those four to five years after his initial attempt to gain a toehold in Berlin.[5]

Even Schuhmann does not entirely avoid the danger of viewing all Brecht's work prior to the unmistakable products of his Marxism as one package. Schuhmann gives due weight to the city poems of the mid-1920s, seeing here the first movement by Brecht towards social analysis and political consciousness and stressing the completely different nature of this poetry from the Augsburg work. Though Schuhmann's own orthodox Marxist position leads him to under-assess the Augsburg poetry—he devotes to it only twenty pages of a three-hundred-page book restricted to the poetry up to 1933—he is right in paying close attention to the period in Berlin *before* Brecht's Marxism. But the distinction Schuhmann properly makes between this period and the Augsburg work is almost taken back again when he comments: "Im Jahre 1926 beendete Bertolt Brecht die Arbeit am Parabelstück *Mann ist Mann*. Noch im September fand am Darmstädter Theater die Uraufführung statt. Damit war zugleich das Finalstadium der ersten Schaffensperiode des Stückeschreibers erreicht."[6] The "first period" of Brecht's work is thus identified as everything prior to his Marxism, say up to 1926. This has the effect of lending to this initial period a continuity that as Schuhmann himself demonstrates does not exist. Part of the problem here is with the terminology. If it is to mean anything useful, the term "early Brecht" should be used for the period before Berlin (i.e., before 1922). But the understandable focus on Brecht's espousal of Marxism has meant that the "early Brecht" has come to be synonymous with the pre-Marxist Brecht.

In this process the delayed publication of the *Hauspostille* plays a contributing role. Looked at in terms of its date of appearance, 1927, the *Hauspostille* seems to bring to an end an era just in time for the new era of the Marxist Brecht to begin. But Brecht had been involved in preparation for the *Hauspostille's* publication since 1922, and if we set aside the *Mahagonny* songs—a late addition—virtually all the poems in it had been written by that year. The collection does mark the end of an era—precisely the Augsburg era, the true early period of

Brecht. The *Hauspostille* gives us the essence of the *pre-Berlin* Brecht, with one crucial exception to which we shall return in the next chapter.

In between the *Hauspostille* poems and Brecht's intensive reading of Marxism-Leninism were some five years during which Brecht left Augsburg, the first time temporarily, the second time for good, and settled in Berlin. This was the time of the big city poems that document the impact of the fast-moving, hard-living German metropolis on the young man from the southern provinces. As the next chapter will attempt to show in detail, *this* was the first watershed in Brecht's life, because it closed off forever the boyhood sphere of Augsburg and confronted the young writer with the big wide world. Unlike the experiences described by the Augsburg work, which tended to be either imagined, vicarious, or comfortably provincial, the big wide world was uncomfortably real, with hard edges. It is this harsh Berlin reality, not the supposed psychological or existential sufferings of the Augsburg Brecht, that we must connect with his espousal of Marxism.

The thesis that the nihilism and anarchism of the young Brecht are dominant factors in a worldview that causes existential or psychological suffering has been put most strongly and in most detail by Peter Paul Schwarz and Carl Pietzcker, the authors, significantly, of two of the three major studies of Brecht's early poetry. Schwarz is less emphatic in his judgments and does not employ psychoanalytic techniques in his analyses, but the conclusions reached in his book *Brechts frühe Lyrik, 1914–1922* add up to a characterization of the young Brecht as a serious nihilist and anarchist-vitalist. These conclusions are already indicated in chapter and section headings such as "Stoische Bejahung des Nichts," "Existentielle Ausgesetztheit in eine Welt ohne Gott," and "Transzendente Orientierungslosigkeit und Untergang"; and Schwarz's summarizing remarks spell them out:

> Im genaueren Sinne ist es die Existenzproblematik des Menschen, die als zweiter, übergreifender Aussagezusammenhang neben der ironischen Struktur der frühen Lyrik Brechts in den Balladen der *Hauspostille* bedeutsam wird.
>
> ... daß "Nihilismus oder Existenzialismus" keine echten Alternativen der frühen Lyrik Brechts darstellen, sondern in einem ursächlichen Zusammenhang stehen. Denn die existentiell verbindlichen Aussagen der frühen Lyrik Brechts lassen sich mit ähnlicher Konsequenz auf die nihilistische Position zurück-

führen wie die ironisch unverbindlichen, so daß erst damit die alternativen Aussagemöglichkeiten der *Hauspostille* und das Zentrum des Werkzusammenhangs genau bezeichnet sind.[7]

My argument with Schwarz's valuable attempt to trace patterns and uncover relationships in the early poetry of Brecht is that his fixation on nihilism narrows his view, and that he takes the young Brecht's nihilism too seriously. Of this more later.

A greater objection must be made to the standpoint taken up by Carl Pietzcker. Pietzcker's book *Die Lyrik des jungen Brecht* is an ambitious attempt to approach the early poetry of Brecht from a theoretical and methodological position that combines Marx and Freud. In its general terms, this position is unexceptionable: "Methodische Voraussetzung der hier vorgelegten Studie ist die Uberzeugung, daß Gedichte individuelle gesellschaftliche Äußerungen sind, Äußerungen eines Individuums, das als solches gesellschaftlich ist und sich von seinem gesellschaftlichen Ort aus zur Gesellschaft verhält— gerade auch, wenn es sich von ihr abzuwenden sucht."[8] The next step, however, toward a more specific "existentielle Standortbestimmung"[9] of the young Brecht already contains problematic features that accompany, and sometimes bedevil, Pietzcker's whole analysis of the early poetry: "Die Studie geht von der These aus, daß Brechts frühe Lyrik vom Leiden an seiner Situation bestimmt ist, die er als allgemein und unveränderbar erfährt und nicht in ihren Ursachen begreift."[10] This is not a methodological statement but an interpretive one, and it is the cornerstone of Pietzcker's enterprise. Implicit in it is the assumption that the "anarchic nihilism" of his subtitle indicates a suffering, alienated response on the part of the young Brecht: "Seine Lyrik spiegelt die Entfremdung eines Autors, der dem Leiden an der Entfremdung dadurch zu entkommen sucht, daß er sich mit ihr einverstanden erklärt oder sich aus ihr hinausphantasiert in Abenteuer, Anarchismus, Untergang und eine Sinnlosigkeit, die ihm als Befreierin erscheint."[11]

I wish to put the contrary proposition that the anarchism, vitalism, and nihilism of the young Brecht are at least as much part of a role-playing process and an experimentation with various guises and identities as they are the reflection of existential distress. Pietzcker himself recognizes, in theory, this important aspect of the *dichtendes Ich*. The author, he says, speaking generally, "erprobt beim Dichten Möglichkeiten seiner selbst, treibt sie ins Extrem, distanziert sie und weist in bewußter, artistischer Gestaltung auf sie hin."[12] Pietzcker then goes on, however, to offer the reading of *Apfelböck oder Die Lilie auf dem Felde* that I described in my introduction, promptly forgetting this theoretical insight and embarking on a psychoanalytical interpretation of the poem that gets under way with the statement: "Brechts Phantasie vom Elternmord holt, wie die der Expressionisten auch, ihre Energie aus dem infantilen Wunsch, den Vater zu töten."[13] Locating the young Brecht in the same latitudes as the Expressionists is a precarious undertaking. Pietzcker—and within the framework of the German critical tradition outlined in the introduction, his case is typical—is a victim of doublethink. On the one hand he perceives the difference between a consciously distanced rendering of a theme and the totally involved pathos of the German Expressionists, but on the other he is unable to resist the underlying conviction that if a twenty-one-year-old poet writes about a young man murdering his parents, *no matter how he writes about it*, he must himself harbor similar desires.

Apfelböck is a good test case for the nature of Brecht's early work. We can perhaps best describe it and pin down its peculiarly enigmatic quality by reference to the Expressionists—but by contrastive reference. The only thing Brecht's poem has in common with Expressionism is its bare subject matter. From Sorge's *Der Bettler* (1912), Hasenclever's *Der Sohn* (1913), and Leonhard Frank's *Die Ursache* (1915) to Arnolt Bronnen's *Vatermord* (1920), German literature presents us with a series of Expressionist murders, near murders, and imaginary murders of fathers and father figures such as teachers. To this series belong Hanns Johst's *Der junge Mensch* (1916); Georg Kaiser's *Rektor Kleist* (1914); numerous autobiographical writings of Heym, Becher, and Benn; and Kafka's *Brief an den Vater* (1919).

It is characteristic of Brecht that *Apfelböck*, written in 1919, tells of events that are neither autobiographical nor the product of a melodramatic imagination. The poem is based on a real murder and trial in Munich in that year,[14] and it describes not so much the actual murder (that is done with in the first stanza) as the subsequent actions, or nonactions, of the young Jakob:

APFELBÖCK
ODER
DIE LILIE AUF DEM FELDE

1
In mildem Lichte Jakob Apfelböck
Erschlug den Vater und die Mutter sein
Und schloß sie beide in den Wäscheschrank
Und blieb im Hause übrig, er allein.

2
Es schwammen Wolken unterm Himmel hin
Und um sein Haus ging mild der Sommerwind
Und in dem Hause saß er selber drin
Vor sieben Tagen war es noch ein Kind.

3
Die Tage gingen und die Nacht ging auch
Und nichts war anders außer mancherlei
Bei seinen Eltern Jakob Apfelböck
Wartete einfach, komme was es sei.

4
Es bringt die Milchfrau noch die Milch ins Haus
Gerahmte Buttermilch, süß, fett und kühl.
Was er nicht trinkt, das schüttet Jakob aus
Denn Jakob Apfelböck trinkt nicht mehr viel.

5
Es bringt der Zeitungsmann die Zeitung noch
Mit schwerem Tritt ins Haus beim Abendlicht
Und wirft sie scheppernd in das Kastenloch
Doch Jakob Apfelböck, der liest sie nicht.

6
Und als die Leichen rochen durch das Haus
Da weinte Jakob und ward krank davon.
Und Jakob Apfelböck zog weinend aus
Und schlief von nun an nur auf dem Balkon.

7
Es sprach der Zeitungsmann, der täglich kam:
Was riecht hier so? Ich rieche doch Gestank.
In mildem Licht sprach Jakob Apfelböck:
Es ist die Wäsche in dem Wäscheschrank.

8
Es sprach die Milchfrau einst, die täglich kam:
Was riecht hier so? Es riecht, als wenn man stirbt!
In mildem Licht sprach Jakob Apfelböck:
Es ist das Kalbfleisch, das im Schrank verdirbt.

9
Und als sie einstens in den Schrank ihm sahn
Stand Jakob Apfelböck in mildem Licht

> Und als sie fragten, warum er's getan
> Sprach Jakob Apfelböck: Ich weiß es nicht.
>
> 10
> Die Milchfrau aber sprach am Tag danach:
> Ob wohl das Kind einmal, früh oder spät
> Ob Jakob Apfelböck wohl einmal noch
> Zum Grabe seiner armen Eltern geht?
>
> (GW, 4:173–75)

It is striking that we are not given even a clue to the motives of the young murderer. He himself can give no reason: "Und als sie fragten, warum er's getan / Sprach Jakob Apfelböck: Ich weiß es nicht." There is no trace in Brecht's poem of the archetypal Expressionist revolt whereby the brutally oppressed or alienated young man attains to independence (and a massive articulateness) through an act of rebellion that cuts the hated bonds of family and society. There is none of the pathos that normally accompanies all this, either. The closest the poem comes to the pathos of youthful sensitivity and vulnerability is the subtitle with its allusion to childlike innocence.

Compare Brecht's flat, noncommittal description with the following final scenes of hectic drama, respectively from Hasenclever's *Der Sohn* and Bronnen's *Vatermord*, perhaps the best-known Expressionist treatments of patricide:

> Der Sohn: Papa . . .
> Der Vater: Sprich den Namen nicht aus!
> Der Sohn: Läßt du mich frei!?
> Der Vater: Frei? *(Er lacht gellend.)* Noch ein Jahr bist du in meiner Gewalt. Noch ein Jahr kann ich wenigstens die Menschheit vor Dir schützen. Es gibt Anstalten zu diesem Zwecke.
> Verlaß jetzt mein Zimmer und betritt es nicht mehr!
> Der Sohn *(mit eiserner Ruhe)*: Das Zimmer ist verschlossen. Hier geht keiner heraus.
> Der Vater *(steht auf und geht langsam, schwerfällig zur linken Seitentür)*.
> Der Sohn *(mit furchtbarer Stimme)*: Halt. Keinen Schritt!!
> Der Vater *(einen Augenblick wie gelähmt von dieser Stimme, setzt sich an den Tisch)*.
> Der Sohn *(zieht den Revolver unbemerkt jetzt ganz aus der Tasche)*.
> Der Vater: Hilfe gegen den Wahnsinn . . . *(Er ergreift das Telephon.)*

Der Sohn *(hebt den Revolver in die Höhe).*
Der Vater *(am Telephon)*: Bitte das Polizeiamt.
Der Sohn: Sieh hierher! *(Er zielt auf ihn und sagt mit klarer Stimme)*: Noch ein Wort—und du lebst nicht mehr.
Der Vater *(macht unwillkürlich eine Bewegung, sich zu schützen. Er hebt den Arm, das Telephon entfällt ihm. Er läßt den gehobenen Arm sinken. Sie sehen sich in die Augen. Die Mündung der Waffe bleibt unbeweglich auf die Brust des Vaters gerichtet.—Da löst sich der Zusammengesunkene, ein Zucken geht durch seinen Körper. Die Augen verdrehen sich und werden starr. Er bäumt sich kurz auf, dann stürzt das Gewicht langsam über den Stuhl zu Boden. Der Schlag hat ihn gerührt).*

(*Der Sohn,* 124–26)

Fessel *stößt mit einem Fleischschlegel den Revolver in der Hand das Fenster auf zielt zittert aber sehr so kommt er ganz herein atemlos greift sich ans Herz und kann keinen Laut ausstoßen indessen springt* Walter *auf mit dem Rücken gegen ihn so daß er knapp vor dem Vater steht ohne ihn zu sehen* Fessel *will alles zugleich tun erschlagen treten würgen schießt ohne zu treffen verliert den Schlegel*
Walter *springt weg wild aufschreiend dann ohne zu denken nackt unbewaffnet auf ihn zu:* Jetzt—
Fessel *fällt zu Boden dabei das Gangfenster zudrückend will schließen*
Walter: Er lebt le le le lebt noch *Brüllt auf sucht nach dem Messer packt es sticht wiederholt auf den Vater los der voll Wut und Haß aber ganz geschwächt sich erhoben hat und schießen will er stirbt ohne zum Atmen zu kommen* Walter *sinkt neben ihn*
Frau Fessel *in ein Leintuch gehüllt kommt ins Zimmer setzt sich auf Walters Bett spricht nach einiger Zeit mit klagender Stimme*: Walter Walter Walter Walter Walter Walter Walter Walter Walter
Walter *erhebt sich steht in der Türe*: Was ist / Was willst du
Frau Fessel: Komm zu mir o o ohh komm zu mir
Walter: Ich hab genug von dir / Ich hab genug von allem / Geh deinen Mann begraben du bist alt / Ich bin jung aber / Ich kenn dich nicht / Ich bin frei / Niemand vor mir niemand neben mir niemand über mir der Vater tot / Himmel ich spring dir auf ich flieg / Es drängt zittert stöhnt klagt muß auf schwillt quillt sprengt fliegt muß auf muß auf
       Ich
       Ich blühe

(*Vatermord,* 53)

Hasenclever's and Bronnen's murders take place in the context of social and personal rebellion, with the familiar Expressionist mix of tempestuous emotion and rhetorical self-assertion on the part of the young heroes. Bronnen gives us the further dimension of an oedipal relationship between mother and son. Both murders are acts of social, psychological, and existential liberation. The plays end with self-emancipation, with the removal of an insupportable obstacle to the self-fulfillment of the son. His true life, independent, free, and vital, begins with the fall of the curtain.

With Brecht there is no liberation but the opposite, no dawning of a new and better life in freedom but self-imprisonment and entrapment, no blissful victory but bewilderment. All reference to parental cruelty and authoritarianism, to the paralyzing hypocritical morality of the time—constant themes of Expressionism—is lacking in Brecht's poem. As to the mode of expression, nothing could be more distant from the turbulence and exaggeration of Expressionism. Brecht's language is laconic to the point of flatness. It stays very close to everyday speech. Only the occasional peculiarity of phrasing or syntax with biblical or Moritat overtones ("Und als sie einstens in den Schrank ihm sahn") and very simple lyrical lines ("Es schwammen Wolken unterm Himmel hin / Und um sein Haus ging mild der Sommerwind") differentiate Brecht's text from a prosaic account.

This closeness to the ordinary, the mundane, is taken to almost comic lengths in the final stanza:

> Die Milchfrau aber sprach am Tag danach:
> Ob wohl das Kind einmal, früh oder spät
> Ob Jakob Apfelböck wohl einmal noch
> Zum Grabe seiner armen Eltern geht?

Stylistically, this is quintessential Brecht: very simple yet subtle, with the unobtrusive biblical Moritat flavor of the first line, the deftly suggested speech and tone of the milk lady, the finely calculated retarding effect of the third line leading into the surprise conclusion. As for the naive question, far from representing a grotesque whimsy of the young Brecht, it too is taken from everyday life. Willett and Manheim report that "Marthe Feuchtwanger, wife of the novelist, drew Brecht's attention to the Apfelböck story in the press, and it was her cleaning woman who made the remark attributed to the milk woman."[15] One has to admire the psychological astuteness of the young poet, who sees that in real life the mundane converges with the appalling, with consequences that are sometimes, if we are honest, comical. One must admire also Brecht's dramatic and artistic sense of the capital to be made of this fact. It is a dramatic and artistic sense diametrically opposed to the reigning one of the day, that of the Expressionists (Carl Sternheim possibly excepted). If we want to seek out the nature of the young Brecht's contribution to German poetry, we can begin right here with his insight into the great effect that can be derived from the juxtaposition of the ordinary and the startling, and with his courage in writing with reserve and with great spareness. Brecht the calm observer of the strangeness of human behavior, Brecht the *realist*, never had far to look for material: it was constantly about him.

Far from highlighting in dramatic detail its hero's youthful motivation for rebellion and murder, *Apfelböck* derives much of its effect from the apparent pointlessness of Jakob's deed and from the absence of a guiding framework—social, political, or psychological. The poem's anticlimactic nature gives it an unresolved quality that is disturbing and unsatisfying, in the positive sense that after we have finished it the poem goes on working on us—a favorite Brechtian ploy. Instead of an answer, a conclusion, a rounded ending, there is the comment of the milk woman, half-farcical, half-moving. Ultimately, the poem suggests that in real human affairs there is no satisfying play of clear-cut question and answer, but rather a disorderly mixture of the apparently logical and the apparently absurd. Life is at once more mundane and more shattering than art. (Of course, it takes a considerable artist to convince us of this.)

The sociopolitical dimension, which plays a certain role in Brecht's early work and might be expected, on the face of it, to provide an explanation for Jakob's actions, is missing from *Apfelböck*. Helmut Lethen[16] and Carl Pietzcker[17] are both unable to argue—though one senses they would like to—that the Apfelböcks are a bourgeois family. (This assertion would need to be taken seriously if Jakob's deed were to be given the sociopolitical significance of revolt against the corrupt and authoritarian bourgeois system.) The poem does not suggest this, and the real Apfelböck, first name Josef, came from a working-class family. Rather, the impression we are left with is of an act without context, an inexplicable and senseless act, bare even of tragedy.

Pietzcker's shifting of *Apfelböck* into the orbit of Expressionism is entirely inappropriate and flies in the face of the whole nature of Brecht's early work. Even if we leave aside the equation of Brecht with the Hasenclevers, Bronnens, and Franks, Pietzcker's reading of *Apfelböck* as the expression of a suppressed hatred of Brecht's parents will scarcely bear examination. Not only does the external evidence, to be outlined later in this chapter, indicate Brecht's unusually relaxed relationship with his family, making it highly unlikely that he was driven by this kind of motive, but more important, the tenor of the poem itself does not point to a suppressed murderous desire. The facts of Jakob Apfelböck's murder of his parents and subsequent events are presented with a laconic calmness that is characteristic of Brecht from the beginning (if we set aside the juvenilia) and that gives the lie to accounts of his early work as the expression of a troubled psyche. This notably sober style, pushing understatement and simplicity almost to their limit, is the most striking aspect of the young Brecht's poetry if we put it in the context of what was being written in Germany at this time. Before *Neue Sachlichkeit* came to be the dominant new mode, in the midst of a still flowering Expressionism characterized by pathos, the poetry of the young Augsburger, though it was not to be published in collection until 1927, was changing the face of German literature.

Even in the case of the one piece of common ground shared by Brecht and the Expressionists, this difference holds. The vitalism so much in vogue in Germany in the first two decades of this century affected Brecht strongly. We might expect some euphoria and rhapsody from Brecht when he expounds on the essential life force, the powerful union of man and nature, the free expression of man's vital powers. Certainly that is what the Expressionists offer us:

> [Der expressionistische Überwinder der Dekadenz hat] den Mut des Spielers und Verschwendergewißheit und segelt bewußt in den unsichern blutdunklen Raum. . . . Was er tut, tut er um eines Dinges willen: um der Steigerung seiner Lebensintensität willen. . . . Alles, was in ihm funktionieren kann, will er rege haben, Energien sollen sich ausstrahlen, alle Gestaltungskräfte in Tätigkeit sein. Denn, was er jetzt bewußt verlangt, ist mehr denn je: Umfangendstes Erleben und Aufleben, brutalstes Sich-lebendig-Fühlen und hochwogendes Bewußtsein der eigenen Kraft.
>
> (Erwin Loewenson,
> Aufruf im *Neuen Club*, 18 November 1909,
> cited from Martens, 192)

Der Atem der Natur, der Wind, die Phantasie der Erde,
Erträumt die Götterwolken, die nach Norden wehn,
Der Wind, die Phantasie der Erde, denkt sich Nebelpferde,
Und Götter sehe ich auf jedem Berge stehn!

Ich atme auf und Geister drängen sich aus meinem Herzen.
Hinweg, empor! Wer weiß, wo sich ein Wunsch erkennt!
Ich atme tief: ich sehne mich, und Weltenbilder merzen
Sich in mein Innres ein, das seinen Gott benennt.
Natur! nur das ist Freiheit, Weltalliebe ohne Ende!
Das Dasein aber macht ein Opferleben schön!
Oh Freinatur, die Zeit gestalten unsere Werkzeugshände,
Die Welt, die Größe, selbst die Überwindungshöhn!
    (Theodor Däubler, *Der Atem der Natur*, cited from Pinthus, 154)

Ich bin ein Korso auf besonnten Plätzen,
Ein Sommerfest mit Frauen und Bazaren,
Mein Auge bricht von allzuviel Erhelltsein.
Ich will mich auf den Rasen niedersetzen
und mit der Erde in den Abend fahren
O Erde, Abend, Glück, o auf der Welt sein !!
    (Franz Werfel, *Der schöne strahlende Mensch*)

Es treiben mich brennende Lebensgewalten,
Gefühle, die ich nicht zügeln kann,
Und Gedanken, die sich zur Form gestalten,
Fallen mich wie Wölfe an!

Ich irre durch duftende Sonnentage . . .
Und die Nacht erschüttert von meinem Schrei.
Meine Lust stöhnt wie eine Marterklage
Und reißt sich von ihrer Fessel frei.

Und schwebt auf zitternden, schimmernden Schwingen
Dem sonn'gen Thal in den jungen Schoß,
Und läßt sich von jedem Mai'nhauch bezwingen
Und giebt der Natur sich willenlos.
    (Else Laske-Schüler, *Trieb*)

This little selection indicates the various aspects of Expressionist vitalism: glorification of the vital powers of the individual, the representation of nature as a vital organic unity into which man merges, and the euphoric experience of a heightened consciousness.

Brecht's vision of vitalism contains these elements too, but with a key difference:

VOM SCHWIMMEN IN SEEN UND FLÜSSEN

1
Im bleichen Sommer, wenn die Winde oben
Nur in dem Laub der großen Bäume sausen
Muß man in Flüssen liegen oder Teichen
Wie die Gewächse, worin Hechte hausen.
Der Leib wird leicht im Wasser. Wenn der Arm
Leicht aus dem Wasser in den Himmel fällt
Wiegt ihn der kleine Wind vergessen
Weil er ihn wohl für braunes Astwerk hält.

2
Der Himmel bietet mittags große Stille.
Man macht die Augen zu, wenn Schwalben kommen.
Der Schlamm ist warm. Wenn kühle Blasen quellen
Weiß man: ein Fisch ist jetzt durch uns geschwommen.
Mein Leib, die Schenkel und der stille Arm
Wir liegen still im Wasser, ganz geeint
Nur wenn die kühlen Fische durch uns schwimmen
Fühl ich, daß Sonne überm Tümpel scheint.

3
Wenn man am Abend von dem langen Liegen
Sehr faul wird, so, daß alle Glieder beißen
Muß man das alles, ohne Rücksicht, klatschend
In blaue Flüsse schmeißen, die sehr reißen.
Am besten ist's, man hält's bis Abend aus.
Weil dann der bleiche Haifischhimmel kommt
Bös und gefräßig über Fluß und Sträuchern
Und alle Dinge sind, wie's ihnen frommt.

4
Natürlich muß man auf dem Rücken liegen
So wie gewöhnlich. Und sich treiben lassen.
Man muß nicht schwimmen, nein, nur so tun, als
Gehöre man einfach zu Schottermassen.
Man soll den Himmel anschaun und so tun
Als ob einen ein Weib trägt, und es stimmt.
Ganz ohne großen Umtrieb, wie der liebe Gott tut
Wenn er am Abend noch in seinen Flüssen schwimmt.

(*GW*, 4:209–10)

The characteristic vitalist features are all present here: the experience of all life as an organic whole, the loss of personal identity in fusion with nature, the reduction of life to the physical and elemental, and the combination of heightened physical awareness with loss of individuality. But what distinguishes Brecht's poem and sets it apart from the material quoted previously is the sensual, not euphoric, character of the fusion of the body with nature, a fusion that Brecht makes as literal as possible. The Expressionist dimension of spiritual ecstasy and rhapsody is completely absent. The language of the poem is factual, as is appropriate for practical advice handed out to the reader ("muß man," "man muß"). What is being preached here is not the Expressionist *Aufbruch*, the setting out for distant existential shores, but lassitude, not the powerful unfolding of the self, but a letting go of oneself. Even the cold shock recommended in the third stanza aims merely at a brief revivifying of the body in preparation for more lying on one's back and drifting along.

Brecht's vitalism is characterized, in other words, by a confinement to the purely physical and material. His avoidance of everything spiritual and metaphysical points to the typical mistrust of the *materialist*. Lying all day in lakes and rivers, letting the body drift, soaking up sky, sun, and foliage is just that and no more—the connection with intellect, even emotion, is rejected, conspicuous by its absence. Vaudeville jokes like "Man macht die Augen zu, wenn Schwalben kommen" emphasize the pure materiality of the experience being recommended, mocking those readers inclined to waft away into ethereal realms. Even God is mentioned, at the end of the poem, as just another drifter in the river. In this respect the inclusion of *Vom Schwimmen in Seen und Flüssen* in the section of the *Hauspostille* entitled "Exerzitien" is done with parodistic intent. "Exerzitien," Brecht explains in the "Anleitung zum Gebrauch" that prefaces the poems, are "geistige Übungen." Any doubt about the parodistic nature of the heading is removed when one looks at other poems included under "Exerzitien": *Vom Klettern in Bäumen* (the aboveground pendant to *Vom Schwimmen in Seen und Flüssen*), *Orges Antwort, Orges Wunschliste*, and *Großer Dankchoral*:

> Lobet das Gras und die Tiere, die neben euch leben und sterben!
> Sehet, wie ihr
> Lobet das Gras und das Tier
> Und es muß auch mit euch sterben.
>
> (GW, 4:215)

It is not my primary purpose here to discuss the relationship and the differences between Brecht and the Expressionists. These have been spelled out repeatedly,[18] and Brecht himself explains his objections to Expressionism—noisy rhetoric, emotionalism, and lack of distancing—in comments collected in *GW*, 7.[19] My aim is rather to use the contrast with Expressionism to help pinpoint the nature of the young Brecht's work and its function as self-expression and self-projection. What claims our attention in poems such as *Vom Schwimmen in Seen und Flüssen* is the element of *distancing*, a curious detachment in the midst of the lively rendering of experience. It is almost as if Brecht is playing melodies that at any time he can drop. Vitalism is a philosophy that attracts the young man but does not sweep him off his feet. He adopts it as a congenial viewpoint, as part of a role that fits well with his models (in poetry and in life) Villon and Rimbaud and that serves, as it has for many young men, as a kind of badge of identity.[20]

The laconic, sometimes brusque tone of the early Brecht is traceable to a skeptical reserve, an indifference, that is, however, as much the reflection of role perception as of profound inner tendency. It is above all the playful dimension of this poetry, its status as youthful experiment, that needs to be recognized, before we attribute to it an existential agony or despair and extract from it alarming readings of Brecht's psychic state. That is what Carl Pietzcker does, for example, in interpreting *Vom Schwimmen in Seen und Flüssen* as an involuntary expression of Brecht's masochism. Pietzcker analyzes the poem as follows:

> Ist das Verhältnis zur Natur hier sexuell bestimmt und läßt sich der Schwimmende wie von einer Mutter tragen, liegt die Vermutung nahe, das "dichtende Ich" phantasiere auch hier unbewußt den Inzest mit der Mutter, das Bild des Schwimmers in der Natur verberge die Inzestphantasie und werde seinerseits von ihr geprägt. Diese Vermutung wird bestärkt, wenn sich von ihr aus der böse und gefräßige Haifischhimmel erklären läßt: mit ihm geht die Strafe in die verbotene Wunscherfüllung ein. Er repräsentiert die verinnerlichte Kastrationsdrohung. Das Ich phantasiert die Kastration, die Strafe für den Inzest, mit der Befriedigung seines Wunsches gleich mit. Der nackte Schwimmer, der sich auf dem Rücken treiben läßt, gibt dem Himmel seinen Penis schutzlos preis, wie der nackte Mazeppa den Geiern; auch in der "Ballade auf vielen Schiffen" kommt der von Haien Bedrohte "nackt" zu den Schiffen geschwommen.[21]

From the calmly sensuous description of floating naked in the water (an activity in which the young Brecht and his cronies frequently indulged in the Lech and its ponds), we arrive by way of Pietzcker's overriding theory of a psychically distressed young Brecht at the masochistic wish that his exposed penis be cut off as punishment for incestuous desires. It is an arbitrary reading. Very little interpretation is necessary, for example, to see that the coming of the "Haifischhimmel" refers simply to dusk falling (the darkness that will devour river and bushes) and that, far from being a fearful event, "alle Dinge sind, wie's ihnen frommt." Quite apart from this arbitrariness, and the crudeness of his psychoanalysis, Pietzcker ignores the relaxed and detached tone of the poem, its matter-of-fact style. This tone indicates not psychic turbulence but a distanced attitude, as Schwarz has pointed out.[22] It points not to a *poète maudit*, the victim of existential or psychological pressures, but to a confident young man in control of his life, who likes to write in ways somewhat shocking to the bourgeoisie and is still experimenting with a new lyrical style of great power.

The cool indifference and calm detachment of the Augsburg Brecht are perhaps nowhere projected so strikingly as in his contribution to the series of Ophelia poems written by German writers in the early part of this century in imitation of Rimbaud's famous *Ophélie*.

VOM ERTRUNKENEN MÄDCHEN

1
Als sie ertrunken war und hinunterschwamm
Von den Bächen in die größeren Flüsse
Schien der Opal des Himmels sehr wundersam
Als ob er die Leiche begütigen müsse.

2
Tang und Algen hielten sich an ihr ein
So daß sie langsam viel schwerer ward.
Kühl die Fische schwammen an ihrem Bein
Pflanzen und Tiere beschwerten noch ihre letzte Fahrt.

3
Und der Himmel ward abends dunkel wie Rauch
Und hielt nachts mit den Sternen das Licht in Schwebe.
Aber früh ward er hell, daß es auch
Noch für sie Morgen und Abend gebe.

4
Als ihr bleicher Leib im Wasser verfaulet war
Geschah es (sehr langsam), daß Gott sie allmählich vergaß
Erst ihr Gesicht, dann die Hände und ganz zuletzt erst ihr Haar.
Dann ward sie Aas in Flüssen mit vielem Aas.

(GW, 4:252)

By the time Brecht wrote this in 1920, German poetry about the fate of the sad but beautiful maiden had run from Paul Zech's Expressionist reworking of Rimbaud to Georg Heym's vitalist *Ophelia* of 1910 and Gottfried Benn's maliciously cynical *Schöne Jugend* of 1912.[23] Like Heym's drowned girl, Brecht's corpse is surrounded by a powerfully evoked but beneficent nature that accompanies her on her journey down the river. Her body seems to blend with the elements. Like Benn, on the other hand, Brecht insists on describing in physical detail what corpses are actually like. This is delayed, however, until the end of the poem. For three stanzas Brecht lulls his reader into the false expectation that this is to be another vitalist-materialist treatment of the life-death cycle, with the familiar poetic effects. For three stanzas Brecht's poem *is* this, and brilliantly so, but the final stanza spells out with calm deliberation the actual physical reality of dead bodies in water. The shock of this is intensified by the dark, lyrical beauty of the foregoing verses. The reader feels duped almost when, reading the final lines, he gradually realizes what is meant by God's "forgetting" the drowned girl: the stages by which he forgets her represent the stages of decomposition of the various parts of the corpse. Finally the once human body is nothing but an unrecognizable mass, indistinguishable from any other matter: "Aas in Flüssen mit vielem Aas."

But if this final line—and therefore the whole of the poem, which, as we see in retrospect, was merely leading us up to it—is a statement about the nothingness (*Nichtigkeit*) of human life, are we not compelled to concur with Peter Paul Schwarz that this is a demonstration of Brecht's nihilism? Similarly, must we not conclude from poems like *Vom Schwimmen in Seen und Flüssen* that its author was a thoroughgoing asocial vitalist, irresponsible sensualist, anarchic wild man—a Baal type, in a word? And that *Apfelböck oder Die Lilie auf dem Felde*, with its demonstration of purposelessness and even absurdity, is an expression of Brecht's deep conviction of the senselessness of existence? Are we not forced to conclude, in other words, that the thesis of the young Brecht's anarchism and nihilism is right after all?

We must so conclude, certainly, if we assume that these poems, and others like them (as well as the early plays, especially *Baal*), present in a direct way Brecht's innermost feelings. But as I argued in the introduction, we cannot assume that, as a matter of principle. And in the specific instances just referred to, we cannot assume them to be direct expressions of his feelings because of the indications in these poems that Brecht is busy projecting an image, fashioning a role, donning a mask. In the case of *Vom Schwimmen in Seen und Flüssen* this ought to be clear enough. The voice speaking to the reader is the voice in the "Anleitung zum Gebrauch" that precedes the poems of the *Hauspostille*, a voice we are constrained to understand as a fabricated entity whose existence is confined to the pages of that collection. Like a dramatic role, it is defined and marked out by characteristic gestures and habits of tone:

Diese Hauspostille ist für den Gebrauch der Leser bestimmt. Sie soll nicht sinnlos hineingefressen werden.

Die erste Lektion (Bittgänge) wendet sich direkt an das Gefühl des Lesers. Es empfiehlt sich, nicht zuviel davon auf einmal zu lesen. Auch sollten nur ganz gesunde Leute von dieser für die Gefühle bestimmten Lektion Gebrauch machen. . . .

Die zweite Lektion (Exerzitien = geistige Übungen) wendet sich mehr an den Verstand. Es ist vorteilhaft, ihre Lektüre langsam und wiederholt, niemals ohne Einfalt, vorzunehmen. Aus den darin verborgenen Sprüchen sowie unmittelbaren Hinweisen mag mancher Aufschluß über das Leben zu gewinnen sein.

(GW, 4:169)

Just as we do not take these injunctions seriously as earnest advice from Bertolt Brecht, so we probably decline to follow literally the advice about *Vom ertrunkenen Mädchen*: "ist mit geflüsterten Lippenlauten zu lesen." And we do not take as literal, serious advice either the various exhortations to a readership addressed as "ihr" in *Vom Schwimmen in Seen und Flüssen*. Rather, we read these addresses as elements in a total text, one of whose functions is a self-portrait by the poet, a portrait that has strong elements of stylization and role-playing in it.

The authorial role is less visible in *Vom ertrunkenen Mädchen*, but it is still present. The poet does not address his reader directly here, but nevertheless the speaker we apprehend behind the words has a familiar face. It is the face of the Baal type (the poem is of course used in the play), the fascinating dealer in powerful lyrical images who turns out to be the ultimate nihilist, seeing in destruction and decay the only lasting truth. But we can no more identify the speaker of *Vom ertrunkenen Mädchen* with the real Bertolt Brecht than we can the character from the play. Both, the speaker and the character, are artistically heightened versions of Brecht, the result of a process in which imagination, wish fulfillment and self-dramatization play an important part.

In the case of *Apfelböck*, the artistic role erected behind the poem, so to speak, is least visible of all. Oddly, Schwarz—against whose thesis of Brecht's pervasive nihilism I have argued—does not use this poem as an example of this nihilism but sees it (quite wrongly, in my view) as "eine gesellschaftskritische Studie Brechts, die in enger Anlehnung an die Moritaten Wedekinds die Widersprüche des bürgerlichen Lebens ironisch gegeneinander ausspielt, aber sich der eigenen Stellungnahme enthält."[24] The last part of this, as we have seen, is accurate, and it is crucial. It is precisely the detached and dispassionate account of Jakob's fate that creates our sense of the speaker of the poem. *That* is Brecht's role, his mask, for this poem: the detached and laconic observer who sees no sense or purpose in things and does not expect to.

That Brecht adopts masks and creates roles for himself in his early poetry is not a new insight. Schwarz himself recognizes it—his discussion of *Vom Schwimmen in Seen und Flüssen* indicates this[25]—but he does not draw general conclusions and so takes at face value those poems where he does not discover an obvious ironic tone. But overt irony is only one indication of the nonidentity of poem statement and author's self, and its absence does not guarantee that we are hearing the innermost secrets of the poet's soul. The laconic detachment of Brecht's account of young Apfelböck's deeds, the languid sensuousness of *Vom Schwimmen in Seen und Flüssen*, and the unemotional description of death and decay in *Vom ertrunkenen Mädchen* are of course carefully calculated. Ever the cool customer, admired by his cronies for his sangfroid, the young Brecht presents to us an image of the indifferent nihilist, the amoral sensualist, the asocial anarchist. These are largely masks, built up in more or less equal portions from the vagabond François Villon and the scandalous Arthur Rimbaud. There is another mask, pulled on with equal ease by the young Augsburger, borrowed from the roistering ballads of Kipling. The question we now have to address is what the function of these masks might be.

If Schwarz's book suffers from his underestimation of the importance of role-playing and self-dramatization in the early poetry of Brecht, Carl Pietzcker's study takes the roles and masks the wrong way, and in a sense too seriously. Recognizing that poets "project images of their potential selves, heighten them and draw artistic attention to them," as he describes it,[26] Pietzcker goes on to ask what it is that makes the young Brecht choose the images of himself he does choose. It is a legitimate question, but Pietzcker's answer to it is constructed with a good deal of tenuous argument, as I have indicated. It is not his use of a psychoanalytic approach that is at fault. It is rather that the assumption is implicitly made from the beginning that the purpose of masks is to conceal something and that the truth behind the mask is therefore to be sought in the other direction, so to speak—in the mask's opposite. Hence Pietzcker's reading of Brecht's studied indifference as the desperate defense of a threatened psyche, of his anarchic vitalism as the self-destructiveness of an alienated personality, and of his lying lazily in a stream as indicating a desire to have his penis cut off.

But masks can serve a quite different purpose. One can try on masks not to conceal one's true face from the world but just for the pleasure and excitement of adopting different guises. In this case one is and is at the same time not the mask; one lives the role but also lives outside it, in an imaginative process that is the very essence of art. Though the element of display is important—Brecht was from the beginning very aware of how he came across to his audience—we should see this kind of masking less as a defense than as an experiment, even as play, in the Schillerian sense. Of course there is bravado here, and an overly defiant determination to be a winner and not to be hurt, which betrays the sensitive young man still seeking his way. Brecht's guises—the cool, uncaring nihilist, the asocial sensualist and anarchist—are not exactly uncommon in young men. To posit behind every such mask a deeply troubled personality, or even a serious nihilistic position, would be to assume a youthful population largely made up of neurotics and desperados.

Brecht's early poetry is fundamentally shaped by his role-playing and self-projection. This is not to deny the existence of poems from the Augsburg period that bear clear testimony to events in the young Brecht's life that caused him genuine suffering. An obvious example is *Lied von meiner Mutter*, written in 1920 on the occasion of his mother's death and included in the *Psalmen*.

1. Ich erinnere mich ihres Gesichts nicht mehr, wie es war, als sie noch nicht Schmerzen hatte. Sie strich müd die schwarzen Haare aus der Stirn, die mager war, die Hand dabei sehe ich noch.

2. Zwanzig Winter hatten sie bedroht, ihre Leiden waren Legion, der Tod schämte sich vor ihr. Dann starb sie, und man fand einen Kinderleib.

3. Sie ist im Wald aufgewachsen.

4. Sie starb zwischen Gesichtern, die ihr zu lang beim Sterben zugeschaut hatten, da waren sie hart geworden. Man verzieh ihr, daß sie litt, aber sie irrte hin zwischen diesen Gesichtern, vor sie zusammenfiel.

5. Viele gehen von uns, ohne daß wir sie halten. Wir sagten ihnen alles, es gab nichts mehr zwischen ihnen und uns, unsere Gesichter wurden hart beim Abschied. Aber das Wichtige haben wir nicht gesagt, sondern gespart am Notwendigen.

6. Oh, warum sagen wir das Wichtige nicht, es wäre so leicht und wir werden verdammt darum. Leichte Worte waren es, dicht hinter den Zähnen, waren herausgefallen beim Lachen, und wir ersticken daran in unsrem Halse.

7. Jetzt ist meine Mutter gestorben, gestern, auf den Abend, am 1. Mai! Man kann sie mit den Fingernägeln nicht mehr auskratzen!

(GW, 4:79)

There is no image projection or self-stylization going on here. The poem gives simple and straightforward expression to Brecht's grief, virtually without rhetoric, with pathos muted and low key.

Such poems remain exceptions, however. Even the other psalms of 1920, whose tone is often more somber and where perhaps one might seek the serious and direct expression of existential distress, reveal themselves as belonging rather to the mode I have delineated as typical of the early first-person poetry, the mode of self-stylization and role-playing. The psalm that immediately precedes the poem on his mother's death presents the poet in his role as the dissolute and nihilistic womanizer.

GESANG VON EINER GELIEBTEN

1. Ich weiß es, Geliebte: jetzt fallen mir die Haare aus vom wüsten Leben, und ich muß auf den Steinen liegen. Ihr seht mich trinken den billigsten Schnaps, und ich gehe bloß im Wind.

2. Aber es gab eine Zeit, Geliebte, wo ich rein war.

3. Ich hatte eine Frau, die war stärker als ich, wie das Gras stärker ist als der Stier: es richtet sich wieder auf.

4. Sie sah, daß ich böse war, und liebte mich.

5. Sie fragte nicht, wohin der Weg ging, der ihr Weg war, und vielleicht ging er hinunter. Als sie mir ihren Leib gab, sagte sie: Das ist alles. Und es wurde mein Leib.

6. Jetzt ist sie nirgends mehr, sie verschwand wie die Wolke, wenn es geregnet hat, ich ließ sie, und sie fiel abwärts, denn dies war ihr Weg.

7. Aber nachts, zuweilen, wenn ihr mich trinken seht, sehe ich ihr Gesicht, bleich im Wind, stark und mir zugewandt, und ich verbeuge mich in den Wind.

(GW, 4:78)

Despite the somber tone, and the indication of real regret at the end of the poem, we must see this poem in the context of all those other texts by the Augsburg Brecht that cast him in the same role as hard-hearted lover, the dissolute macho type. This goes on right up to the very last poem of the *Hauspostille*, in which the poet assures his women, "In mir habt ihr einen, auf den könnt ihr nicht bauen."

In questioning the ultimate seriousness of Brecht's anarchism and nihilism, I am not making a moralistic judgment, or seeking to demean the early poetry by trivializing it. We do not think less of the young Brecht's intelligence because he experiments creatively with various worldviews and attitudes rather than totally identifying with them. On the contrary. Nor is it an attack on the sincerity of the young poet to doubt the absoluteness with which he holds these views and attitudes. The notion we need here is in any case not sincerity but authenticity,[27] and by the latter criterion Brecht's early work is to be praised highly. Its authenticity is assured by the sensitive and intelligent appropriation of all manner of ideas, philosophies, and viewpoints, and by the sophisticated imaginative process by which they are turned into art. We are only justified in passing moral judgments on such a process and its result where the *purpose* seems to us reprehensible. Such a judgment, not flattering to Brecht, is made in chapter 5 of this book. In the case of the Augsburg Brecht with his anarchist, vitalist, and nihilist roles, their purpose is bound up with the imaginative self-expression of a young writer experimenting with life and experimenting with himself. There is nothing reprehensible in that.

Finally, lest my remarks are felt to contain, after all, a degree of condescension towards the young Brecht, I should perhaps state here my belief that the Augsburg poetry, in particular the *Hauspostille*, is an astonishing achievement. Comparisons are invidious, but how many major poets, of any language, can boast a first collection of such consistently excellent work? In German literature we may have to go back to Strassburg in 1771.

My argument for an experimental Brecht who tries on favorite masks rather than a neurotic Brecht who erects defense mechanisms is strengthened by what we know of his life in Augsburg. From the numerous accounts of his friends and his own diaries, everything points to a Brecht who led a remarkably carefree life.[28] He was given a great deal of freedom, appears to have had little trouble attracting girls (circumstances that produced numerous affairs and an illegitimate child by the time Brecht was twenty-one), and managed to surround himself with cronies who acknowledged him as their leader and superior. Brecht's jaunts along the quiet river Lech with this chosen band of boyhood friends, the evenings in his own private attic room where the admired budding poet and dramatist read out his latest work, and the forays into Augsburg's taverns are part of a youth that has a great deal of the idyllic about it. Here is one of the select group, Hans Otto Münsterer, quoting from his own diary for 1919:

> "Nachts in den Lechauen. Wir saßen am Boden, Bert, Otto Müller und ich. Der Himmel ist hoch, weit und herrlich blau, langsam in Orange übergehend, schließlich violett. Unten der gläserne, weißsprühende Fluß und fern die schwarze Silhouette der Stadt mit ihren Türmen und Giebeln. Das Gras war naß vom Tau. Brecht sang."

Fünf Tage später lehnen wir an der Lechbrücke:

> "Die Ufer verschwimmen in blauen Nebeln. Und ich denke, das ist ein fremdes Schiff und wir stehen am Heck, gebeugt über die gelbe Ganga, denn die Schneeschmelze des Himalaja hat den Fluß trüb gemacht vom Lehm, und wir fahren in eine ferne indianische Nacht. Brecht schrieb. . . ."

> An den heißen Nachmittagen schwimmen wir im Hahnreibach, liegen nackt im Gras der Wolfszahnau oder klettern auf Bäume, wie es in einem der *Evangelien* heißt, das mir Brecht am 11. Juni dort vorliest.[29]

The descriptions we have of the young Brecht's domain on the upper floor of the family dwelling in the Bleichstraße also confirm that he was given a great deal of leeway and allowed to do almost as he pleased up there. One of his acquaintances, Johann Harrer, has given us a revealing account of Brecht's quarters:

> Wenn ich bei den Brechts nach Eugen fragte, wurde mir vom Dienstmädchen oder von Fräulein Roecker in einer etwas blasierten Art gesagt: "Er ist wieder oben!" Wie ich dann hörte, war Fräulein Roecker damals nicht besonders gut auf Eugen zu sprechen, weil sie den Damenbesuch, den er zuweilen tagsüber empfing, nicht dulden wollte. . . . Das Dachzimmer hatte eine Doppeltür und war in einen größeren Wohnraum und ein kleineres Schlafgemach unterteilt. An der inneren Tür prangten mit einer Nadel angeheftet *Zwölf Suren für meine Besucher.* . . . In einer Ecke des Zimmers stand lange ein Notenständer mit einer aufgeschlagenen *Tristan*-Partitur, dazu ein Taktstock. Bert erzählte mir, er müsse nach seinen dichterischen Gedankenflügen dirigieren, um sich zu besänftigen. Ich habe ihn allerdings niemals dirigieren sehen. Aber der Notenständer hat uns sehr beeindruckt. An der eisernen Bettstelle hing eine Gitarre. Die Wände des Zimmers waren vielfach mit Bildern und Zeichnungen seiner rasch wechselnden Ideale bedeckt. Einige Zeit schwärmte er leidenschaftlich für Napoleon. . . . Dann wiederum war Nietzsche, ein andermal Hauptmann oder Wedekind, mit dazugehörigen Motiven von Neher mit Kohle gezeichnet, zu sehen. Einmal hängte er seine eigene Gipsmaske auf, die er sich bei einem Bildhauer hatte abnehmen lassen, der im Hof des Johannisvereins wohnte.[30]

The young Brecht's love of self-presentation, and his habit of appropriating in rapid succession various role models, is clearly apparent from this.

As for family background, Brecht's youth and early manhood, spent with his family in Augsburg, were characterized by permissiveness on the part of the parents (for all their occasional disapproval of Eugen Berthold's lifestyle), and by Brecht's relatively relaxed attitude toward family and social environment. He achieved independence and freedom of movement with little friction, and the accounts we have of these early years bespeak a happy youth, not the savagely oppressed and tortured existence so familiar from other contemporary sources, especially the Expressionists. As Hans Mayer long ago argued:

> Es gibt aber bei Brecht keinen Vaterkomplex und keine literarisch zu erhöhende Familientragödie. Die Vater-Sohn-Konflikte aus der Jugend Walter Hasenclevers, Johannes R. Bechers, Franz Kafkas oder Arnolt Bronnens, die als reales Familiendrama begannen, um als expressionistische Literaturmode weiterzuwirken, fehlten in Brechts Elternhaus wie in seiner Literatur.[31]

We might in fact speculate that it is the very absence of stress and turmoil in the young Brecht's existence that stirred him to create, as a kind of compensation, the wilder and more savage aspects of his writing. The texts exemplifying what we could call the Baal syndrome, and especially the poems and stories about pirates and adventurers, might be the expression of Brecht's need to experience, albeit vicariously, something more exciting and dangerous than the provincial pleasures of Augsburg. We might also see the early texts about the big city in this light: as a reflection of the small-town boy's fascination with the fast-growing metropolises he knew only from books. It is significant that when Brecht finally got to Berlin all this stopped, not just the poems about imagined or fictive big cities, but those about the pirates, vagabonds, and romantic outcasts too. They stopped because they were no longer needed, because the young man from Augsburg now had his hands full with challenging experiences—not vicarious and not romantic either—in a real big city, which provided him with all the action and turmoil he could wish for. In a similar way it is significant that the only early play that deals with actual political and social events of the day, *Trommeln in der Nacht*, is not characterized by extravagant language and imagery, but is relatively sober and restrained. It seems that the exuberance of the young Brecht's language increases with the degree of distance from reality, and decreases where actual events and persons are described.

Apart from Augsburg and its meadows, the recurring landscapes and locales of Brecht's early poetry are the sea, the American frontier, the East Indies, and at the end the "jungle of the cities." The lifestyles described again and again are those of vagabonds, pirates, conquerors, adventurers—hard men, all. These point to a youthful imagination fueled by books, which gave Brecht a sensed affinity with the wastrel student, part-time criminal, and brothel house dweller François Villon and an admiration for the scandalous and nihilistic youth Arthur Rimbaud (both of whom, as it happened, also wrote very good poetry); these models inspired him too with the inclination to create in his own writing desperado figures—murderers, brigands, and anarchists—and aggressively asocial types à la Baal. But about all this is a certain aura of youthful discovery, of fun, and of innocence. This aura of innocent fun surrounds even the wildest and potentially most objectionable of the young Brecht's ballads.

BALLADE VON DEN SEERÄUBERN

1
Von Branntwein toll und Finsternissen!
Von unerhörten Güssen naß!
Vom Frost eisweißer Nacht zerrissen!
Im Mastkorb, von Gesichten blaß!
Von Sonne nackt gebrannt und krank!
(Die hatten sie im Winter lieb)
Aus Hunger, Fieber und Gestank
Sang alles, was noch übrigblieb:
 O Himmel, strahlender Azur!
 Enormer Wind, die Segel bläh!
 Laßt Wind und Himmel fahren! Nur
 Laßt uns um Sankt Marie die See!

2
Kein Weizenfeld mit milden Winden
Selbst keine Schenke mit Musik
Kein Tanz mit Weibern und Absinthen
Kein Kartenspiel hielt sie zurück.
Sie hatten vor dem Knall das Zanken
Vor Mitternacht die Weiber satt:
Sie lieben nur verfaulte Planken
Ihr Schiff, das keine Heimat hat.
 O Himmel, strahlender Azur!
 Enormer Wind, die Segel bläh!
 Laßt Wind und Himmel fahren! Nur
 Laßt uns um Sankt Marie die See!

3
Mit seinen Ratten, seinen Löchern
Mit seiner Pest, mit Haut und Haar
Sie fluchten wüst darauf beim Bechern
Und liebten es, so wie es war.
Sie knoten sich mit ihren Haaren
Im Sturm in seinem Mastwerk fest:

Sie würden nur zum Himmel fahren
Wenn man dort Schiffe fahren läßt.
   O Himmel, strahlender Azur!
   Enormer Wind, die Segel bläh!
   Laßt Wind und Himmel fahren! Nur
   Laßt uns um Sankt Marie die See!

. . . .

5
Sie morden kalt und ohne Hassen
Was ihnen in die Zähne springt
Sie würgen Gurgeln so gelassen
Wie man ein Tau ins Mastwerk schlingt.
Sie trinken Sprit bei Leichenwachen
Nachts torkeln trunken sie in See
Und die, die übrigbleiben, lachen
Und winken mit der kleinen Zeh:
   O Himmel, strahlender Azur!
   Enormer Wind, die Segel bläh!
   Laßt Wind und Himmel fahren! Nur
   Laßt uns um Sankt Marie die See!

. . . .

7
Sie tragen ihren Bauch zum Fressen
Auf fremde Schiffe wie nach Haus
Und strecken selig im Vergessen
Ihn auf die fremden Frauen aus.
Sie leben schön wie noble Tiere
Im weichen Wind, im trunknen Blau!
Und oft besteigen sieben Stiere
Eine geraubte fremde Frau.
   O Himmel, strahlender Azur!
   Enormer Wind, die Segel bläh!
   Laßt Wind und Himmel fahren! Nur
   Laßt uns um Sankt Marie die See!

. . . .

9
Doch eines Abends im Aprile
Der keine Sterne für sie hat
Hat sie das Meer in aller Stille
Auf einmal plötzlich selber satt.

Der große Himmel, den sie lieben
Hüllt still in Rauch die Sternensicht
Und die geliebten Winde schieben
Die Wolken in das milde Licht.
  O Himmel, strahlender Azur!
  Enormer Wind, die Segel bläh!
  Laßt Wind und Himmel fahren! Nur
  Laßt uns um Sankt Marie die See!
. . . .

11
Noch einmal schmeißt die letzte Welle
Zum Himmel das verfluchte Schiff
Und da, in ihrer letzten Helle
Erkennen sie das große Riff.
Und ganz zuletzt in höchsten Masten
War es, weil Sturm so gar laut schrie
Als ob sie, die zur Hölle rasten
Noch einmal sangen, laut wie nie:
  O Himmel, strahlender Azur!
  Enormer Wind, die Segel bläh!
  Laßt Wind und Himmel fahren! Nur
  Laßt uns um Sankt Marie die See!
                                              (GW, 4:224–28)

Powerful and exhilarating, the ballad of the pirates is perhaps Brecht's most extravagant evocation of the uninhibited, anarchic lifestyle. Schwarz refers to a "von der Ekstase der Trunkenheit getragene 'Ausbruch ins Überdimensionale.'"[32] There is nothing the pirates shrink from, including their own destruction. A complete nihilism seems to possess them. They love only total freedom from restraint, imaged in the poem by the vastness of the open sea and sky, which, ultimately, is all they desire.

On one level the poem is a piece of youthful romanticism, a twenty-year-old's fantasy of absolute freedom and license. What saves such extravagance from being simply foolish, and the description of the pirates' animality from being just distasteful, is the poem's joyous expansiveness, a kind of liberated and liberating gusto. It is this gusto and a feeling of sheer fun that we find intoxicating, not nihilism or anarchism in any serious sense. The poem's gesture, we may say, is not the clenched fist so much as the outflung arms. Brecht does not take it all too seriously, in any case. Flashes of the ludicrous or the grotesque are not lacking, indicating the poet's awareness that the pirates and their life-style have their silly side. Lines like "Nachts torkeln trunken sie in See / Und die, die übrigbleiben lachen / Und winken mit der kleinen Zeh" have the function of drawing attention to the fact that, at bottom, all this is not deadly serious. The comic always has a distancing effect, and, like the joke about the swallows in *Vom Schwimmen in Seen und Flüssen*, the comic element here prevents us from identifying ourselves, or the young Brecht, too intensely and too naively with the pirates.

This roaring ballad serves as an answer to the question of what the young Brecht writes when all the stops are out. The suspicion we perhaps have that behind that reserve and brusqueness noted elsewhere lurks a repressed turbulence or savagery is dispelled here. The savagery shows no sign of having been repressed; there is nothing inhibited about this poem. It is a text whose author is on top of his imagined worlds, and in this sense not entrapped in them. If I have suggested that the young Brecht had the typical landlubber's romantic view of the seafaring life, the typical small-town boy's ambivalent fascination with the great metropolis, and the typical Central European's attraction to exotic places across the ocean, it must also be made clear that Brecht himself was not unaware of this. What I have described as the *relaxed* feel of Brecht's early poetry, for all its extravagance and its power, is due in no small measure to this intelligent awareness, and to the ability it gave him to stay on top of his material. It is thus not only the memoirs of friends and the entries in Brecht's own diaries, but the work itself that gives us a young Brecht who was not careworn but carefree. The early work is characterized not by stress and insecurity but by a relaxed confidence. Not until he went to Berlin did the young man from Augsburg have to confront the harshness of the world. Only then did he need to look for explanations and remedies for such harshness. Only then were there questions that urgently required answers.

3. Autobiography and Poetry: Conquering the Big Bad City

Unter ihnen sind Gossen
In ihnen ist nichts, und über ihnen ist Rauch.
Wir waren drinnen. Wir haben nichts genossen.
Wir vergingen rasch. Und langsam vergehen sie auch.
—Brecht, *Über die Städte*

Darin ist kein Strich enthalten der nicht erlebt, aber kein Strich, wie er erlebt worden.
—Goethe to Eckermann, speaking of *Die Wahlverwandschaften*,
   17 February 1830

That Brecht was fascinated by the big city, not by any particular city so much as by the idea and the image of the metropolis, is abundantly clear. His imagination stirred at an early age by Upton Sinclair's Chicago novel *The Jungle*,[1] the young man from Augsburg saw the metropolis, even before he had experienced one, as a cold and hostile "swamp" or "jungle," in which human beings battled for survival. This initial conception of the metropolis was still thoroughly romantic. It is significant that the young Brecht absorbed nothing of Sinclair's socialist ideas, nothing of the fire in the belly that characterizes the American's depiction of the tragic battle for survival of an immigrant family in the slaughter yards district of Chicago. What Brecht got from Sinclair was the excitement and naked drama of life in the metropolis, where individuals sank, rose to the surface, and sometimes sank again forever in a nerve-tingling struggle with a ferociously hostile environment. Chicago: the name came to be used by Brecht to designate precisely this aspect of the big city. It was essentially an existential view of life in the metropolis, not at all a political one. This view was modified once Brecht actually went to live in *his* Chicago—Berlin. Not unexpectedly, the romantic tinge very quickly disappeared. What remained was the real experience of a cold, hostile place where one must battle to make one's way.

As well as *Im Dickicht der Städte* and other plays from the 1920s that reflect this fascination with the cold, hard city (*Mahagonny* and the planned *Joe Fleischhacker* and *Dan Drew*, for example), Brecht's poetry from this period is full of his experiences of the metropolis. One must remember that the *Hauspostille*, though it did not appear until 1927, was made up almost entirely of poems written by 1921. By the time it came out, Brecht was putting together a group of poems that belonged not to Augsburg but to Berlin: a "reader for city dwellers."

Though it often seems to have been lost sight of, *Aus einem Lesebuch für Städtebewohner* and related poems represent, as Klaus Schuhmann amply demonstrates,[2] a transition to Marxism. The "anarcho-nihilist" of the Augsburg period gives way to the soberly "objective" poet of Berlin who observes and records human behavior, commenting coldly on man's inhumanity to man in the big city, although apparently not yet perceiving the sociopolitical causes and connections beneath this surface of human behavior. But just as the use of *anarcho-nihilist* to characterize the young Brecht is, as we saw in the previous chapter, problematical, so the term *objective* (*sachlich*) reflects a somewhat one-sided, if not superficial understanding of the Berlin Brecht. What it does not take into account are the personal psychological factors that bring about these texts and determine their nature. These powerful psychological factors emerge clearly if we pay more careful attention than is frequently the case to the details of Brecht's life in the 1920s and if we distinguish between two kinds of big city poem. There is the *Lesebuch für Städtebewohner* and related poems from 1926 to 1927. And there are *earlier* city poems from around 1921 to 1922 that are entirely different. These two diverse groups come from crucially different periods in the young Brecht's life and career, and are divided by his eventually successful conquest of the German literary and theatrical scene where it mattered, in Berlin. Willett and Manheim draw attention to the importance of the big city poems by giving two of their ten groupings in *Poems, 1913–1956* the headings "The Later Devotions and the First City Poems, 1920–1925" and "The Impact of the Cities, 1925–1928." These headings make clear a difference between the early and the later city poems, though Willett and Manheim make an error, as we shall later see, in including the key poem *Vom armen B. B.* in the later section.

The later poems are collected in the *GW* under the headings *Aus einem Lesebuch für Städtebewohner* and *Zum Lesebuch für Städtebewohner gehörige Gedichte*, the latter arranged by Elisabeth Hauptmann. Obviously related to Brecht's ambition to compose a cycle of plays on the theme of "der Einzug der Menscheit in die großen Städte,"[3] these poems reflect on the one hand the current fashion for *Asphaltlyrik*. Frank Warschauer, the author of *Asphaltgesicht*, had befriended Brecht during his first difficult winter in Berlin in 1921–22, and as late as 1934 Brecht defended *Asphaltliteratur*.⁴ On the other hand, Brecht's situation as a *Städtebewohner* was somewhat different from that of most other *Asphaltlyriker*. The big city was for him both fascinating and frightening, an unfamiliar, alien phenomenon; and something of the shock of his initial attempt to gain a foothold in Berlin in 1921-22 remained with him perhaps for all of his life. There had been an earlier, brief visit to Berlin in February 1920, but the stay in 1921-22 was a serious attempt to "conquer" Berlin (*erobern* was Brecht's own word). Brecht's view of the metropolis as a *Sumpf, Dschungel*, or *Dickicht* may have been romantically tinged, conditioned by his reading of Upton Sinclair and Johannes Vilhelm Jensen,⁵ but the actual experience undergone by the young man from Augsburg took the shine off this image, and Brecht quickly came to see the metropolis really as a jungle. Nevertheless, he was determined to be a big city person, to test himself in the crucible and to come through as a tough, successful type:

Berlin war für die Zeichen der Zeit aufgeschlossen. Hier spürte man am ehesten Amerika und die Auswirkungen der modernen Zivilisation. Die Währungskrise war überwunden, die deutsche Wirtschaft erholte sich dank amerikanischer Kapitalinvestitionen. In Berlin versammelten sich die großen und die kleinen Spekulanten, es gab Wettkämpfe und menschliche Existenzkämpfe. Die Stadt als Schlachtfeld.
Brecht fühlte sich nicht als Berliner. Aber er war jetzt Großstädter aus Überzeugung. Er zwang sich, "von der Natur einen sparsamen Gebrauch zu machen". Auch dem landschaftlichen Dekor der Stadt widerstand er. "Man kann sich keinen Betrachter vorstellen, der den Reizen der Stadt, sei es dem Häusermeer, sei es dem atemraubenden Tempo ihres Verkehrs, sei es ihrer Vergnügungsindustrie, fühlloser als Brecht gegenüberstünde."⁶

Of course, even this ambition to make it in the big city betrays the lad from the provinces. Brecht was after all a small-town boy. In 1925, by which time he had made Berlin his home, the capital had a population of just under 4 million. Munich, the only large center at all familiar to Brecht before Berlin, had at this time a population of 670,000. Augsburg had 162,000. One must consider what this meant for Brecht. Munich would have seemed an expanded, more exciting version of Augsburg: new and big, but only four times as big. That, as well as the similarity in speech and habits and the fact that it was not far away, made Munich easily manageable. Berlin was a quite different matter. It was almost six times as big as Munich and so many times bigger than Augsburg that comparison was meaningless. Berlin was a real metropolis, bursting with energy, noise, and pace, a boom city that had more than doubled in size since 1900, the first and only real national center Germany ever had, the place where you made it or were never heard of again. In addition, the accent was strange, the food was different, and local habits were unfamiliar. For all his bravado about taking Berlin by storm, Brecht remained in certain not unimportant ways an Augsburger. Even later, in 1924, by which time he had broken through in Munich and returned to Berlin with solid contracts and a post as Dramaturg at the Deutsches Theater, he was still attached to his southern origins in a tangible way:

> Trotz der Begeisterung für die Großstadt und der gewaltsamen Veränderung der "heroischen" Landschaft seiner Jugendzeit blieb Brecht in seinen privaten Gewohnheiten Augsburg und dem Elternhaus verhaftet. Essen wollte er in der Regel nur das, was man in Augsburg zu essen pflegte. Was er einmal persönlich "vereinnahmt" hatte, wollte er bewahren und immer zur Verfügung haben. Die alten Freunde wollte er alle am liebsten in Berlin haben, und auch das Dienstmädchen Marie Hold war eine Augsburgerin, die schon den väterlichen Haushalt in der Bleichstraße besorgt hatte. Den Schneider, bei dem er seine bewußt einfache und abgetragen aussehende Kleidung anfertigen ließ, kannte der Dichter ebenfalls noch von Augsburg her.[7]

This clinging to the familiar surroundings of home betrays the provincial young man seeking warmth and security in the big bad city. This *real* big city, like the real Chicago Brecht had read about, was cold, hard, and impersonal; its inhabitants were unfriendly and brusque. It is this harshness, the lack of human warmth, that Brecht the small-town boy from the South captures in his "reader for city dwellers." What emerges again and again from these poems is a sense of vulnerability, of exposure to a hostile, alien environment:

8

Laßt eure Träume fahren, daß man mit euch
Eine Ausnahme machen wird.
Was eure Mutter euch sagte
Das war unverbindlich.
Laßt euren Kontrakt in der Tasche
Er wird hier nicht eingehalten.

Laßt nur eure Hoffnungen fahren
Daß ihr zu Präsidenten ausersehen seid.
Aber legt euch ordentlich ins Zeug
Ihr müßt euch ganz anders zusammennehmen
Daß man euch in der Küche duldet.

Ihr müßt das Abc noch lernen.
Das Abc heißt:
Man wird mit euch fertig werden.

Denkt nur nicht nach, was ihr zu sagen habt:
Ihr werdet nicht gefragt.
Die Esser sind noch vollzählig
Was hier gebraucht wird, ist Hackfleisch.

(Aber das soll euch nicht entmutigen!)
                                        (GW, 4:274–75)

"Leave your dreams behind"—the city is the place of disillusionment, of bitter disappointment. The various brutal pieces of "advice" tear away the fond hopes and ambitions with which the newcomer, bright-eyed, comes to the big city. In this context, the poem's final parenthetical line has the function of a jeering final kick.

A similar process of disillusionment is described stage by stage in the following poem, number 9 of the *Lesebuch*:

VIER AUFFORDERUNGEN AN EINEN MANN VON
VERSCHIEDENER SEITE ZU VERSCHIEDENEN ZEITEN

Hier hast du ein Heim
Hier ist ein Platz für deine Sachen.
Stelle die Möbel um nach deinem Geschmack
Sage, was du brauchst
Da ist der Schlüssel
Hier bleibe.

Es ist eine Stube da für uns alle
Und für dich ein Zimmer mit einem Bett.
Du kannst mitarbeiten im Hof
Du hast einen eigenen Teller
Bleibe bei uns.

Hier ist deine Schlafstelle
Das Bett ist noch ganz frisch
Es lag erst ein Mann drin.
Wenn du heikel bist

Schwenke deinen Zinnlöffel in dem Bottich da
Dann ist er wie ein frischer
Bleibe ruhig bei uns.

Das ist die Kammer
Mach schnell, oder du kannst auch dableiben
Eine Nacht, aber das kostet extra.
Ich werde dich nicht stören
Übrigens bin ich nicht krank.
Du bist hier so gut wie woanders.
Du kannst also dableiben.

(GW, 4:275–76)

This *Rollengedicht* gives us four speakers addressing in turn the newcomer. The progression from the friendly invitation of the first stanza to the abrupt, dubious offer in the last, and the cleverly suggested downhill path from the cozy "Heim" at the beginning to the seedy "Kammer" at the end, is almost as disheartening as the outspoken discouragement of the previous poem.

The disparity between the rosy hopes of the new arrival beguiled by promises that everything will be all right and the actual bitter reality is given really brutal expression in the two initial poems of *Zum Lesebuch für Städtebewohner gehörige Gedichte*:

1

Die Städte sind für dich gebaut. Sie erwarten dich freudig.
Die Türen der Häuser sind weit geöffnet. Das Essen
Steht schon auf dem Tisch.

Da die Städte sehr groß sind
Gibt es für die, welche nicht wissen, was gespielt wird, Pläne
Angefertigt von denen, die sich auskennen
Aus denen leicht zu ersehen ist, wie man auf dem schnellsten
  Wege
Zum Ziel kommt.

Da man eure Wünsche nicht genauer kannte
Erwartet man natürlich noch eure Verbesserungsvorschläge.
Hier und dort
Ist etwas vielleicht noch nicht ganz nach eurem Geschmack
Aber das wird schleunigst geändert
Ohne daß ihr euch einen Fuß ausreißen müßt.

Kurz: ihr kommt
In die besten Hände. Alles ist seit langem vorbereitet. Ihr
Braucht nur zu kommen.

(GW, 4:277)

2

Tritt an! Warum kommst du so spät? Jetzt
Warte! Nein, du nicht, der da! Du kannst
Überhaupt weggehen, dich kennen wir, das hat gar keinen Zweck
Daß du dich da heranschmeißt. Halt, wohin?
Haut ihm doch bitte in die Fresse, ihr! So
Jetzt weiß er Bescheid hier. Was, er quatscht noch?
Nehmt ihn euch mal vor, er quatscht immer.
Zeigt dem Mann mal, auf was es hier ankommt.
Wenn er meint, er kann brüllen bei jeder Kleinigkeit
Immer auf das Maul, ihr werdet doch noch mit so einem fertig
   werden.
So, wenn ihr mit ihm fertig seid, könnt ihr
Hereinbringen, was von ihm noch da ist, das
Wollen wir behalten.

(GW, 4:277–78)

The actual experience of life among the denizens of the "jungle" described in the second poem is a rude shock for the newcomer, who must bitterly realize that the smooth reassurances of the first poem were either deliberately intended to deceive or maliciously sarcastic ("Erwartet man natürlich noch eure Verbesserungsvorschläge"). The tyro receives his first lesson in the course of instruction entitled "Never give a sucker an even break."

The tone of coldness and mistrust that pervades the *Lesebuch* is set by the very first poem, *Verwisch die Spuren*:

Trenne dich von deinen Kameraden auf dem Bahnhof
Gehe am Morgen in die Stadt mit zugeknöpfter Jacke
Suche dir Quartier, und wenn dein Kamerad anklopft:
Öffne, oh, öffne die Tür nicht
Sondern
Verwisch die Spuren!

(GW, 4:267)

Deny your parents, the message continues, dump your friends, take but don't give, trust nobody, and leave nothing behind you. This is carried *ad absurdum* in the final stanza:

Sorge, wenn du zu sterben gedenkst
Daß kein Grabmal steht und verrät, wo du liegst
Mit einer deutlichen Schrift, die dich anzeigt
Und dem Jahr deines Todes, das sich überführt!
Noch einmal:
Verwisch die Spuren!

(Das wurde mir gelehrt.)

(GW, 4:268)

The newcomer to whom such ruthless advice is given soon learns to act on it:

13

Ich habe ihm gesagt, er soll ausziehen.
Er wohnte hier im Zimmer schon sieben Wochen
Und wollte nicht ausziehen.
Er lachte und meinte
Ich mache Scherze
Als er am Abend heimkam, stand
Sein Koffer an der Tür. Da
Wunderte er sich.

(GW, 4:288)

These are learned attitudes and they reflect the bitter experience of the newcomer in the metropolis, who has decided to do unto others what has been done unto him. Dog eat dog, the law of the jungle.

The *I* in these poems is comparatively one-dimensional and is straightforwardly presented. Compared to the earlier poems from the Augsburg period, or for that matter the later exile poems, there is little attempt in the *Lesebuch für Städtebewohner* and associated poems to construct an authorial identity, to profile the speaker and present him to an audience. This lack of interest in self-portrayal beyond the mere sketching of his social circumstances is revealing. We have seen that, in the Augsburg period, the first-person poetry was used to present various roles and guises, artistic masks of the young Brecht. In the relatively secure and familiar world of Augsburg, Brecht could experiment with his masks, try out his roles. When he was confronted with a new and difficult environment, the reverse happened. There was a withdrawal from self-examination and self-projection and a corresponding concentration on the social milieu. Not only is the language of the city poems from the later part of the 1920s markedly austere and impersonal, there is an almost total absence of those rhetorical devices, particularly the address to the reader, that characterize the earlier poetry. It is as if the time for playing games is past, and the *I* becomes a mere participant among many others in a social environment. The primary aim is the description of this environment, not the portrayal of a multifaceted self. The *I* is always located socially.

This impersonality does not mean that the private world of the poet is totally ignored. On the contrary, the comparative lack of posturing and role-playing in these poems means that we see a poet who, because he is not bothering with his image, perhaps is very close to the historical Brecht, the young man from the provinces who attempted to make his mark in Berlin in 1921–22. This certainly seems true of such poems as *Oft in der Nacht träume ich*, where the pressures on the newcomer in the metropolis are given graphic expression:

7

Oft in der Nacht träume ich, ich kann
Meinen Unterhalt nicht mehr verdienen.
Die Tische, die ich mache, braucht
Niemand in diesem Land. Die Fischhändler sprechen
Chinesisch.

Meine nächsten Anverwandten
Schauen mir fremd ins Gesicht
Die Frau, mit der ich sieben Jahre schlief
Grüßt mich höflich im Hausflur und
Geht lächelnd
Vorbei.

Ich weiß
Daß die letzte Kammer schon leer steht
Die Möbel schon weggeräumt sind
Die Matratze schon zerschlitzt
Der Vorhang schon abgerissen ist.
Kurz, es ist alles bereit, mein
Trauriges Gesicht
Zum Erblassen zu bringen.

Die Wäsche, im Hof zum Trocknen aufgehängt
Ist meine Wäsche, ich erkenne sie gut.
Näher hinblickend, sehe ich
Allerdings

Nähte darinnen und angesetzte Stücke.
Es scheint
Ich bin ausgezogen. Jemand anderes
Wohnt jetzt hier und
Sogar in
Meiner Wäsche.

(GW, 4:281)

This poem reveals very plainly the fears of the individual in the big city, describing a sense of alienation culminating in virtual loss of identity. First is the fear of failure. Brecht (characteristically) adopts the role of a carpenter, whose tables no one wants. The difficulty the southerner in Berlin has with the local dialect is given brief but vivid expression: he may as well be in a foreign country. Amid the general anxiety and insecurity that characterize life in the metropolis, fears assail him that even those closest to him may desert him. The next stage of the anxiety is that he will be lost from view, forgotten, with no trace of him remaining. The final stanza presents a frightening image of alienation and loss of self: his most personal clothing has been taken over by someone else. This has the earmarks of the classic nightmare of loss of identity. Though the picture is not without an element of comedy, it is a grim humor.

Sometimes this fearful sense of vulnerability swings round and turns into vengeful aggression. The set-upon newcomer gets tough and hits back:

20

Ich merke, ihr besteht darauf, daß ich verschwinde
Ich seh, ich esse euch zu viel
Ich verstehe, ihr seid nicht eingerichtet auf solche
    Leute wie ich
Nun, ich verschwinde nicht.

Ich habe euch zugeredet
Daß ihr euer Fleisch hergeben sollt
Ich bin neben euch hergegangen
Und habe euch nahegelegt, daß ihr ausziehen müßt
Zu diesem Zweck habe ich eure Sprache gelernt
Am Ende
Hat mich jeder verstanden
Aber am Morgen war wieder kein Fleisch da.

Einen Tag noch habe ich mich hingesetzt
Um euch die Gelegenheit zu geben, daß ihr noch kämt
Um euch zu rechtfertigen.

Wenn ich wiederkehre
Unter roherem Mond, meine Lieben
Dann komme ich in einem Tank
Rede mit einer Kanone und
Schaffe euch ab.

Wo mein Tank durchfährt
Da ist eine Straße
Was meine Kanone sagt
Das ist meine Ansicht
Von allen aber
Verschone ich nur meinen Bruder
Indem ich ihn lediglich aufs Maul schlage.

(*GW*, 4:293–94)

Such bloodthirsty promises of vengeance can of course be read as the mere wishful thinking of the ill-treated outsider.

All these poems are marked by the experience of the big city as cold, hostile, and alienating. They express the experiences of the newcomer, either brought painfully face to face with unfriendly, exploitative, or cynical metropolitans, or quickly adopting these same characteristics of unfriendliness and cynicism and thus joining—if he survives, and it is a condition of surviving—the ranks of the big city denizens. Either way this poetry reflects the harsh, bitter experiences of the young tyro coming for the first time to "das kalte Chicago." The roles and masks so characteristic of the Augsburg period have given way to an unmediated and direct presentation of actual social experience. But the masks do not disappear until Brecht has overcome the difficulties that he describes in the big city poems of 1926–27. One has to remind oneself that by the time these poems were written, Brecht was well established in Berlin. In his terms, he had "conquered" the capital; the big bad city was his oyster. *Leben Eduards des Zweiten* and *Im Dickicht der Städte* had been produced at the Berlin Staatstheater and the Deutsches Theater respectively in the latter part of 1924, *Mann ist Mann* had been premiered in 1926; Brecht was a member of the Gruppe 1925, which included the best-known younger German writers (Becher, Döblin, Klabund, Kisch, Rudolf Leonhard, and Tucholsky, among others); numerous newspaper pieces, articles, short stories, and poems had kept Brecht's name before the public; and sensational events such as the exchange with Thomas and Klaus Mann in August 1926,[8] the "Matinée in Dresden" affair in March of that year,[9] and Brecht's provocative role as judge of the poetry competition organized by *Die literarische Welt* early in 1927[10] had established him in the eyes of the general public and the *literati* alike as an important figure. Brecht had made it in Berlin. And *only when he had made it* did he give overt expression to the harsh experiences of his attempt to gain a foothold in the big city: the cold shoulders, the rejection of his work, the hunger, the perpetual search for somewhere to sleep, the usually disappointed need for human warmth.

This attempt to gain a foothold in Berlin went back six years, when Brecht had made a determined but unsuccessful attempt to establish himself in the capital, center of the German theater and cultural focal point of Europe. It was a failure. Brecht, who had gone to Berlin early in November 1921 full of confidence, was forced to return to Augsburg in April 1922, after only a few months, defeated and discouraged. There had been some good moments, and the new friendship with Arnolt Bronnen provided some warmth. Both needed it. That winter they were both cold and hungry, and Brecht landed in the hospital suffering from malnutrition and a bleeding bladder.

> Berlin und die Theater insgesamt verfluchend, aßen die unglücklichen Eroberer ihre Erbsensuppe bei Aschinger. Brecht hatte das Erlebnis der Großstadt gesucht, er hatte den Dschungel unternehmungslustig betreten, bekam aber keinen festen Boden unter die Füße. "Chicago" stieß ihn ab. Wie Garga in seinem gleichnamigen Drama schien der Dichter an der Stadt zu scheitern, in ihr seine Menschlichkeit zu verlieren.[11]

Looking back on this time later, Brecht wrote:

> Ich habe mich schwer an die Städte gewöhnt. Ich hatte kein Geld und zog immerzu um. Dann wohnte ich einen Monat lang in einem schon fertig gestellten Zimmer. Die Zimmer waren zu häßlich und zu teuer. Um es in ihnen auszuhalten, hätte ich viel schwarzen Kaffee und Kognak trinken müssen, aber ich hatte nicht einmal genügend Geld zum Rauchen. In einer guten Zeit wäre es amüsant gewesen, durch alle diese Zimmer durchzugehen und diese Nachtlager morgens zu vergessen. Aber in dieser Zeit hatte niemand genug ego in sich, um etwas machen

zu können. Man kam dazu, sich selber zu bewohnen, und dadurch kam eine Spaltung in einen selber hinein; wahrscheinlich deshalb habe ich immer das Gefühl gehabt, ich sei eine besonders provisorische Sache.[12]

These all too clear indications of the painfulness of Brecht's first attempt to make his mark in the big city contradict careless statements like Schumacher's: " 'Die große Angst vor dem kalten Chicago', das für ihn Berlin war, sollte ihn nicht packen."[13] Schumacher's confident assertion that the only thing that clouded Brecht's first stay in Berlin was his treatment in literary circles, "was ihn ergrimmte,"[14] maintains the legend of Brecht's self-assurance and keeps afloat the image of the brash, aggressive cool customer taking the cultural world of Berlin by storm. But this image—the accepted one in Brecht scholarship by now—is above all an image projected assiduously by Brecht himself. And it was projected most of all at a time when in reality his ego was taking a beating, when he was assailed by—let us not shrink from the terms—anxiety and trauma. At precisely the low point of this first venture into the big city, coming back defeated to the security and familiarity of Augsburg on the night train on 26 April 1922, the young Bertolt Brecht wrote perhaps his most famous poem. Certainly it is the key to an understanding of the twenty-four-year-old poet's attempt to conquer the metropolis:

VOM ARMEN B. B.

1
Ich, Bertolt Brecht, bin aus den schwarzen Wäldern.
Meine Mutter trug mich in die Städte hinein
Als ich in ihrem Leibe lag. Und die Kälte der Wälder
Wird in mir bis zu meinem Absterben sein.

2
In der Asphaltstadt bin ich daheim. Von allem Anfang
Versehen mit jedem Sterbsakrament:
Mit Zeitungen. Und Tabak. Und Branntwein.
Mißtrauisch und faul und zufrieden am End.

3
Ich bin zu den Leuten freundlich. Ich setze
Einen steifen Hut auf nach ihrem Brauch.
Ich sage: Es sind ganz besonders riechende Tiere
Und ich sage: Es macht nichts, ich bin es auch.

4
In meine leeren Schaukelstühle vormittags
Setze ich mir mitunter ein paar Frauen
Und ich betrachte sie sorglos und sage ihnen:
In mir habt ihr einen, auf den könnt ihr nicht bauen.

5
Gegen Abend versammle ich um mich Männer
Wir reden uns da mit "Gentlemen" an.
Sie haben ihre Füße auf meinen Tischen
Und sagen: Es wird besser mit uns. Und ich
   frage nicht: Wann?

6
Gegen Morgen in der grauen Frühe pissen die Tannen
Und ihr Ungeziefer, die Vögel, fängt an zu schrein.
Um die Stunde trink ich mein Glas in der Stadt aus
   und schmeiße
Den Tabakstummel weg und schlafe beunruhigt ein.

7
Wir sind gesessen, ein leichtes Geschlechte
In Häusern, die für unzerstörbare galten
(So haben wir gebaut die langen Gehäuse des
   Eilands Manhattan
Und die dünnen Antennen, die das Atlantische Meer
   unterhalten).

8
Von diesen Städten wird bleiben: der durch sie
   hindurchging, der Wind!
Fröhlich machet das Haus den Esser: er leert es.
Wir wissen, daß wir Vorläufige sind
Und nach uns wird kommen: nichts Nennenswertes.

9
Bei den Erdbeben, die kommen werden, werde ich
   hoffentlich
Meine Virginia nicht ausgehen lassen durch Bitterkeit
Ich, Bertolt Brecht, in die Asphaltstädte verschlagen
Aus den schwarzen Wäldern in meiner Mutter in früher Zeit.
                                          (GW, 4:261–63)

Even if we take only stanzas 1, 2, 6 and the last half of 9, all that remain intact from the original[15]—which was written, if we can trust

Brecht's notebook, "nachts 1/2 10 im Dezug"—it is clear that the poem gives us, not a vision of the metropolis as a cold monster swallowing the vulnerable and the inexperienced, but rather a picture of the cool, detached, sardonic young man for whom the hard, tough city is his natural environment and who has no illusions about it, himself, or the future. This picture is a mask in virtually every respect. Brecht was certainly not "at home" in the "asphalt city," was not at all "content" at this stage, and was not, according to eyewitness reports "friendly to people." (See, for example, Bronnen's report in *Tage mit Bertolt Brecht* of Brecht's handling of the rehearsals for *Vatermord*.)[16]

Unlike the other masks we have seen, moreover, this one is defensive. *Vom armen B. B.* and a handful of other, lesser poems written about the city in that winter of 1921–22 are the crucial exceptions to my argument for the experimental as against the neurotic and defensive Brecht. What makes them the exception is that they belong neither to the secure world of Augsburg nor to the later feeling of having conquered Berlin, but to the difficult period of transition. Unable to admit in his work the traumatic effect this transition had on him (until later, when he could afford to admit it), Brecht reached for his characteristic Augsburg tools of trade in order this time not so much to try on yet another brilliant variation of his favorite masks, but to transform this traumatic experience into something manageable. If we are justified in speaking of defense mechanisms anywhere in the work of the young Brecht, it is here. Of course even in *Vom armen B. B.* attention is drawn to the mask. Even in this poem, which we must understand as an attempt to cope with unpleasant and deflating experiences through the creation of a role that rises above these experiences, Brecht admits with the other hand, as it were, that this *is* a created role. The artist stands beside his self-portrait, smiling sardonically. The very title immediately directs our attention to this ironic dimension, and likewise the first line, with its mock-official "Ich, Bertolt Brecht."

Nonetheless, *Vom armen B. B.* crosses the line between the mask whose primary function is artistic experimentation with versions of the self, and the mask that, however ironically donned, is created to help its wearer manage his life. We cannot insist on the rigidity of this distinction: in practice, in the texts, it is fluid and shifting. But there is a sense in which Brecht's most famous poem is an exercise in survival.

Stanza 6 of *Vom armen B. B.* is, from the point of view of role creation, especially interesting. The violently antinature stance expressed by "pissen die Tannen" and "ihr Ungeziefer, die Vögel, fängt an zu schrein" is the more striking because of its contrast to the earlier (but not much earlier) vitalist celebration of nature that we associate with the *Hauspostille*. The powerful evocations of a sensually experienced nature give way in this last poem of the collection to a completely negative attitude. The violence of this attitude is what is significant. It is the violence that accompanies a forced, willed change of style. When Brecht left Augsburg for Berlin in 1921, he left behind the world of his boyhood and youth, and many of the experiences that hitherto had stamped his work. The soft, languorous life of wanderings along the quiet river Lech and its meadows, of hours whiled away with his bosom pals, had to cease. The Augsburg idyll had to be finished with, and a new life-style embarked upon, one that was appropriate to the metropolis.

Vom armen B. B. is thus a transition poem, marking the conscious giving up of one life-style for another, and it is appropriate that it is the closing poem of the *Hauspostille*, marking the end of the Augsburg years. Willett and Manheim are only technically correct in including *Vom armen B. B.*, whose final version was written in 1925, in "The Impact of the Cities, 1925–1928." In tone and attitude, as well as in origin, the poem belongs to the "First City Poems." The self-image of the poet is very much the tough and cool figure of the earlier poetry with its relaxed bravado and romantically tinged nihilism, not the later cold, tense character who is aware of man's vulnerability in the big city and who documents its destructive effect.

Willett and Manheim's notes, useful and indeed at times indispensable as they are, provide another example of the lack of distinction in Brecht criticism between the city poetry belonging to Brecht's first attempt to succeed in Berlin (early November 1921 to late April 1922) and the later poems written about "das kalte Chicago" in 1926–27 after Brecht had thoroughly established himself. Pointing out that *Früher dachte ich* appears in Brecht's *Tagebuch* under 19 December 1921, with the title "Anderes Gedicht" and that it is therefore wrongly included in the group *Zum Lesebuch für Städtebewohner gehörige Gedichte* in *GW*, Willett and Manheim note that the poem nevertheless "anticipates remarkably" the later collection.[17] But it does *not* anticipate these. *Früher dachte ich* is on the contrary conspicuous among the *Lesebuch* poems in *GW* precisely because its tone, and the nature of the image of himself projected by the poet, are quite different.

Früher dachte ich: ich stürbe gern auf eignem Leinenzeug
Heute
Rücke ich kein Bild mehr gerad, das an der Wand hängt
Ich lasse die Stores verfallen, ich öffne dem Regen die Kammer
Wische mir den Mund ab, mit fremder Serviette.
Von einem Zimmer, das ich vier Monate hatte
Wußte ich nicht, daß das Fenster nach hinten hinausging
  (was ich doch liebe)
Weil ich so sehr für das Vorläufige bin und an mich nicht recht
  glaube.
Darum hause ich, wie's trifft, und friere ich, sage ich:
Ich friere noch.
Und so tief verwurzelt ist meine Anschauung
Daß sie mir dennoch erlaubt, meine Wäsche zu wechseln
Aus Courtoisie für die Damen und weil
Man gewiß nicht ewig
Wäsche benötigt.

(GW, 4:278–79)

This is much more akin, as one would expect, to other poems written around the same time—*Vom armen B. B., Brief an die Mestizen, Epistel, Sentimentale Erinnerungen, Man sollte nicht zu kritisch sein, Bericht anderswohin*—than to the later *Lesebuch für Städtebewohner* group. The heedless attitude toward his environment ("Wußte ich nicht, daß das Fenster nach hinten hinausging") and even to his own well-being ("Ich lasse die Stores verfallen, ich öffne dem Regen die Kammer"), the sardonic joke at the end, the studied rudeness of behavior (not toughness in self-defense but the gratuitous rudeness so typical of the young Brecht)—all place this poem clearly in the period before 1924.

Two of the poems mentioned above also appear, like *Früher dachte ich*, in the *Tagebuch* for 19 December 1921: *Brief an die Mestizen* (under the title "Noch ein Gedicht") and *Epistel* (which began in the *Tagebuch* simply as "Gedicht" before being given the typescript title "2. Brief an die Moskauer, eine weitere Ermahnung" and then finally its present title). A third poem, now known by its first line, *Man sollte nicht zu kritisch sein*, originally bore the title "An die Menschenfresser. Brief an die Moskauer 1." Its typescript is dated 1922 by the Bertolt-Brecht-Archiv der Deutschen Akademie der Künste (hereinafter BBA), suggesting that Brecht added it to the three poems that he had written into the *Tagebuch* a little earlier in the order (using GW titles) *Epistel*, *Früher dachte ich*, and *Brief an die Mestizen*.

The somewhat confusing titling history does not conceal the close relationship between these poems. Even if we did not know that three of them appear in the *Tagebuch* under the same date, their thematic and stylistic similarity, their common tone, tell us that they are cut from the same cloth. The first of them, *Epistel*, has that detached, uncaring view of his own life and fate with which the reader of Brecht's early poetry is familiar:

> Einer kann herkommen aus Ulm und mich abschlachten.
> Dann erbleicht in der Luft ein Tag
> Das Zittern einiger Grashalme, das ich vor Zeiten bemerkte
> Kommt nun endlich zum Stillstand.
> Ein toter Mensch, der mit mir befreundet war
> Hat keinen mehr, der weiß, wie er aussah.
> Mein Tabakrauch
> Der inzwischen durch Milliarden Himmel gestiegen ist
> Verliert seinen Gottesglauben
> Und
> Steigt weiter.
>
> (GW, 4:106–7)

This is so coolly remote as to constitute practically a case of that detachment from one's body advocated by oriental religions. Not that the poet here could be called serene: he is merely switched off, unable to get excited about his own fate. It is an example of that nihilistic attitude that is so common in Brecht's early work, relieved here as so often by a sardonic irony that is directed as much at himself as it is outward. It is the same irony that pervades the last lines of *Früher dachte ich* and that is present also in the third poem of 19 December 1921, *Brief an die Mestizen, da erbittert Klage geführt wurde gegen die Unwirtlichkeit*:

> Ich bin vollkommen überzeugt, daß morgen ein heiteres Wetter ist
> Daß auf Regen Sonnenschein folgt
> Daß mein Nachbar seine Tochter liebt
> Mein Feind ein böser Mann ist.
> Auch daß es mir besser geht als fast allen andern
> Daran zweifle ich nicht.
> Auch hat man mich nie sagen hören, es sei
> Früher besser gewesen
> Die Rasse verkomme
> Oder es gäbe keine Frauen, denen ein Mann reicht.
> In all dem

Bin ich weitherziger, gläubiger, höflicher als die Unzufriedenen
Denn all dies
Scheint mir wenig zu beweisen.

(GW, 4:106)

Like the "Muskovites" in the earlier titles of *Epistel* and *Man sollte nicht zu kritisch sein*, the "mestizoes" or halfbreeds here refer to the unfriendly and discontented Berliners. Though the poem leaves little doubt that Brecht is not finding life in the metropolis exactly easy, there is no indication that he allows this to disconcert him. On the contrary, the basic impression the poem manages to convey is that the poet, having no illusions, is incapable of disappointment or frustration, and so drifts along accepting what life brings, not getting too upset about a world he has no hopes for, and sardonically commenting on the deficiencies of an all too imperfect society.

It is the same image as is communicated by *Vom armen B. B.*, and like that famous piece of poetic "autobiography," these three poems from the early part of Brecht's first winter in Berlin assiduously promote the impression of careless self-sufficiency, of life in the metropolis lived heedlessly but in the end contentedly. Even when the poet mentions the harshness of life in the city, there is a nonchalant tone to these poems, appropriate to the dissolute, drifting life-style the poet describes. There is no sign of the psychic pressures and tensions or of the sheer physical wretchedness that, as numerous *Tagebuch* entries and comments by contemporaries such as Bronnen testify, assailed Brecht that winter. On the very same day he put the three poems in his diary, Brecht has another entry, telling a different story: "Wieder diese apokalyptischen Gespensterstürme, die warm, genäßt die Dächer bürsten, das Grippewetter, das einen vergiftet, man legt Eier in die Ofenecken und raucht sich zu Tode. In aller Frühe hat man seinen Herzkrampf, stolziert dann herum wie aus Glas, kann wegen der Eiskälte im Zimmer nicht arbeiten."[18] And one week earlier: "Aber man weckte mich um 10, und es war eine solche Qual in mir, eine wäßrige Qualle zwischen den Rippen, daß ich aufstand. Es ist keine Luft in dieser Stadt, an diesem Ort kann man nicht leben. Es schnürt mir den Hals zu, ich stehe auf, fliehe in ein Restaurant, fliehe aus dem Restaurant, trabe in der eisigen Mondnacht herum, krieche wieder hier herein, schreibe mit Unlust, muß wieder in die Klappe, kann nicht schlafen."[19] The disparity between the bleak and depressing reality of the young Augsburger's very unromantic experiences in the big city in 1921–22 and the nonchalant image projected in the poetry of this time draws our attention once again to the *indirect* way in which Brecht transformed his experiences into poetry.

Of course, the seemingly factual entries in the diary such as the two cited above must also be seen as subject to the constraints I have emphasized in this book: they are "autobiographical" only in the provisional sense, like any other diary entry. In weighing them against the poems, with their very different message, we can only make judgments on the basis of probability. In this case the weight of biographical evidence, such as we have from Brecht's friends and acquaintances of the time, strongly supports an account of Brecht's first winter in Berlin as a chastening experience. In addition, psychological common sense leads us to posit a (real) traumatic experience coped with by means of a (fictive) role as heedless and sardonic cool customer, rather than the opposite. If poems such as *Vom armen B. B.* and *Früher dachte ich* give us the truth, what is the function and purpose of the diary entries telling of bleak despair and discomfort? A careful reading of the poems, the *Tagebuch*, and the biographical material produces a clear case of Brecht's ability to create in his work roles for himself that enable him to overcome psychological and physical difficulties—here his initial failure in Berlin. The daunting, harsh conditions that assailed the young Augsburger in the metropolis *are* present in these poems: they are only transformed from destructive conditions that threaten to overwhelm the vulnerable stranger into conditions that are calmly acknowledged and sardonically remarked upon from a (created, fictive) position of strength.

Particularly in the case of *Früher dachte ich* and *Vom armen B. B.*, it is a tribute to the power of the twenty-four-year-old Brecht's writing that this transformation is so complete and assured. The tone is exactly right, the verbal gestures perfect. The effect is of unshakable composure, a kind of shoulder shrugging calm. Using a blend of the factual—his Schwarzwald origins in *Vom armen B. B.*, the actual mention of "freezing" in *Früher dachte ich*—with the artistically imaged and assumed role, Brecht smuggles into our consciousness, so to speak, the image of himself as the cool, sardonic, detached dweller in the doomed metropolis, the very embodiment of the "mich kann keiner" type: self-assured, self-sufficient, and cynical. Far from writing, under the impact of his difficult first encounter with the metropolis, poems that directly reflect his sense of vulnerability, his despair, and his sheer discomfort, Brecht typically masks these experiences, processes them in ways that provide distance and therefore control. That is the function of the role, the mask. Looked at in this light, the famous poem about "poor B. B." (the title is actually ironic in multiple ways) is not simply self-stylization: it is an artistic tour de force. Later, when the initial trauma had passed and the difficulties had been overcome, *then* more direct expression of such experiences could be given. So Brecht in 1926, having returned to the big city and become a success, wrote a series of poems, the *Lesebuch für Städtebewohner* and related pieces, that explicitly describe the coldness and hostility of the metropolis—but only when he could afford to admit the psychic impact that "das kalte Chicago" had had on him, five years earlier.

4. The Poet in Dark Times: Messages from Exile

Homer hatte kein Heim
Und Dante mußte das seine verlassen.
Li-Po und Tu-Fu irrten durch Bürgerkriege
Die 30 Millionen Menschen verschlangen
Dem Euripides drohte man mit Prozessen
Und dem sterbenden Shakespeare hielt man den Mund zu.
Den François Villon suchte nicht nur die Muse
Sondern auch die Polizei.
"Der Geliebte" genannt
Ging Lukrez in die Verbannung
So Heine, und so auch floh
Brecht unter das dänische Strohdach.
—Brecht, *Die Auswanderung der Dichter*

In den finsteren Zeiten
Wird da auch gesungen werden?
Da wird auch gesungen werden.
Von den finsteren Zeiten.
—Brecht, Epigraph to *Svendborger Gedichte II*

When Brecht left Germany on 28 February 1933, the day after the Reichstag fire, he was just 35 and at the height of his powers. He was an established writer in two senses. He already had an impressive opus behind him, and since the success of the *Dreigroschenoper*, he had been internationally well known. Second, he was *settled* as a writer, had worked out what kind of author he wished to be and knew what his role was. The turn to Marxism, with all that this entailed for Brecht's work, was complete in the sense that its implications had been absorbed and acted upon. Most of the *Lehrstücke* were complete and a good part of the theater theory also.

It is tempting to see a causal connection between this clear sense of role, of mission, and Brecht's unbroken output during his fourteen years of exile, an output achieved in the face of a difficult and frustrating alien existence. But this is true and at the same time untrue. It is true for the work brought forth by the immediate need during this time to comment on the events of the day and to contribute to the anti-Nazi literature coming from the emigrés. Much of the poetry Brecht wrote during the Nazi era is occasional poetry, and much of it is propaganda. This does not mean that these occasional or propaganda poems are second-rate. Some of them are excellent. Bearing out the point made long before him by Heine, that good propaganda must be good literature, Brecht made many fine contributions to the anti-Nazi cause. He was at his best in a satirical vein:

DIE VERBESSERUNGEN DES REGIMES

1
Wenn man herumfragt, so hört man: es gibt viele Verbesserungen.
Viele, die lange keine Arbeit hatten
Haben jetzt Arbeit. Freilich
Sie hungern noch immer. Dabei
Sind die Löhne nicht gesunken, allerdings
Die Lebensmittel sind teurer geworden. Aber einzelne Fleischer
Hat man aus ihren Läden geholt und eingesperrt
Als sie zu schnell aufschlugen. Das weiße Mehl
Das sich übrigens nicht mehr rühren läßt
Kostet nicht viel mehr als früher, nur
Muß man zu jedem Pfund Weißmehl auch ein Pfund Schwarzmehl nehmen
Das sich zu nichts verwenden läßt. Andrerseits
Gibt es einige Fabriken, wo das Mittagessen
Nur zwanzig Pfennig kostet und reichlich ist, das
Ist eine große Verbesserung, schade
Daß diese Fabriken selten sind. Immerhin
Viele kennen einen oder den andern, der in einer solchen Fabrik arbeitet.
. . . .

2
Der Führer wacht auch über die Preise. Nur darum
Ist zum Beispiel ein Mantel noch für den alten Preis zu haben, wenn er auch
Nicht mehr so lange hält wie früher. Ohne den Führer
Wäre er aber teurer geworden. Überhaupt
Soll der Führer den Kapitalisten auf die Finger sehen. Natürlich
Haben sich die Dividenden erhöht, aber es heißt
Daß die Kapitalisten ihre Profite
Nur noch von Furcht erfüllt einstecken, und sie müssen

Mindestens einmal im Jahr, am Ersten Mai
Auf Staatsbefehl vor den einfachen Arbeitern
Die die schwere Arbeit für sie machen, öffentlich den Hut ziehen.

3
Das Regime sorgt auch für Vergnügungen.
Die Ferienfahrten auf eigenen Schiffen sind beliebt. Wenige
Denken, wenn sie auf dem Schiff sitzen, noch an die
    Abgaben.
Das Geld, das man ihnen abzog
Hatten sie schon für verloren gegeben. Die Abzüge
Waren zwangsweise, die Ferienfahrten
Scheint ein freiwilliges Geschenk des Staates.
Wer Geld verloren hat, freut sich auch
Wenn er einen Teil zurückbekommt.

4
So gibt es überall Verbesserungen, und die Rede davon
Stopft auch dem Hungrigen den Mund, wenn es
Statt einem Tropfen auf den heißen Stein jetzt zwei
    Tropfen gibt
Ist das nicht eine Verbesserung?

. . . .

(GW, 4:701–3)

One of the "Deutsche Satiren" that make up the fifth section of the *Svendborger Gedichte*, this poem is a successful exposure of the much-vaunted "improvements" made by the Nazi regime. These satires present persuasive attacks on all aspects of Nazi Germany, and they are the more persuasive for being, artistically, of a good standard. Brecht had a talent for satire that has been neglected or underrated. As far back as the brilliant early poem *Legende vom toten Soldaten* (1919), he had used an effective mixture of simple forms and cutting images to ridicule the crimes and the stupidities of various German regimes.

However, though one might expect to find a preponderance of such work in these years, this is not the case. Equally as noticeable as the volume of propaganda verse in the exile period is the large number of poems where Brecht speaks directly of himself, surveying his life and defining his role as a writer. Here we are dealing with a marked increase in comparison with the poetry written up to 1933, and to the poetry we must add other texts of a clearly, if problematically, autobiographical nature, such as the *Flüchtlingsgespräche*, the

Keunergeschichten, the relevant portion of the *Arbeitsjournal*, and *Leben des Galilei* (with whose autobiographical implications Brecht criticism must sooner or later seriously concern itself). This part of Brecht's work during the exile years—a very large part—will not allow us to uphold the easy connection between impressive productivity and certainty of role, because it is precisely that role that is repeatedly subjected to examination. It seems that exile—and in this he was not alone—if anything sharpened Brecht's need to define his identity and his function as a writer. Again and again he returns to this identity: as German, as communist, as exile, as writer. The latter self makes the point more than once that this is a "bad time for poetry." Of course he makes the point in poetry:

SCHLECHTE ZEIT FÜR LYRIK

Ich weiß doch: nur der Glückliche
Ist beliebt. Seine Stimme
Hört man gern. Sein Gesicht ist schön.

Der verkrüppelte Baum im Hof
Zeigt auf den schlechten Boden, aber
Die Vorübergehenden schimpfen ihn einen Krüppel
Doch mit Recht.

Die grünen Boote und die lustigen Segel des Sundes
Sehe ich nicht. Von allem
Sehe ich nur der Fischer rissiges Garnnetz.
Warum rede ich nur davon
Daß die vierzigjährige Häuslerin gekrümmt geht?
Die Brüste der Mädchen
Sind warm wie ehedem.

In meinem Lied ein Reim
Käme mir fast vor wie Übermut.

In mir streiten sich
Die Begeisterung über den blühenden Apfelbaum
Und das Entsetzen über die Reden des Anstreichers.
Aber nur das zweite
Drängt mich zum Schreibtisch.

(GW, 4:743–4)

Written in 1939 in Skovsbostrand (the sound referred to is the Svendborg sound that features in several of the Danish poems), this forswearing of beauty and the merely aesthetic has become famous as an expression of Brecht's artistic credo. The poem seems to state so much of what we commonly think of as Brecht's position, a position characterized by a dedication to social relevance and political responsibility, whereby "mere" art is rejected and instead an art in the service of political enlightenment is called for. This is the message of the latter part of the poem, the last three stanzas, in which the beauties of life and art are ignored as images of social injustice and political barbarity press in upon the poet. The first two stanzas make a somewhat different point, one that is familiar to us from an equally famous Brecht poem, the slightly earlier *An die Nachgeborenen*, in whose third and most quoted section appear the lines:

Dabei wissen wir doch:
Auch der Haß gegen die Niedrigkeit
Verzerrt die Züge.
Auch der Zorn über das Unrecht
Macht die Stimme heiser.

(GW, 4:725)

Together, the two parts of *Schlechte Zeit für Lyrik* spell out the message that in these dark times the poet cannot afford the luxury and self-indulgence of writing beautifully about beautiful things. He must write about ugliness, and write about it without aesthetic adornment, even though he knows the result will itself be unattractive. The same message, the same statement of present aims, had been given in a third poem, written at the beginning of Brecht's exile in 1934:

AUSSCHLIESSLICH WEGEN DER ZUNEHMENDEN UNORDNUNG

Ausschließlich wegen der zunehmenden Unordnung
In unseren Städten des Klassenkampfs
Haben etliche von uns in diesen Jahren beschlossen
Nicht mehr zu reden von Hafenstädten, Schnee auf den
   Dächern, Frauen
Geruch reifer Äpfel im Keller, Empfindungen des
   Fleisches
All dem, was den Menschen rund macht und menschlich
Sondern zu reden nur mehr von der Unordnung
Also einseitig zu werden, dürr, verstrickt in die Geschäfte
Der Politik und das trockene "unwürdige" Vokabular
Der dialektischen Ökonomie
Damit nicht dieses furchtbare gedrängte Zusammensein
Von Schneefällen (sie sind nicht nur kalt, wir wissen's)

Ausbeutung, verlocktem Fleisch und Klassenjustiz eine
  Billigung
So vielseitiger Welt in uns erzeugte, Lust an
Den Widersprüchen solch blutigen Lebens
Ihr versteht.

(GW, 4:519)

This is a proclamation, a statement of what literature is to be like under the historical circumstances of late capitalism and fascism. Not so much in the form of an apology here, but in the same spirit of urgent practical need that marks the end of *Schlechte Zeit für Lyrik*, the identical point is made: under the circumstances, given the chaos and barbarity into which Europe is slithering, Brecht and those of like mind have decided to turn from the traditional subjects of poetry—the beauties of the seasons, the pleasures of the flesh—in order henceforth to write in a "one-sided" and "dry" manner of such unpoetic things as economic and political relations.

These poems are brilliantly devious. Under cover of an apparently forthright statement about what needs to be done, and an apology for its being necessary, a point quite different from the surface message is made. The statements of these poems are rhetorical, in the double sense that they are not the whole truth but artistically pointed and slanted ("one-sided") statements, and that the reader is implicitly invited to see beyond the surface to the more complex "whole truth." We get to this more complex true state of affairs in two ways. First, a moment's reflection or a quick look through Brecht's work in these years will produce a significant amount of poetry—proportionately at least as much as in other periods—about girls' breasts and apple blossom, to use Brecht's own shorthand. Some of this poetry is rhymed. Faced with this contradiction, we must conclude that poems like *Ausschließlich wegen der zunehmenden Unordnung* and *Schlechte Zeit für Lyrik* are consciously and transparently one-sided statements, made not to conform to an actual state of affairs (the complete eschewing of poetry about love, nature's beauties, and the like) but to drive home forcefully an urgent sense of the artist's political responsibilities.

Second, the poems themselves are living proof that, contrary to what is said in them, writing about contemporary social and political history, or about the duty to do this, does not have to mean a lack of aesthetic beauty. Indeed, *Ausschließlich wegen der zunehmenden Unordnung*, *An die Nachgeborenen*, and *Schlechte Zeit für Lyrik* must be reckoned among the best poetry Brecht wrote. Aesthetically, artistically, they are excellent by any standards—any, that is, except the superannuated if still influential ones ("Ein garstig Lied! Pfui! ein politisch Lied," *Faust I*, 68) that Brecht had never accepted and that, from the beginning of his career, he had set out to discredit. We are surely not intended to think that Brecht is lamenting his inability to write poetry along traditional lines—love poems, verse about the beauties of a landscape, and poetry about "all that makes a man round and human." That kind of poetry he never wrote. His forswearing of such verse, defiant in *Ausschließlich wegen der zunehmenden Unordnung*, apologetic in *Schlechte Zeit für Lyrik*, is therefore rhetorical, in the sense in which I use that term throughout these studies of Brecht's poetry: it is an artistic construct, an argumentative strategy that aims to win the reader over—by art and argument—while not necessarily hiding from view its strategic and constructed nature, rather in the way we are convinced by an actor's (not just a Brechtian actor) transmitting an idea or an emotion while we simultaneously note and enjoy the artistic means employed. Thus we are moved by the force of Brecht's argument in *Ausschließlich wegen der zunehmenden Unordnung* though we can see the actor's (poet's) gestures for what they are. We note that the very first word of the poem has that rhetorical forcefulness that is necessary to argumentation and does not need to conform to the actual truth. This truth is of course that Brecht wrote the way he did not *solely* because of the increasing "disorder" (Brecht's peculiarly intellectual word for capitalism run amok) but for other reasons as well. How else is a Marxist poet to write, in any situation imaginable except possibly an eventual utopia, than in the way the poem describes?

Even the pre-Marxist Brecht, the Brecht say of the *Hauspostille*, had not written of apple blossom and women very often, and where he had it had been in a noticeably unconventional manner: love poems characterized by ambiguity of language and a strikingly offhand attitude toward the beloved, and nature poetry belonging to a rather brutal vitalism, not to the tradition stretching back to Goethe or the Romantics. And the lyricism of this earlier Brecht, powerful as it is, has so little in common with German poetry before him that one hesitates even to use the word lyrical, so attached is it to that central tradition evoked by names like Goethe and Hölderlin, Eichendorff and Rilke, and characterized by delicacy of feeling, contemplative musing, language exalted or fragile—and the strict avoidance of anything "merely" political.

In the act of forswearing, in *Ausschließlich wegen der zunehmenden Unordnung*, an art that he never would have considered anyway,

Brecht demonstrates the kind of art he does approve of. It is not, however, monotonous or dry. Brecht's deliberately derogatory terms *dürr, trocken,* and *einseitig* are contradicted by the poem that contains them. It is a small masterpiece of construction, its phrasing, line arrangement, and syntax cleverly managed to produce a single, virtually unpunctuated sentence that hustles the reader breathlessly through it. Having reached the end, however, he is confronted by the two words "Ihr versteht." Not sure that he *has* followed the swift and concentrated argument, the reader returns to the beginning and reads the whole thing again.

Ausschließlich wegen der zunehmenden Unordnung is thus another example of the poet Brecht's highly developed sense of his reader's presence on the receiving end of the text, so to speak. Whether the individual reader considers himself directly addressed by the "Ihr" of the final line or not scarcely matters in this case. He is bound to find this "Ihr versteht" challenging and even slightly intimidating, the more so since it is without even a question mark to soften the implicit demand for full and instantaneous comprehension. It is also of little or no importance whether the reader perceives the artistic and rhetorical means used to do this, whether he is able to reflect on the nature of the author-reader relationship being set up here. By a paradox, the subsequent or even near-simultaneous apprehension of the artistic means by which the message and its emotional and aesthetic effects are produced does not diminish this message or our appreciation of it. On the contrary, it is enhanced. Our critical awareness is thus not a "seeing through" of artistic constructs and strategies but rather an appreciative re-creation. This situation, fundamental to art and its reception, perhaps needs to be emphasized here in case the impression arises that my comments on *Ausschließlich wegen der zunehmenden Unordnung,* and the discussion of *Schlechte Zeit für Lyrik* and *An die Nachgeborenen* that follows, are an attempt to unmask these poems as some kind of fraud. If this is fraud, then so is all art.

Ausschließlich wegen der zunehmenden Unordnung is a forerunner of *Schlechte Zeit für Lyrik* in its "abandonment," purportedly for immediate historical and political reasons, of an art with which the author had no sympathy in any case. In both poems it is clear what kind of art this is. The first poem speaks scathingly of "Billigung so vielseitiger Welt," "Lust an den Widersprüchen solch blutigen Lebens," vehemently rejecting any rejoicing at the colorful multifariousness of the world, any acceptance of life's contradictions and disharmonies, because this rejoicing and this acceptance is made in the face of actual social and political circumstances in which multifariousness and contradiction include persecution and exploitation. The poem represents a stern Marxist-Leninist rejection of a spectacularly rich but vicious and unjust world, an attack on the Saint-Simonist affirmation of life with all its beauties and all its faults; or in general terms the condemnation of an art (for Brecht, most art) perceived to be amoral because ultimately it cared more about elegantly turned phrases than about social evil.

The famous lines of *Schlechte Zeit für Lyrik*, "In meinem Lied ein Reim / Käme mir fast vor wie Übermut," make the same point. This later poem, however, is different in tone from *Ausschließlich wegen der zunehmenden Unordnung*. Whereas the latter is defiant, even aggressive in its insistence on social comment rather than lyrical beauty, *Schlechte Zeit für Lyrik* is apologetic. But the strategy of both poems is basically the same. In *Ausschließlich wegen der zunehmenden Unordnung* an art is rejected that covers over with an aesthetic gloss the evils of the time; in *Schlechte Zeit für Lyrik* the poet apologizes for not being able to write about attractive things because his attention is claimed by suffering and injustice. In both cases the kind of poetry thus rejected is cleverly described in such a way as to make us feel that its loss is no loss at all. In the later poem there is a frivolousness about the "green boats and the merry sails of the sound" that is calculated to prejudice us, so that we are inclined to dismiss the apology for not writing about such things. This apology, made in the first two stanzas, itself already invites demur, since the propositions made there are clearly open to contradiction. One of Brecht's favorite ploys is to support a statement by advancing arguments that turn out to not hold water or to provoke contradiction, thus undermining the statement and allowing the poet's true message to emerge. In the present case, the very first proposition is not very convincing. Even if it is true that "only the fortunate (or happy) man is popular," this is, morally speaking, of dubious status, and so is the fact that people only like to look at handsome or beautiful things. And the argument that follows in the second stanza is still more dubious. To state that a tree grown twisted because it is rooted in poor soil is rightly called a cripple is to invite contradiction. A moment's reflection, moreover, will convince us that Brecht of all people, champion of the poor and disadvantaged, defender of those whose social background and class position meant they never had a chance, could not seriously advance such an argument. Our attention is thus drawn to the *unconvincing* nature of the poem's argument in the first two stanzas, and by extension to the analogous proposition implied by the title: that poetry is successful only when it is "beautiful" and is rightly called ugly when it reflects the ugly times in which it is written. Quite apart from the question begged by the word *schön*, the last line of this is diametrically opposed to Brecht's whole philosophy and aesthetic. At the very least we are forced to reexamine—and this is the *real* aim of the poem—conventional and facile notions about the function of art and about artistic values. By the time we arrive at the end of the poem, we are ready to applaud the poet's urgent move to his desk to write not about apple blossom but about the evils and dangers of Nazism.

The regret at having to deny himself the pleasure of writing about life's pleasures is thus largely rhetorical. Brecht did write of such things, even in dark times—though never in a conventional lyrical manner. The truth was that, though in an obvious sense it was indeed a "bad time for poetry"—a certain kind of poetry—it was a good time for another sort, precisely Brecht's kind of poetry.[1] The complexities here can be seen in a nutshell in the lines "In meinem Lied ein Reim / Käme mir fast vor wie Übermut." *Übermut* has a range of meanings from frivolity or wantonness to pride or arrogance.[2] In any case the clear implication is that in dark times conventional aesthetic embellishments are to be eschewed because of the implicit accompanying neglect of serious matters. But this kind of embellishment had always been rejected by Brecht, who either avoided rhyme and regular meter for reasons described in the famous essay "Über reimlose Lyrik mit unregelmäßigen Rhythmen" (1939), or, when he did use them, did so for some good purpose. It is often forgotten that Brecht, the most important innovator in German poetry in our century, nevertheless used traditional lyrical forms and devices throughout his career. Formally, he is a brilliant experimenter (the Lukácsian suspicion of Brecht's formalism is, in Lukács's terms, well-founded), but he is also a master of conventional formal structure—which he uses in times good and bad.

If the protestation that a rhyme would seem frivolous or impertinent in a song written in such dark times only makes sense as a rhetorical gambit used to make a point (since any literal understanding of that statement is impossible), the ultimate irony and paradox of *Schlechte Zeit für Lyrik* is that it is precisely a *poem*. Moreover it is a poem that, while not rhymed, has most of the other recognizable attributes of lyrical poetry, from its shape on the page to its mixture of pictorial images and philosophical or expository comment—all expressed in that condensed fashion that has been a trademark of poetry from its beginnings. It is also a good poem, which gives intellectual and aesthetic pleasure and would do so in good times or bad. Part of this pleasure comes from recognizing the clever way the poet makes his point and the strategy by which the kind of poetry writing favored and expertly handled by the poet is apologized for in such a way as actually to privilege it. The same strategy emerges from the poem that immediately follows in the *GW* and that is linked through its title to *Schlechte Zeit für Lyrik*:

SCHLECHTE ZEIT FÜR DIE JUGEND

Statt im Gehölz zu spielen mit Gleichaltrigen
Sitzt mein junger Sohn über die Bücher gebückt
Und am liebsten liest er
Über die Betrügereien der Geldleute
Und die Schlächtereien der Generäle.
Wenn er das Wort liest, daß unsere Gesetze
Es den Armen und den Reichen verbieten, unter den
  Brücken zu schlafen
Höre ich sein glückliches Lachen.
Wenn er entdeckt, daß der Schreiber eines Buches bestochen
  ist
Leuchtet seine junge Stirn. Ich billige das
Aber ich wollte doch, ich könnte ihm
Eine Jugendzeit bieten, in der er
Ins Gehölz spielen ginge mit Gleichaltrigen.

(GW, 4:744)

By having recourse to the excuse of bad times, Brecht can justify the necessity for the kind of poetry he would write anyway and for the reading matter he would give his son anyway. He can then simultaneously express his regret and his preference for a different situation—one in which he could write rhymed poetry about breasts and blossom, and provide a carefree childhood for his son.

As I emphasized before, the cleverness and effectiveness of these poems lies partly in the fact that the reader is allowed to perceive the rhetorical strategy used. As with irony, the full effect of the text depends on the reader's awareness of more than one level. Such poems as these draw our attention to the complex and ambiguous nature of experience and the communication of experience. This in no way prejudices Brecht's firmness of purpose as a committed writer. These poems are paradoxical, but their serious point remains. When Brecht wishes at the end of *Schlechte Zeit für die Jugend* that his son could spend his childhood engaged in careless pastimes with his friends, he perhaps envisages a time, after the dark times have passed, when it will no longer be necessary for children to learn about injustice and corruption. This is a serious perspective, just as the urgent move to the desk at the end of *Schlechte Zeit für Lyrik* is serious. But the statements that lead up to these serious conclusions are made in the framework of a literary text, carefully arranged, phrased, and pointed. They are artistically and rhetorically put, in full knowledge of their limited applicability for that poem, for that situation, for that readership. This knowledge of limited truth is the knowledge of the intelligently self-conscious artist, and it remains intact alongside all earnestness of purpose.

Ausschließlich wegen der zunehmenden Unordnung, Schlechte Zeit für Lyrik, and *Schlechte Zeit für die Jugend* all involve self-presentation on Brecht's part. The image he puts forward of himself is governed to a large extent by the "finstere Zeiten" he so often refers to in the exile years. These years are dark not so much because of his personal fate as an exile living in difficult and at times repugnant circumstances but because of the catastrophic political situation in Europe. Purely personal statements about his exile are infrequent. Private concerns are linked to public affairs, and in this way Brecht's own life and writing come more and more to be presented in terms of the fight against fascism and the anxious hopes and fears of the exile, not so much for himself but for the future of mankind. Occasionally the self-perception of Brecht the banned writer, on the run and isolated, comes very close to the bone:

GEDANKEN ÜBER DIE DAUER DES EXILS

I

Schlage keinen Nagel in die Wand
Wirf den Rock auf den Stuhl.
Warum vorsorgen für vier Tage?
Du kehrst morgen zurück.

Laß den kleinen Baum ohne Wasser.
Wozu noch einen Baum pflanzen?
Bevor er so hoch wie eine Stufe ist
Gehst du froh weg von hier.

Zieh die Mütze ins Gesicht, wenn Leute vorbeigehn!
Wozu in einer fremden Grammatik blättern?
Die Nachricht, die dich heimruft
Ist in bekannter Sprache geschrieben.

So wie der Kalk vom Gebälk blättert
(Tue nichts dagegen!)
Wird der Zaun der Gewalt zermorschen
Der an der Grenze aufgerichtet ist
Gegen die Gerechtigkeit.

II

Sieh den Nagel in der Wand, den du eingeschlagen hast:
Wann, glaubst du, wirst du zurückkehren?
Willst du wissen, was du im Innersten glaubst?

Tag um Tag
Arbeitest du an der Befreiung
Sitzend in der Kammer schreibst du.
Willst du wissen, was du von deiner Arbeit hältst?
Sieh den kleinen Kastanienbaum im Eck des Hofes
Zu dem du die Kanne voll Wasser schlepptest!

(GW, 4:719–20)

The two-part structure much favored by Brecht allows him to present, with as much pathos as he ever permitted himself, the moving plight of the emigré who is at first able to convince himself that his exile will be merely temporary, a few weeks, but then gradually succumbs to the terrible knowledge that it will last a long time, and may go on forever. This knowledge literally killed numbers of Brecht's fellow exiles. Perhaps even more bitter for Brecht, who seems actually to have had little illusion about the duration of exile, was the thought that his unceasing work against fascism was like a drop of water on a hot stone. Brecht is not known for being downcast. Even in his diaries he usually managed, in these difficult years, to remain of good hope, though the period from 1933 to 1941 was one long retreat, for Brecht and his household and for the cause with which he identified. *Gedanken über die Dauer des Exils* represents a low point in Brecht's spirits, a moment where all role fashioning is abandoned and the poet stands naked and afraid.

This poem is in its way more bitter toward its author than the entry in the *Arbeitsjournal* for 16 September 1940:

Es wäre unglaublich schwierig, den gemütszustand auszudrücken, in dem ich am radio und in den schlechten finnisch-schwedischen zeitungen der schlacht um england folge und dann den *puntila* schreibe. Dieses geistige phänomen erklärt gleichermaßen, daß solche kriege sein können und daß immer noch literarische arbeiten angefertigt werden können. Der puntila geht mich fast nichts an, der krieg alles; über den puntila kann ich fast alles schreiben, über den krieg nichts. Ich meine nicht nur "darf," ich meine auch wirklich "kann". Es ist interessant, wie weit die literatur, als praxis, wegverlegt ist von den zentren der alles entscheidenden geschehnisse.[3]

These moments of real self-criticism or gloom are infrequent. I say "real" to differentiate such utterances from texts that use a *mock* humility or self-criticism to engender a response that will bolster the poet's ego. In the second part of *Gedanken über die Dauer des Exils* there is no signal for this response, no textual indication that we are to read the apparent despair as in fact an expression of hope, as the apparent apology of *Schlechte Zeit für Lyrik* turns out to be a persuasive assertion or as the proclamation of the abandonment of "beauty" in *Ausschließlich wegen der zunehmenden Unordnung* is actually a statement about a superior kind of art.

In general it is the image of the confident persuader, the unbowed fighter, that dominates Brecht's exile work. The *Flüchtlingsgespräche*, begun in Finland in 1940 during a particularly uncertain stage of Brecht's flight, allowed him to write semiautobiographically of the refugee's plight, using a marvelous humor that rises above the frustrations and dangers of his situation. This was one way for the artist to cope with dark times. Another—familiar to us from the beginning of Brecht's career—was to assert, now under cover of a seeming modesty, his own importance. The famous exile poems give us a Brecht who, far from feeling forgotten and cast aside, seems very conscious of who he is, of his status, of his historical position. As chapter 7 of this book attempts to show, it is in Brecht's apparently modest self-portraits that we must look for the assertion of his lasting importance, in poems that deal with the poet's reputation and achievements. The greatest, perhaps, of the exile poems falls into this category too.

AN DIE NACHGEBORENEN

I

Wirklich, ich lebe in finsteren Zeiten!
Das arglose Wort ist töricht. Eine glatte Stirn
Deutet auf Unempfindlichkeit hin. Der Lachende
Hat die furchtbare Nachricht
Nur noch nicht empfangen.

Was sind das für Zeiten, wo
Ein Gespräch über Bäume fast ein Verbrechen ist
Weil es ein Schweigen über so viele Untaten einschließt!
Der dort ruhig über die Straße geht
Ist wohl nicht mehr erreichbar für seine Freunde
Die in Not sind?

Es ist wahr: ich verdiene noch meinen Unterhalt
Aber glaubt mir: das ist nur ein Zufall. Nichts
Von dem, was ich tue, berechtigt mich dazu, mich
    sattzuessen.
Zufällig bin ich verschont. (Wenn mein Glück aussetzt,
    bin ich verloren.

Man sagt mir: Iß und trink du! Sei froh, daß du hast!
Aber wie kann ich essen und trinken, wenn
Ich dem Hungernden entreiße, was ich esse, und
Mein Glas Wasser einem Verdurstenden fehlt?
Und doch esse und trinke ich.

Ich wäre gerne auch weise.
In den alten Büchern steht, was weise ist:
Sich aus dem Streit der Welt halten und die kurze Zeit
Ohne Furcht verbringen
Auch ohne Gewalt auskommen
Böses mit Gutem vergelten
Seine Wünsche nicht erfüllen, sondern vergessen
Gilt für weise.
Alles das kann ich nicht:
Wirklich, ich lebe in finsteren Zeiten!

II

In die Städte kann ich zur Zeit der Unordnung
Als da Hunger herrschte.
Unter die Menschen kam ich zu der Zeit des Aufruhrs
Und ich empörte mich mit ihnen.
So verging meine Zeit
Die auf Erden mir gegeben war.

Mein Essen aß ich zwischen den Schlachten
Schlafen legte ich mich unter die Mörder
Der Liebe pflegte ich achtlos
Und die Natur sah ich ohne Geduld.

So verging meine Zeit
Die auf Erden mir gegeben war.

Die Straßen führten in den Sumpf zu meiner Zeit.
Die Sprache verriet mich dem Schlächter.
Ich vermochte nur wenig. Aber die Herrschenden
Saßen ohne mich sicherer, das hoffte ich.
So verging meine Zeit
Die auf Erden mir gegeben war.

Die Kräfte waren gering. Das Ziel
Lag in großer Ferne
Es war deutlich sichtbar, wenn auch für mich
Kaum zu erreichen.
So verging meine Zeit
Die auf Erden mir gegeben war.

III

Ihr, die ihr auftauchen werdet aus der Flut
In der wir untergegangen sind
Gedenkt
Wenn ihr von unseren Schwächen sprecht
Auch der finsteren Zeit
Der ihr entronnen seid.

Gingen wir doch, öfter als die Schuhe die Länder
  wechselnd
Durch die Kriege der Klassen, verzweifelt
Wenn da nur Unrecht war und keine Empörung.

Dabei wissen wir doch:
Auch der Haß gegen die Niedrigkeit
Verzerrt die Züge.
Auch der Zorn über das Unrecht
Macht die Stimme heiser. Ach, wir
Die wir den Boden bereiten wollten für Freundlichkeit
Konnten selber nicht freundlich sein.

Ihr aber, wenn es so weit sein wird
Daß der Mensch dem Menschen ein Helfer ist
Gedenkt unsrer
Mit Nachsicht.

(GW, 4:722–25)

This poem is actually three poems, and we would be able to see this even if its genesis were not known. Part I is another lament about dark times along the lines of *Schlechte Zeit für Lyrik*, an apology by the poet for not being able, due to the circumstances, to be better than he is, together with an expression of the survivor's bad conscience. It was written after the other two sections, probably late in 1938 or even 1939 (when *Schlechte Zeit für Lyrik* was written).[4] Part II goes back to 1934 at least. BBA 345/28 has a 1934 version that differs only in minor detail from the final one, but the poem is strongly reminiscent of the early Brecht of *Vom armen B. B.* and has the same character of *Lebensbericht* or life portrait. This suggests that its origins may lie even further back, and that Brecht superimposed the Marxist references to political and class struggle later. Part III takes up the apology of part I and builds it into an envoi or farewell directed at a later generation. It started as a short poem entitled "Bitte an die Nachwelt um Nachsicht" dating from around 1937:

Ihr Nachgeborene, wenn ihr lest, was ich schrieb ,
Bedenkt auch, Freundliche, die Zeit, in der ich schrieb
Was immer ihr denken möget, vergesst nicht
Diese Zeit.

(BBA 345/29)

The finished version of the whole poem thus represents a skillful blending of three different but related texts. (When it appeared in *Gedichte im Exil*, the poem was not even divided into parts and followed the order III, I, II.)

Even if we did not know the intertextual relationships—if we had not read *Schlechte Zeit für Lyrik*, for example, and were not aware of the use Brecht makes elsewhere of the lament and the apology—a careful reading would lead us to see that there is a multiplicity of meanings, even a fundamental ambiguity, in *An die Nachgeborenen*. It is a poem made rich by a mixture of role-playing and soul baring, of fact and fantasy, of self-revelation and self-concealment. The portrait that emerges, however, is calculated to place the poet in a favorable light, for all its ambiguity. This ambiguity begins with the title. The relationship of the reader of the poem to the "Nachgeborenen" of the title is difficult to pinpoint, and may be shifting. Do we feel ourselves to be, more than a quarter of a century after Brecht's death, *Nachgeborene*, members of a later generation? To put the question more assertively: Do we not feel ourselves to be, in the act of reading the poem, contemporaries of the poet, just as much as Brecht's real contemporaries who read the poem in 1938 or in 1948 in *Gedichte im Exil* or in 1951 in *Hundert Gedichte*? The reader does not perform historical orientations and calculations while engaged in reading the poem. While reading *An die Nachgeborenen*—in 1938, 1948, 1988, or 2088— the reader is the poet's contemporary. (In the same way we remain the contemporaries of Claudius in Robert Graves's book *I, Claudius*, impervious to the relativizing and disorienting knowledge of Graves's fiction that what we are reading has been discovered after 1900 years, having been hidden by its author Claudius in 41 A.D., as revealed in the early pages of the novel.) This means that it is even possible for the reader reading *An die Nachgeborenen* in 2088 to wonder how the later generations addressed by the poet (the characterized readers) will react to this address. For him, while he is reading the poem, the time is the present—the poem's present, the present of the reading act.

If the title of *An die Nachgeborenen* confronts us with a complexity and ambiguity of poet-reader relationships, its first line is ambiguous in the sense that we do not know whether to take the sigh embodied in "Wirklich, ich lebe in finsteren Zeiten!" completely seriously. This uncertainty may not exist at first, but as so often in Brecht's poetry, we have to modify our initial reaction. The final stanza of part I is a lament or apology for the poet's inability to be "wise," with the excuse that the "dark times" make this impossible. However, beneath the apology there is a clear, if indirect, assertiveness, expressed through the four definitions of *weise sein*. To stay away from strife, to avoid violence, to turn the other cheek, to suppress one's desires: these quietist sentiments with their echoes of a meek and mild Christianity are unrecognizable as anything Brecht seriously could consider acceptable. Both by temperament and by political persuasion, he was not the man—and so much of his work elsewhere makes this point—to embrace such a code of behavior. At best it could only be seen as politically naive, at worst as craven. We are given further indications that these examples of "wisdom" are not to be taken seriously. "Alte Bücher" are hardly a recommendation of validity from Brecht, who was an iconoclast long before he had a philosophy of history to confirm him in his aggressiveness against the old and established; and the world *gilt* in the third last line is equivocal: saying that something "passes for wise" does not inspire confidence in it. When, therefore, Brecht says that he is incapable of being wise if this is what wise is, he is in fact praising himself.

This puts the final line of the poem's first part in a strange light. "Wirklich, ich lebe in finsteren Zeiten!" is part of the poet's *pretended* lament and apology. The regretful sigh with which the words are spoken is part of a rhetorical argument; it is a gesture belonging to a role. Though Brecht did indeed live in dark times, that is not the sole reason—so the covert argument of the text seems to run—for his acting as he does. He is as he is, and writes as he writes, not "ausschließlich wegen der zunehmenden Unordnung," or merely because of the dark times, but because of his temperament and his political and artistic beliefs.

This reading of the last lines of *An die Nachgeborenen*, part I—a reading, it should be emphasized, dictated to us by the verbal structures of the text as well as by our knowledge of the writer Brecht and the gambits he liked to employ—has implications for the rest of the poem. We are first of all forced to reconsider the first section of part I, since it begins the way the last section ends. Yet it is not clear that the sigh "Wirklich, ich lebe in finsteren Zeiten!" at the beginning of the poem is an actor's gesture, and our knowledge that these were in fact dark times prevents us from reading the line merely as a pose. Of course, we might say that for Brecht the "naive word" was *always* foolish, not just in dark times. Carefree behavior and an untroubled mien could always be interpreted as lack of compassion or awareness. And we are surely not being asked to believe that Brecht would have preferred a "conversation about trees" to one about dialectics or the latest developments in Germany. Are these examples of bad times then like the examples of wisdom a little later, false examples? Not wholly, since Brecht really was living in dark times, the darkest our century has known, and there are no clear textual indications in these initial lines that we are invited to "see through" them. In particular the end of the second stanza, "Der dort ruhig über die Straße geht / Ist wohl nicht mehr erreichbar für seine Freunde / Die in Not sind?" appears to describe without any element of pose the unpleasant climate of mistrust and uncertainty in which the German exiles found themselves. Times certainly were dark when personal relationships could be marred by such doubts and suspicions.

The ambiguity created by this hovering between confession and strategic argument is maintained in the next two stanzas, the central section of part I, in which Brecht speaks of his situation and expresses guilt at being among those exiles who are better off. There is an appeal to the reader in this expression of guilt. The author-reader psychology here is complex, but we can describe it in the following way. Our response to these central stanzas involves the perception that the reader addressed here ("glaubt mir") is a characterized reader and that what is asked of *us* is disagreement with the poet. That is, the appeal to the characterized reader is the equivalent of a baring of bad conscience ("nichts . . . berechtigt mich," "wie kann ich essen und trinken"), but the underlying invitation to the *implied* reader is to brush this aside in a reassurance that he, Brecht, must not be so foolish as to think this way. In the unspoken dialogue between poet and implied reader that these lines embody, the poet makes self-castigating assertions and the implied reader replies with demurring answers: "It is irrational to punish yourself because you are more fortunate than others." There is even a built-in, anticipated rejoinder from the implied reader, "Iß und trink du! Sei froh, daß du hast!" to which the poet answers, "Aber wie kann ich," to which in turn we implicitly reply further that it is foolish for him to imagine that the food and water he consumes mean that someone must go without.

Up to this point, the rhetorical movement of these two central stanzas of part I has been the display of bad conscience by the poet, encouraging, because it is so obviously irrational, a dissenting response from the reader. But with the final line something quite different happens. "Und doch esse und trinke ich" drops the implied appeal to the reader. It is as though the poet sees that such an appeal is foolish and accomplishes nothing. His bad conscience, pointless though it may be, will not disappear, and nor, as the line wryly admits, will his need to eat and drink.

We are thus given in the central section of part I of *An die Nachgeborenen* a glimpse of the peculiar psychological stresses under which the exiles lived, together with an indication of the poet's awareness of the futile, and ironic, aspects of the typical guilt feelings of the survivor. These guilt feelings emerge even more sharply in a short poem written later during Brecht's exile:

ICH, DER ÜBERLEBENDE

Ich weiß natürlich: einzig durch Glück
Habe ich so viele Freunde überlebt. Aber heute nacht im Traum
Hörte ich diese Freunde von mir sagen: "Die Stärkeren überleben"
Und ich haßte mich.

(GW, 4:882)

Once again the poet tells us that his survival is merely luck. There is therefore no rational reason for a bad conscience. But the dream suggests the real reason for his guilt feelings: he is tough, and the tough survive. When brought into connection with the friends who have perished, because they were not tough but too gentle and vulnerable, survival seems an almost reprehensible thing. "Die Stärkeren" seems to imply a hardness akin to ruthlessness and heartlessness. But the survivor presenting himself to us here is not heartless. Otherwise he would not have a bad conscience and write this poem. The *function* of the poem, like the function of the central two stanzas of the first part of *An die Nachgeborenen*, is thus twofold and paradoxical. It is to express feelings of guilt and bad conscience, and at the same time to seek sympathy.

The lament occasioned by the dark times in which the poet wrote and the apology for his failings make part I of *An die Nachgeborenen* a genre piece. The lament on the age in which the poet lived ("O tempora, o mores!") has a long history, and this historical and generic context is present for us as we read the poem. This goes for parts II and III also, which are likewise genre pieces—*Lebensbericht* and farewell respectively. These are often found together, as the account of the poet's life turns into an appeal to his contemporaries and/or posterity. It is typical of Brecht, however, that the most immediate source for this account of his life and the ensuing valediction is not a classical writer, not even Brecht's beloved Horace, but an outsider, an educated renegade, the antiestablishment vagabond poet François Villon. The influence of Villon on Brecht's poetry did not stop after Brecht had grown out of his early fascination with the romantic milieu of adventurers, bandits, and pirates. The literary *modi* used by Villon in the *Testament* and the *Lais* continued to provide Brecht with models until his return from exile. (After that, in the GDR, Villon as the embodiment of the antigovernment stance was not usable.) In parts II and III of *An die Nachgeborenen* the influence of Villon is unmistakable. The two-line refrain of part II is similar to the structure used by Villon in his *ballades*, and the flavor of "So verging meine Zeit / Die auf Erden mir gegeben war" is vintage Villon. In part III the address to those who come after echoes the beginning of Villon's famous epitaph for himself in the so-called *Ballade des pendus*: "Frères humains qui après nous vivez."(*Oeuvres*, 1:290) Brecht had already used this *Epitaphe Villon*, to give the poem its correct title, in very much the same way in his *Ballade, in der Macheath jedermann Abbitte leistet* from the *Dreigroschenoper*, which begins "Ihr Menschenbrüder, die ihr nach uns lebt, / Laßt euer Herz nicht gegen uns verhärten."(GW, 1:482) Now he uses it again, in a different setting.

As for the *Lebensbericht* of part II, it is strongly reminiscent of *Vom armen B. B.* but contains an explicitly political commentary, whereas the earlier poem is very much in the "anarchist" mode of the tough and cool work of the early 1920s, which is not interested in social analysis in the main. The purpose of the *Lebensbericht* is the reckoning up of the author's life. In Villon this is explicit. His longest work, the *Testament*, is an account of, justification of, and apologia for Villon's life and deeds (as well as a massive payback for his enemies). With Brecht this purpose is less explicit, but clear nevertheless.

It is important that we be aware of this aspect of the poem as a set piece. It is literature as well as autobiography, and the literary form in which it is expressed fundamentally shapes the poem. Sometimes the form or genre gets the upper hand. The picture the poet presents of himself is of the embattled fighter living in times of social and political unrest. In terms of Brecht's biography, we get a mixture of factually accurate statements like that in the first two lines and stylized, if not downright melodramatic, details such as, "Mein Essen aß ich zwischen den Schlachten / Schlafen legte ich mich unter die Mörder." Echoes of earlier self-images are present: "Der Liebe pflegte ich achtlos," and "Die Straßen führten in den Sumpf zu meiner Zeit." But the careless, sardonic voice of the early city poems has been replaced by a humble one, whose claims are deliberately modest: "Ich vermochte nur wenig"; "Die Kräfte waren gering." Such modesty cannot fail to remind us of how great was Brecht's contribution to the fight against Nazism during the dark times, and of his honorable position high on the Nazis' extermination list. Behind the humility is the sure belief that he will be seen to have fought forcefully, to have played an important role. Brecht's modesty is of the kind that can only be afforded by important people.

The mixture of autobiography and role creation, of confession and image projection, is present also in the time perspective of this poem. The poet speaks as a man at the end of his life, looking back on his experiences. His race is run; no future, no continuing career is envisaged: "So verging meine Zeit / Die auf Erden mir gegeben war." Part III then goes on even more explicitly to present a picture of a man at the end of his life. Yet when *An die Nachgeborenen* was put together Brecht was forty years old, and when part II was begun he was a good deal younger. The man was at the height of his powers and certainly determined to be a survivor, to go on living and writing. It is the literary tradition of the valediction, and the specific model of Villon's farewell, that takes over from factuality here.

Perhaps not quite. Precisely the case of Villon, who two years after writing his *Testament* was banished from Paris, never to be heard of again, would have served as an example of what can happen to poets in uncertain times. Sitting on the Danish island of Fünen as he composed *An die Nachgeborenen*, within range of the heavy artillery of the Third Reich, Brecht had every reason to reflect on the appropriateness of writing farewell poems while still in one's thirties. We have only to posit the following hypothetical situation to convince ourselves of this appropriateness: In April 1940, two years after writing the poem *An die Nachgeborenen*, Brecht is still in Denmark, fails to get out in time, and is captured by rapidly advancing German troops. He is handed over to the Gestapo and never heard of again. This is an entirely plausible scenario; it describes the fate of many of Brecht's fellow exiles. But the potential factuality of *An die Nachgeborenen* must not distract us from its essential *literary* nature, its status as poetic set piece. After all, Brecht began writing farewell poems at a very early age, long before there was any cause to wonder if he would survive the next year. What is *Vom armen B. B.* if not a sardonic farewell from a poet dwelling in the doomed metropolis? That poem was written when Brecht was just twenty-four and there was no immediate likelihood of the world's coming to an end.

The status of *An die Nachgeborenen* as literary genre piece is most evident of all in part III, the valediction and apologia. Here the address to the reader is most urgent, most insistent. "Ihr Menschenbrüder, die ihr nach uns lebt, / Laßt euer Herz nicht gegen uns verhärten"—so Brecht had transcribed Villon a decade earlier in the *Dreigroschenoper*. In this case too the appeal is directed at a later generation, which will arise out of the ruins of the present age. Once again the "Flut, in der wir untergegangen sind" is both poetic metaphor and potential fact. And once again the appeal is made in such a way as to convince us that no appeal is necessary. Using the humble voice of part II, the poet makes a case for "Nachsicht" to be exercised when his faults are recalled. Forbearance is asked for on the grounds that the circumstances were harsh and the times dark. But every poet who ever presented himself in this way to his readers for judgement has stressed this. It is part of the set piece. As for the readers, whether they are indeed happy citizens of a future era where "der Mensch dem Menschen ein Helfer ist" (a veiled reference to Goethe's "Edel sei der Mensch, hilfreich und gut"?),[5] or live in an age not as dark as Brecht's but not perfect either; whether we conceive of them as Brecht's own contemporaries or as members of a later generation—in none of these cases would they be inclined to think censoriously of the fighters in unjust times. The reader will not merely excuse but approve the just hatred and the anger, as he will approve the poet's decision to write about oppression rather than apple blossom; and he will reflect that by apologizing for something that does not need an apology, the poet is able to present himself as a man of modesty and sensitivity.

An die Nachgeborenen is a classic Brecht poem. It contains so much of Brecht the writer, so much of the personality that has become, through his work, part of literary history. But it is, precisely, a literary personality, built up through scores of first-person texts, especially poetry, in which Brecht fashions images of himself using a complex mixture of fact and fantasy, self-revelation and role projection. In *An die Nachgeborenen* the play of factuality and potentiality, of history and poetry, of apparent self-disparagement and actual self-assertiveness, is most marked. In one sense Brecht's great autobiographical poem is the last place to go for reliable information. In another sense it tells us a great deal about Brecht, the man and the writer.

5. Poetry, Conscience, and False Consciousness: The *Buckower Elegien*

The various groupings of Brecht's poems, as he himself or Elizabeth Hauptmann arranged them and as they appear in *GW*, 4, have varying status and significance as collections. Inclusion in a large collection like the *Hauspostille* implies very little about the nature or intention of a poem: Brecht merely selected what he clearly considered to be the best of his verse up to that time, and set about imposing on this very heterogeneous collection a retrospective ordering. Even the resulting *Lektionen* of the *Hauspostille* contain very diverse poems. To take only the first *Lektion*, entitled "Bittgänge," it is difficult to see what, say, *Apfelböck* and *Morgendliche Rede an den Baum Griehn* have in common, or in what sense either is a *Bittgang*. Likewise with the other big collection, the *Svendborger Gedichte*: originally entitled *Gedichte im Exil*, these range from the "phototexts" (*Phototexte*) of the *Deutsche Kriegsfibel* to complex *Lehrgedichte* such as *Legende von der Entstehung des Buches Taoteking* and the great autobiographical poem *An die Nachgeborenen*. One would of course not look for homogeneity in such large collections. In smaller groupings, from the *Psalmen* of 1920 to the *Sonette* of 1933–34 and the *Hollywood-Elegien* of 1942, one expects, and finds, considerable similarity among the individual poems. But this similarity is in large part the result of a common form or genre (*Psalmen* and *Sonette*) or of a narrow geographic and thematic focus (*Hollywood-Elegien*).

In this respect the *Buckower Elegien* occupy a special position. A relatively large collection of poems—twenty-four in all—these "elegies" are cut from the same cloth, although that is not evident at first glance. Paradoxically the two unifying factors suggested by the title, one geographic and one generic, are both misleading. Only a few of these poems fit the conventional definition of *elegy*, and some of the best-known poems in the collection cannot be called elegiac by even the most liberal definition. As for the locale, it is of only minor importance. These are not poems describing, eulogizing, or musing on a particular place. As with the *Svendborger Gedichte*, the place of composition is only of incidental significance.

Temporally, on the other hand, the Buckow elegies are of a piece: all were composed in the summer of 1953. And it is the events of that summer that produce, in a collection of different kinds of poems, the largest coherent group. There are twenty-one poems plus an epigraph under *Buckower Elegien* in GW, 4, which follows exactly the *Aufbau Gedichte 7*. *Die neue Mundart* and *Lebensmittel zum Zweck* were originally included in the collection but were removed by Elizabeth Hauptmann before publication.[1] These two poems were subsequently printed for the first time in *Sinn und Form* 32 (1980), although a pirated version of *Die neue Mundart* appeared in *Rote Fahne*, the mouthpiece of the West German communist party (KPD), in 1978 (No. 25). Of the total of twenty-four poems, eight refer to the uprising of 17 June and its aftermath. A further seven are about the situation in the GDR generally.

This needs to be set against the conventional view of the Buckow elegies as quietly contemplative poems. Strictly speaking there are only four or five of these: *Der Rauch, Tannen, Rudern, Gespräche, Bei der Lektüre eines spätgriechischen Dichters*, and perhaps the "motto." Two further poems (*Der Blumengarten* and *Laute*) are little "moral" poems, the one about *Freundlichkeit*, the other reminiscent of *Der Rauch* with its point about the value of human company. Even if one counts all these together as relatively short, quietly styled private reflections, there are only seven. This does reflect, of course, the increased proportion in Brecht's later poetry of more private or personal verse, but that too has been exaggerated. The fact is that even in this last collection that has come to be associated most with the "private" style of the late period, less than half the poems are actually in the personal contemplative mode, and at least some of these refer in any case to the events of June 1953. The real unifying factor in the *Buckower Elegien* is in fact precisely those events. These are poems written within a comparatively short space of time, under the direct influence of the most severe crisis Brecht was ever exposed to. It was a crisis both political and personal, raising fundamental questions about the young German communist state with which Brecht identified, and about his role within that state.

The temporally and referentially concentrated nature of the *Buckower Elegien* makes the extraction of one or two poems for analysis a dangerous undertaking. Even apparently obvious poems, as I attempt to demonstrate below with *Böser Morgen*, cannot always be successfully read without the context of the other poems in the collection. And some of these other poems are totally neglected: *Der Himmel dieses Sommers* and *Die Wahrheit einigt*, for example, two very dissimilar poems that provide important material for an overall, that is, adequate, understanding of the collection.

There has also been a tendency in Brecht criticism to concentrate on precisely those poems from the *Buckower Elegien* that appear to have no bearing on June 1953, even though they are in the minority. Attracted by the formal beauty and simplicity of *Der Rauch, Rudern, Gespräche, Laute,* and *Der Blumengarten*, critics have admired their epigrammatic precision while neglecting to ask questions about the presence of such peaceful and simple verse in a collection in which the majority of poems bear witness to the poet's alternatively bitter and contorted response to what he thought he saw as, or thought he had to see as, an attempted counterrevolution. Similarly, it is a digression from what the Buckow elegies mainly and plainly are about to write an essay, as Hugo Dittberner does, on the topic of "Die Philosophie der Landschaft in Brechts *Buckower Elegien*," just as it is for Gerhard P. Knapp to examine the "Ironie und Resignation" of Brecht's late poetry on the basis of, among others, two Buckow elegies extracted from their context (leading to a completely inadequate interpretation of *Der Radwechsel*); and just as it is for Paul Kersten to include *Der Rauch*, again without any surrounding context, in a discussion of "Bertolt Brechts Epigramme." The fact that one can find these three articles side by side in the second of the *Text + Kritik* special editions on Brecht,[2] which is devoted largely to the poetry and possesses after all a certain representative status, confirms the impression that there is a tendency for Brecht scholars to write on what the *Buckower Elegien* are only marginally about.

The present chapter looks at all twenty-four poems in Brecht's last collection, and looks at them with the consciousness that all of these poems are connected, directly or indirectly, with the events of June 1953 and their aftermath.[3] The procedure used is to examine individual poems in the light of all the other poems, to group poems that illuminate each other either because of their similarity or because of their apparent contradiction, and to attempt an assessment of the Buckow elegies as Brecht's only clear artistic response to the crisis of 1953.

It is a response that represents, in the body of Brecht's poetry, a revealing exception. As I have tried to make clear in my analyses of Brecht's poetry thus far, it is a serious error to make too easy an equation between the *I* of the poems and the historical Bertolt Brecht. In fact, in the majority of poems that use the first person or engage the reader in implicit dialogue, we do better if we assume a nonidentity, and attend to the rhetorical structure and image projection going on in the text. The *Buckower Elegien* are the most concentrated and striking exception to this. No other group or sequence of poems by Brecht reveals such a degree of identity between the *I*, or the personal voice in the poetry, with the man Brecht.

This identity, this direct relationship, can be established in two ways. One is to compare the known biographical and historical facts—judiciously sifted and assessed, it goes without saying—with what the poems say. The other is to search the poem for textual evidence of irony, posturing, image projection, transparent rhetoric (rhetoric meant to be recognized for what it is), or outright dissemblance. With the city poems the first approach establishes that there is no direct correlation between experience and poetry: Brecht's chastening experiences in Berlin during his first stay in 1920–21 precisely are *not* reflected in the poetry of this time. They emerge in a direct way only later. In the case of poems like *An die Nachgeborenen*, it is the rhetorical structure of the poem itself that will not allow us to take it—at least not all of it—as a straightforward statement of Brecht's feelings. When we come to the *Buckower Elegien*, however, neither of these negative criteria is present. We have enough information, in the form of diary and letters, to indicate that Brecht's experience of the crisis of 1953 emerges directly in the poems. And a careful reading of the poems fails to unearth the kind of irony or openly rhetorical structures that would make us doubt the identity of the *Ich* with the historical Brecht. The *Buckower Elegien* are unique among the larger groups of Brecht's poetry precisely in this respect. Brecht is nowhere more vulnerable in his first-person poetry than in this late collection. The author of the *Hauspostille* is a role creator of considerable talent and diversity. The poetry there, and in the twenties generally, is visibly experimental, exploring various modes, genres, styles, voices, and running through various possibilities of communication with the poet's audience. The author of the *Svendborger Gedichte*, while more settled as a writer, still indulges in that kind of subtle and shifting relationship with his audience. It is now one basic role on which he has settled, and it is of course much more than just a role; but the play of self-revelation and self-concealment goes on nevertheless. The exiled sage speaks to us sometimes in ways that betray an all-too-intense awareness of his status as exiled sage. Sometimes this awareness is expressed with a certain amusement, and at these moments we sense the tongue in the cheek, the "verschmitztes Lächeln." This is not to say, of course, that the Brecht of these earlier periods is not sometimes earnest, with no trace of dissemblance or irony in the voice that addresses us. But there is no group of poems except the *Buckower Elegien* where such direct earnestness is maintained unbroken, over so many poems. Why this should be so is a question that will be addressed at the end of this chapter.

Brecht's response to the events of June 1953, as expressed in the *Buckower Elegien*, is sometimes direct but more often indirect. One group of poems singles out aspects of life in the GDR, or certain members of the populace, and subjects them to a critical and suspicious gaze. It is as if the incidents of June 1953 had made Brecht acutely aware of the unconverted elements of the GDR population. In particular he focuses on three old enemies: German, specifically Prussian, militaristic behavior (*Gewohnheiten, noch immer*), the church (*Heißer Tag*), and fascists (*Vor acht Jahren*). *Der Einarmige im Gehölz* is in a different category. There is an almost neutral coolness of observation in this poem, so that the ex-SS man is rather a photographic object than a target for hatred:

DER EINARMIGE IM GEHÖLZ

Schweißtriefend bückt er sich
Nach dem dürren Reisig. Die Stechmücken
Verjagt er durch Kopfschütteln. Zwischen den Knieen
Bündelt er mühsam das Brennholz. Ächzend
Richtet er sich auf, streckt die Hand hoch, zu spüren
Ob es regnet. Die Hand hoch
Der gefürchtete SS-Mann.

(GW, 4:1013)

The disclosure in the final line and a half of the one-armed man's identity, though we are not prepared for it and are therefore perhaps surprised, is made laconically and without comment. The fact is registered, nothing more, through the frozen, snapshotlike image of the Hitler salute. Of course, stopping like this as it does, the poem invites us to ask why, in an antifascist state, an SS man is apparently still at large, if in reduced circumstances. Or we may simply reflect with satisfaction on the present humble state of a person who formerly had been powerful and "gefürchtet." Either way, there is little if any overt hostility and anger in this poem.

There is a good deal more hostility expressed in *Vor acht Jahren*:

Da war eine Zeit
Da war alles hier anders.
Die Metzgerfrau weiß es.

Der Postbote hat einen zu aufrechten Gang.
Und was war der Elektriker?

(GW, 4:1013)

The time "when everything was different here" is precisely indicated: 1945, the last year of Nazi rule. Even without the title, the poem's meaning is plain. Possibly the second line is a kind of quotation: "Da war alles anders hier" was (and still is) a stock phrase in the mouths of the unrepentant, those who had learned nothing and looked back approvingly on the past. Brecht was under no illusion about the continued survival of these attitudes in the new German socialist state. "Hier" may refer to the first instance to Buckow, which Brecht called a "mißgünstiges Kleinbürgernest," but it is also the whole country. Brecht's impatience with the survival of attitudes and practices that in theory are not tolerated in a communist state appears also in *Heißer Tag*:

Heißer Tag. Auf den Knien die Schreibmappe
Sitze ich im Pavillon. Ein grüner Kahn
Kommt durch die Weide in Sicht. Im Heck
Eine dicke Nonne, dick gekleidet. Vor ihr
Ein ältlicher Mensch im Schwimmanzug, wahrscheinlich ein
    Priester.
An der Ruderbank, aus vollen Kräften rudernd
Ein Kind. Wie in alten Zeiten! denke ich
Wie in alten Zeiten!

(GW, 4:1011)

One is made to feel here, particularly in the last two lines, Brecht's bitterness that such sights are still to be seen in a communist state.
Heißer Tag has a structure that Brecht employs frequently in his later poetry, especially in the Buckow elegies. It is the structure of a picture with commentary. Sometimes the picture is a moving one, as here; sometimes it is a still (*Tannen*). (And in *Der Einarmige im Gehölz* a moving picture is frozen in the penultimate line.) The commentary that follows the picture is often separated from it typographically and is in each case brief and pointed. This structure with its emblematic and epigrammatic elements largely accounts for the distilled effect of the *Buckower Elegien* and their blending of the visual with the meditative or expository.

The aggressive, critical poems of this collection are not restricted to those aspects of life in the GDR that Brecht the ruthless undergrowth clearer detested because they represented a hangover from the capitalist, bourgeois, and fascist past. This group is balanced by those poems that criticize the bureaucracy and leadership of the GDR for having lost touch with the populace and for their self-imprisonment in dogma and propaganda. Of these the best known example is *Die Lösung*.

> Nach dem Aufstand des 17. Juni
> Ließ der Sekretär des Schriftstellerverbands
> In der Stalinallee Flugblätter verteilen
> Auf denen zu lesen war, daß das Volk
> Das Vertrauen der Regierung verscherzt habe
> Und es nur durch verdoppelte Arbeit
> Zurückerobern könne. Wäre es da
> Nicht doch einfacher, die Regierung
> Löste das Volk auf und
> Wählte ein anderes?
>
> (GW, 4:1009–10)

This is a famous poem, not just because it makes bold and specific reference to the rebellion, but because it is a classic example of Brechtian writing: perfectly proportioned, perfectly paced. The long opening sentence followed by the "solution" starts as something tentative but ends with sudden and decisive force. Brecht had from the beginning a very fine sense of the way in which verbal inaccuracy or absurdity betrays a stupid or corrupt mind. Kurt Barthel's now immortal proposition, as secretary of the writers' association, needed only to be taken to its logical conclusion in order to unmask it—a classic satirical technique. But there is an added sting in the tail of this poem. The notion of a government's dissolving the people and electing another promotes inevitably in the reader's mind the opposite procedure on which this absurdity is based. And that, as Brecht well knew, was a procedure that, in mere mention, was taboo. It is a measure of Brecht's anger at the more stupid and dogmatic elements of the GDR regime that he responded not just with a very aggressive poem but with an implied proposal—free elections—with which he himself, in sober moments, was not in agreement.[4]

The late publication of *Die neue Mundart* makes it much less well known than *Die Lösung*. But it is just as good a poem, and just as devastating in its criticism of the party bureaucracy:

> Als sie einst mit ihren Weibern über Zwiebeln sprachen
> Die Läden waren wieder einmal leer

Verstanden sie noch die Seufzer, die Flüche, die Witze
Mit denen das unerträgliche Leben
In der Tiefe dennoch gelebt wird.
Jetzt
Herrschen sie und sprechen eine neue Mundart
Nur ihnen selber verständlich, das Kaderwelsch
Welche mit drohender und belehrender Stimme gesprochen wird
Und die Läden füllt—ohne Zwiebeln.

Dem, der Kaderwelsch hört
Vergeht das Essen.
Dem, der es spricht
Vergeht das Hören.

(*Gedichte aus dem Nachlaß*, 428)

Once again Brecht uses the structure outlined above, an epigrammatic ending set apart from the foregoing, which in this case is not so much a picture as a narrative comparison between then and now. The final four lines deliver the *Spruch*-like judgment on the object of Brecht's disgust: those party bosses who once understood and communicated with their fellows in shared want and oppression, and now from their new positions of power speak "mit drohender und belehrender Stimme" a "cadre jargon" (the brilliant pun is not really translatable) that is the sign of their lack of desire to truly communicate with their fellows. Communication means both making oneself understood and listening to the response. Neither of these processes takes place.

Brecht's criticism in this poem is in a way more wholesale than in *Die Lösung*. In that poem he attacks, at least on the face of it, only the stupidity of one party functionary. Here the "sie" referred to can only mean the party functionaries and bureaucracy in toto. It is a sweeping criticism, and it is made more biting by Brecht's reference in the first stanza, through the then/now contrast, to a potentially explosive issue: the rise to power of an elite, a party vanguard, that having assumed power, loses touch with, increasingly alienates, and eventually even betrays the people in whose name it acts. If the measure of Brecht's anger in *Die Lösung* is the implicit suggestion of free elections, in *Die neue Mundart* it is his raising of this sensitive point about the new German socialist state. It is sensitive not just because, as Brecht knew, large numbers of the population actually did feel this way about the GDR elite, but because, theoretically, such a process of alienation was not possible. The whole issue within Marxism of the role within a socialist society of the intelligentsia—I use the word in the Marxist sense to mean not principally artists and academics but the leading decision-making planners and managers in all sectors of society—has never been resolved. That Brecht was extremely sensitive to this problem I have tried to show elsewhere.[5] His barbed reference in this poem to the GDR bureaucracy is the more striking because it is so unusual. Brecht rarely lifts the lid off.

Lifting the lid off, talking openly about taboo matters, is a sign of revolt or of desperation. Brecht must have been feeling very rebellious or very desperate to write *Die neue Mundart*. The same goes for the other poem removed from the Buckow elegies before publication, *Lebensmittel zum Zweck*:

> An die Kanonen gelehnt
> Teilen die Söhne Mac Carthys Schmalz aus.
> Und in unendbarem Zug, auf Rädern, zu Fuß
> Eine Völkerwanderung aus dem innersten Sachsen.
>
> Wenn das Kalb vernachlässigt ist
> Drängt es zu jeder schmeichelnden Hand, auch
> Der Hand seines Metzgers.
>
> *(Gedichte aus dem Nachlaß, 428)*

Picture and epigrammatic commentary again, an exemplification of the structure central to the Buckow elegies. Here the picture is dramatic, and bitter. The "Schmalz" being doled out is both nourishment and cheap pap, and those doling it out are the hated Americans, caught with photographic precision in the familiar lounging attitude. They are lounging on artillery guns, and their political and military functions are pinpointed in the succinct description of them as "sons of Mac Carthy [sic]."

The scene in the second half of the first stanza is also vividly sketched: an interminable column heading west from the heart of the GDR. This image of the "unendbarer Zug" must have been, as it is still, a particularly poignant and painful one for Germans. The picture of the endless procession of people in wagons, on bicycles, on foot pushing handcarts, all moving slowly west is graven in the memories of people who experienced the events of 1945. That the same exodus was taking place all over again, from the German state that described itself as the haven of the peaceful, the oppressed, and the exploited, is bitter indeed.

This exodus was another source of acute embarrassment to the GDR regime. No amount of reference to "unrepentant fascists," "petit bourgeois elements," and the like could conceal the extent of the problem, which was not "solved" until the building of the Berlin wall in 1961. Far from attempting to conceal it, Brecht describes it here as a "Völkerwanderung." Like that other demographic phenomenon to which the term is usually applied, it was nothing less than a mass migration. "Voting with one's feet" is the appropriate phrase for what the poem describes.

Of course, those who so vote are, from Brecht's point of view, wrong—misguided and ignorant wretches unwittingly delivering themselves up to their class enemy. Lured by the superficially attractive but essentially trivial "Schmalz" of the West, they abandon the promise of an eventual future of equality and humanity. The neglected calf, in Brecht's terms, rushes to the hand that caresses it, not seeing that it is the hand that will slaughter it.

Quite apart from the arguable first part of this proposition, the image of the calf, striking as it is, is not very flattering to the participants in the *Völkerwanderung*. To compare the workers' and peasants' grievances (Brecht himself referred to "berechtigte Unzufriedenheit") to a calf's reaction to being "neglected" (a euphemism if ever there was one) is to trivialize those grievances and insult the intelligence of those who draw their conclusions. Calling such people "calves" is quite revealing of Brecht's attitudes. Though on the one hand he is critical—at times even bitterly satirical—of the regime and bureaucracy that has ignored the mood and the opinions of the people, on the other hand he shares to a large extent that regime's attitude toward the ordinary people of the GDR. They are not yet educated in socialism; they are still vulnerable to bourgeois enticements and not really trustworthy in a crisis; they must be protected against themselves, kept firmly under control until such time as the state is stabilized and secure, and socialism reigns in the minds of the people as well as in the laws and statutes. This little poem thus contains in concentrate Brecht's conflicting reactions to the events of and around June 1953, reactions that are given separate expression in other poems from the Buckow collection. In poems like *Vor acht Jahren* we see the mistrustful Brecht looking around him at an unconverted population. In *Die Lösung* it is a stupid and dogmatic ruling group that attracts his anger and derision. In *Lebensmittel zum Zweck* these attitudes come together to make it a touchstone for Brecht's views.

But he did not release it for publication. A copy of the typescript (BBA 97/09) bears a handwritten comment by Elizabeth Hauptmann: "Dieses Gedicht wollte Brecht *nicht veröffentlichen*, gab statt dessen *Jakobs Söhne ziehen aus* an die Berliner Zeitung."[6] Perhaps he was aware of the insult implicit in the image of the immature, foolish calf, or perhaps the description of a taboo subject—mass flight from the GDR—seemed too bold or politically undesirable. *Jakobs Söhne*, the poem published in place of *Lebensmittel zum Zweck*, though not with the *Buckower Elegien*, is both less explicit and less insulting:

> Vater, warum sprichst du nicht?
> Die Esel scharren schon.
> Wir gehn die Hände schütteln
> Mit deinem andern Sohn.
>
> Gebt ihr ihm die Hand
> Steckt sie schnell wieder ein:
> Euer Bruder in Ägyptenland
> Wird ein Ägypter sein.
>
> Vater, warum lachst du nicht?
> Wolle nicht bitter sein!
> Mehl gibt leckere Kuchen
> Und süß schmeckt der Wein.
>
> Für ein Fäßlein Wein
> Für ein Säcklein Mehl
> Ward mancher schon ein Kriegsknecht
> Verkauft war Leib und Seel.
>
> (GW, 4:1017)

The poem, balladesque in its style, describes in the form of a parable the departure of the foolish sons in search of "leckere Kuchen" and "süßer Wein." But although the sons are here also presented as naive and foolish, the father, representative of wiser, less corruptible, politically more astute counsel, is not so much patronizing as merely sad.

Of the other *Buckower Elegien*, three further poems may be seen as—perhaps indirect—criticisms of the leadership in the GDR: *Der Himmel dieses Sommers*, *Die Kelle*, and *Große Zeit, vertan*. The first of these may merely express a general fear of armed conflict:

> Hoch über dem See fliegt ein Bomber.
> Von den Ruderboten auf
> Schauen Kinder, Frauen, ein Greis. Von weitem
> Gleichen sie jungen Staren, die Schnäbel aufreißend
> Der Nahrung entgegen.
>
> (GW, 4:1015)

Poetry, Conscience, and False Consciousness 131

This is a picture without the commentary that is usually provided. As such, it invites us to supply the interpretation. We cannot take the poem merely at face value, just as a little picture. The title refers to "this summer," and the emphasis must direct our attention to the events of 1953. The first line gives us the ominous bomber and the contrasting peacefulness of the lake. Then, from the mundane picture of people looking up as the plane goes over, is drawn the startling analogy of baby birds opening their beaks for food. The comparison is entirely inappropriate, since the "food" that comes from this plane is bombs. The irony is rather unpleasant.

One other detail attracts our attention. Brecht specifically omits able-bodied men from his third line: "Schauen Kinder, Frauen, ein Greis." Where are the men? Perhaps in the bomber and similar vehicles of war. Whatever the answer, their absence, together with the other details of the poem, helps to produce an atmosphere of foreboding. Whether the bomber is meant to be a sign of the conflict within the GDR or whether it rather indicates the imminence of a Western-inspired attempt to "reunify" Germany (a widespread fear in the GDR after June 1953), the plane is a bird of ill omen. The sky is not clear, sunny, and beautiful this summer.

Die Kelle is more direct in its reference to the events of 1953. It has the same general structure as *Der Himmel dieses Sommers*, consisting of a short but vivid picture whose meaning is not explicit. In the case of *Die Kelle* the picture is a dramatic one:

> Im Traum stand ich auf einem Bau. Ich war
> Ein Maurer. In der Hand
> Hielt ich eine Kelle. Aber als ich mich bückte
> Nach dem Mörtel, fiel ein Schuß
> Der riß mir von meiner Kelle
> Das halbe Eisen.
>
> (GW, 4:1015)

Brecht employs a favorite device here, used three times in the *Buckower Elegien*: the dream in which a message emerges. This poem is unusual in that the dream action is rather indirect in its meaning. Nevertheless we can interpret it without difficulty by reference to 17 June. The shot that shatters the bricklayer's trowel must come from the security forces, the police, or from a Russian soldier. (The latter possibility would represent the only reference in the whole of the *Buckower Elegien* to the presence in the GDR of Russian tanks and troops.) In any event the productive work being achieved is rudely curtailed. It is typical of Brecht that he uses the image of the bricklayer, a worker, to refer to himself. As far back as 1926 he had appeared as a carpenter to make a point about the alienating impact of the big cities, in *Oft in der Nacht träume ich*. More important, however, is the fact that the mason and his tools have a key symbolic function in the iconography of the communist world. That the representative worker of the "workers' and peasants' state" has his trowel shot away is, on this symbolic level, an explicit comment. The violence that is potential and implicit in *Der Himmel dieses Sommers* becomes actual and explicit in *Die Kelle*. The reference to the events of June 1953 is very clear. It was of course the building sector where the trouble started. The shot that strikes the builder's trowel is not only a grim reminder that this is a dangerous situation in which people get killed, but tips the scales of sympathy heavily in favor of the rebellious workers and against the regime and the measures it took to quell the uprising. The bricklayer is presented as getting on with a useful task in which he is peacefully absorbed. The shot, on the other hand, is purely destructive.

Like *Der Himmel dieses Sommers*, the direction of attack of *Große Zeit, vertan* is uncertain:

Ich habe gewußt, daß Städte gebaut wurden
Ich bin nicht hingefahren.
Das gehört in die Statistik, dachte ich
Nicht in die Geschichte.

Was sind schon Städte, gebaut
Ohne die Weisheit des Volkes?

(GW, 4:1010)

What are the cities referred to here? If one relates the poem to *Lebensmittel zum Zweck* or *Jakobs Söhne ziehen aus*, it seems they are the new cities in the West, particularly in West Germany, whose shine and glitter are a beacon to the deluded people who flock to them, not seeing that they are the new bastions of big business and exploitation. Built "ohne die Weisheit des Volkes," these monuments to Western money and technology are worthless.

But it is more logical to link *Große Zeit, vertan* with the group of *Buckower Elegien* that criticize the actions and performance of the GDR government, and to see the new cities as products of the reconstruction in the GDR that began after the war and was still in full swing in 1953. The charge that the GDR leadership was obsessed with technology was after all not an uncommon one at the time, and Brecht refers on at least one other occasion in his poetry (*Unglück-*

licher Vorgang) to the senselessness of throwing up buildings without heed to their human function or consultation with those who will use them.

This reading of *Große Zeit, vertan* may be the more plausible because the poem appears, in the order presented in the *Aufbau Gedichte 7* and *GW*, between *Die Lösung*, a poem explicitly critical of the leadership, and *Böser Morgen*. The order of these poems may not reflect Brecht's intentions, if any, but a more weighty indication that it is GDR cities that are meant is that *all* the other poems in this collection are concerned with the GDR. There are certainly anti-West poems from this period, beginning in 1947 with *Der anachronistische Zug*, but they do not appear in the *Buckower Elegien*.

Brecht's rejection in this poem of the narrow policy of building and developing at all costs and as fast as possible is another aspect of his disillusionment with the GDR. There is something approaching contempt in his curt dismissal of the much-vaunted, endlessly publicized achievements of "reconstruction": "Das gehört in die Statistik, . . . / Nicht in die Geschichte." The remark is particularly cutting because it is the capitalist West, not socialism, that is supposed, according to Marxist opinion, to be guilty of the quantity-not-quality approach and to ignore human considerations in the blind pursuit of "more and bigger." Also cutting, and bitter, is the poem's title. One is perhaps first inclined to apply the notion of "waste of opportunity" contained in *vertan* to the poet, who has lived through a "great time" without experiencing or viewing its achievements. But the poem makes clear that this is meant dialectically, that the time was not *groß* at all and so there was nothing to miss—or alternatively that there was indeed a (potentially) "große Zeit," the birth of a communist Germany, that was however wasted. Either way the title is sarcastic.

Of this relatively large group of poems within the *Buckower Elegien* criticizing the GDR leadership and bureaucracy, none was published in Brecht's lifetime. The six poems included in *Versuche 13* (1954) were *Der Blumengarten, Gewohnheiten, noch immer, Rudern, Gespräche, Der Rauch, Heißer Tag*, and *Bei der Lektüre eines sowjetischen Buches*. They are without exception harmless poems, in the sense that they are either critical of retrograde elements of the GDR population (*Heißer Tag*), eulogistic of communism (*Bei der Lektüre eines sowjetischen Buches*), or nonspecific expressions of unexceptionable sentiments. The only one of these six poems that could be taken as a criticism of the regime is *Gewohnheiten, noch immer*, in which the continued presence in the GDR of Prussian attitudes is sardonically noted. One is led to wonder about the function the *Buckower Elegien* had for Brecht, given this extremely cautious release. Either the majority of poems were clearly never intended for immediate public consumption, or a process of self-censorship quickly developed. Whatever the case, the result was that precisely those poems that attempted to come to grips with the uprising of 1953 were held back—two of them indefinitely. In this way Brecht—to put it unkindly—was able to have his cake and eat it too. He could give expression, in his art and in private—presumably these unpublished poems were shown to Brecht's friends—to his frustrations and anger about the GDR leadership while maintaining the public image of the astute, reliable, and committed socialist writer.

But one cannot ever really have one's cake and eat it too. While Brecht's public reticence about the uprising of 17 June and its handling by the leadership may have satisfied the latter, the masses expected something more of their hero. Brecht's inability to please both the party to whom he felt bound in allegiance and the "common" people whose esteem meant so much to him created the severe *personal* crisis of 1953. How he handled this crisis one can read also in the *Buckower Elegien*. The litmus paper test is in the little poem *Böser Morgen*:

> Die Silberpappel, eine ortsbekannte Schönheit
> Heut eine alte Vettel. Der See
> Eine Lache Abwaschwasser, nicht rühren!
> Die Fuchsien unter dem Löwenmaul billig und eitel.
> Warum?
> Heut nacht im Traum sah ich Finger, auf mich deutend
> Wie auf einen Aussätzigen. Sie waren zerarbeitet und
> Sie waren gebrochen.
>
> Unwissende! schrie ich
> Schuldbewußt.
>
> (GW, 4:1010)

This poem makes it clear why the events of 17 June 1953 "alienated" Brecht's "entire existence."[7] It was not just that these events demonstrated to him how minimal support for communism among the populace actually was, it was also that Brecht's own standpoint, and his actions during this period, were marked by a basic and unresolved dilemma: suspicion of the motives for the uprising and support for the hard stance of the regime on the one hand, sympathy with the ordinary worker and contempt for much of the party and its dogmatic rigidity on the other. The *Arbeitsjournal* entry for 20 August 1953, whose beginning refers to 17 June as having "alienated" Brecht's "entire existence" is a good example of this conflict. The entry (1017) reads in full:

buckow. TURANDOT. daneben die BUCKOWER ELEGIEN. der 17. juni hat die ganze existenz verfremdet. in aller ihrer richtungslosigkeit und jämmerlicher hilflosigkeit zeigen die demonstrationen der arbeiterschaft immer noch, daß hier die aufsteigende klasse ist. nicht die kleinbürger handeln, sondern die arbeiter. ihre losungen sind verworren und kraftlos, eingeschleust durch den klassenfeind, und es zeigt sich keinerlei kraft der organisation, es entstehen keine räte, es formt sich kein plan. und doch hatten wir hier die klasse vor uns, in ihrem depraviertesten zustand, aber die klasse. alles kam darauf an, diese erste begegnung voll auszuwerten. das war der kontakt. er kam nicht in der form der umarmung, sondern in der form des faustschlags, aber es war doch der kontakt.—die partei hatte zu erschrecken, aber sie brauchte nicht zu verzweifeln. nach der ganzen geschichtlichen entwicklung konnte sie sowieso nicht auf die spontane zustimmung der arbeiterklasse hoffen. es gab aufgaben, die sie unter umständen, unter den gegebenen umständen, ohne zustimmung, ja gegen den widerstand der arbeiter durchführen mußte. aber nun, als große ungelegenheit, kam die große gelegenheit, die arbeiter zu gewinnen. deshalb empfand ich den schrecklichen 17. juni als nicht einfach negativ. in dem augenblick, wo ich das proletariat—nichts kann mich bewegen, da schlaue, beruhigende abstriche zu machen—wiederum ausgeliefert dem klassenfeind sah, dem wieder erstarkenden kapitalismus der faschistischen ära, sah ich die einzige kraft, die mit ihr fertig werden konnte.

The rationalizing going on here is truly hair-raising, but in addition, Brecht's actions and statements during the crisis of June 1953 and its aftermath reveal the classic symptoms of the man caught between the grindstones of opposing attitudes. He swings between a mistrust of the populace every bit as intense, and even paranoid, as that of the party leadership, and an opposing dislike of precisely that leadership and its inflexible resolve not to change its preconceived views. There is abundant evidence for this dislike, but one should not underestimate Brecht's suspicion of the masses or the events of 17 June either. In a letter to Peter Suhrkamp he maintained that there was a danger that these events could have led to a new Nazi revolution:

among the workers demonstrating on the streets were "allerlei deklassierte Jugendliche" and ex-Nazis "die durch das Brandenburger Tor, über den Potsdamer Platz, auf der Warschauer Brücke, kolonnenweise eingeschleust waren."[8] In another note on the uprising, this point is expanded:

> Die Demonstrationen des 17. Juni zeigten die Unzufriedenheit eines beträchtlichen Teils der Berliner Arbeiterschaft mit einer Reihe verfehlter wirtschaftlicher Maßnahmen.
> Organisierte faschistische Elemente versuchten, diese Unzufriedenheit für ihre blutigen Zwecke zu mißbrauchen.
> Mehrere Stunden lang stand Berlin am Rande eines dritten Weltkrieges.
> Nur dem schnellen und sicheren Eingreifen sowjetischer Truppen ist es zu verdanken, daß diese Versuche vereitelt wurden.
> Es war offensichtlich, daß das Eingreifen der sowjetischen Truppen sich keineswegs gegen die Demonstrationen der Arbeiter richtete. Es richtete sich ganz augenscheinlich gegen die Versuche, einen neuen Weltbrand zu entfachen.[9]

This makes abundantly clear just where Brecht stood with regard to the handling of the uprising by the Russians. As for his attitude toward the GDR populace, it comes close at times to paranoia. The *Arbeitsjournal* entry for 7 July 1954 reads:

> das land ist immer noch unheimlich. neulich, als ich mit jungen leuten aus der dramaturgie nach buckow fuhr, saß ich abends im pavillon, während sie in ihren zimmern arbeiteten oder sich unterhielten. vor zehn jahren, fiel mir plötzlich ein, hätten alle drei, was immer sie von mir gelesen hätten, mich, wäre ich unter sie gefallen, schnurstracks der gestapo übergeben.
> (1017)

This, be it noted, is said about his own young protégés.

Brecht's dilemma over what should be his response to the uprising of 17 June is the central and unifying factor in an apparently heterogeneous collection of poems. His anguish comes from the fact that, as he sees it, the populace is both genuinely aggrieved *and* not to be trusted, the government is both right to act quickly to quell the rebellion *and* out of touch with the mood and mind of the people. The poems in the *Buckower Elegien* reflect this clearly. One can chart the vacillation in attitude from poem to poem and pinpoint those poems where the clash of such opposing attitudes is most in evidence. One of these is the previously quoted *Böser Morgen*. This is the only poem in the *Buckower Elegien* that refers to Brecht's own involvement in the crisis of June 1953. The details of this involvement are by now well known. Brecht's telegram to Walter Ulbricht, sent on 17 June, was both an appeal for a "große Aussprache mit den Massen" and an assurance of support for the government. Only the last sentence of the telegram, however, was made public on 21 June: "Es ist mir ein Bedürfnis, Ihnen in diesem Augenblick meine Verbundenheit mit der Sozialistischen Einheitspartei Deutschlands auszusprechen." Though Brecht subsequently wrote a renewed request for the "nötige Aussprache über die allseitig gemachten Fehler," the impression created by the publication of that last sentence out of context was that Brecht supported unconditionally the brutal measures of the government and the Russian military, and that this was the full extent of his reaction. It looked to many people as if Brecht had betrayed the common man. *Böser Morgen* is the only evidence we have of the effect that this had on Brecht. But the painful exclamation "Unwissende!" does not merely refer to the affair of the telegram, with its suppressed first part supporting a dialogue between government and workers. Irrespective of the telegram, Brecht's attitudes toward the crisis, as demonstrated above, were as much determined by his fear of a "Nazi revolution" or a Western-inspired reunification of Germany—and by his doubts about the capacity of the rebellious workers to resist subversion by Western *agents provocateurs*—as they were by sympathy with the "justified grievances" of the masses and dislike of the highhandedness and rigidity of the government. What the exclamation "Unwissende!" expresses is Brecht's conviction that the masses, the ordinary people, did not understand the situation, did not see the full picture. But this conviction made him feel guilty, because it implied a knowledge and status superior to those of the poor deluded or ignorant common man, and because the fact that the masses did not understand was partly the fault of that minority that did. Brecht was always sensitive to his status as writer and intellectual and to his relationship with the masses. The dream image of the broken, worn fingers of the workers pointing at him "wie auf einen Aussätzigen" is very powerful, and captures the pain of someone for whom it had always been important to be accepted by the common people.

However, something else takes place in this poem besides Brecht's protest that he is (unjustly) reviled. In his admission that he nevertheless has a bad conscience lies an implicit appeal to the reader, an attempt to gain sympathy. We can detect this by asking the question that has frequently directed the interpretations in this book: What does the poem's rhetoric hope to persuade us of? This question is of course present, articulated or not, in the mind of every critical reader of any poem. In most of the other *Buckower Elegien* the answer is straightforward, the direction and thrust of the text self-evident. In a few, notably *Der Radwechsel*, the message is difficult to decipher. But in that case the difficulty lies in choosing among several possible meanings, not in discovering a covert text under the surface, such as we saw in *Schlechte Zeit für Lyrik*, for example. Among the *Buckower Elegien*, *Böser Morgen* is the only example of this latter kind, though to my knowledge it has not been recognized as such. *Exposed* might be a better word, since in my view the poem contains an element of false consciousness, of evasion. This emerges precisely in the final word of the poem. "Schuldbewußt" both expresses Brecht's awareness of his privileged position as an important intellectual vis-à-vis the ordinary people and at the same time seeks exoneration from blame. It seeks exoneration not on rational grounds but by using a purely rhetorical, ultimately emotional appeal, calculated to obtain sympathy for the conscience-stricken writer. First he claims that he is wrongly blamed, then, by admitting that he nevertheless feels guilty, encourages a gesture of demur in his readers. It is a rhetorical strategy that we have seen Brecht use on more than one occasion—in *An die Nachgeborenen* and *Schlechte Zeit für Lyrik*, for example—and that we shall see most clearly of all in *Warum soll mein Name genannt werden?* But whereas in those poems the rhetorical strategy is used to make subtle points that add complexity, in a quasi-ironic way, to Brecht's self-image, in *Böser Morgen* it is used to obscure the truth and to rationalize away a bad conscience. That is, it represents a refusal to spell out the real problems posed by the uprising of 1953 and the gaping credibility gap it caused; it is a flight from real confrontation into rhetoric: poetry *as evasion*.

In other words, though *Böser Morgen* gives dramatic expression to a personal and political crisis, the poem stops short of real self-confrontation. Instead, it swerves into a merely rhetorical protestation of being innocent but feeling guilty. This allows the poet to retain his "good guy" image with the reader, but it is an evasion, because the *reasons* for these guilt feelings are not examined. The poet confesses his feelings of guilt, not guilt itself. The implication the reader is meant to take is that the guilt feelings are irrational, have no basis, and are just an indication of the nice Brecht, who feels guilty even when it is not his fault—or that, even if he is in some sense guilty, his willing admission of guilt still makes him a nice person.

Böser Morgen allows us to see the problematic nature of Brecht's two positions, the position of sympathizer with the justified grievances of the populace against a ruling elite blinded by dogmatism, and the position of responsible and experienced political intellectual who sees a potential counterrevolution developing among a populace either immature and misled or actively antisocialist. Confronted with dilemma, Brecht retreats to poetry, which becomes the vehicle for first one position, then the other. But it is precisely in those poems where the positions collide—*Böser Morgen* and *Der Radwechsel*—that we perceive the nondialectical nature of Brecht's standpoint: self-justification instead of self-analysis in *Böser Morgen*, and in *Der Radwechsel* helplessness stylized into art. However much one sympathizes with the psychological pressures created by years of exile, however readily one pays due respect to the fate of the German Left and takes into account the historical experience of fascism that distorted its perceptions in so many ways, the account of the 17 June crisis offered by Brecht in his comments cited above and in *Böser Morgen* still amount to a rationalization. At a moment when only honesty and scrupulous (self-) criticism could have helped, Brecht—he was of course not alone—chose to put up the shutters, chose the retreat to rhetoric instead of the advance to true analysis.

Those *Buckower Elegien* that represent a direct response to the June 1953 crisis are negative, resigned, or helpless. One exception to this is discussed below. It is significant that though this single exception, *Die Wahrheit einigt*, is a *positive* poem, in the sense of offering optimistic images of socialism, it is close to disastrous as art. Just as significantly, the *successful* positive poems among the Buckow elegies are poems of a general, not a specific, character, expressing general ideals rather than responding directly to a specific crisis. *Der Rauch* and *Laute* are examples of this; *Rudern, Gespräche* is another:

Es ist Abend. Vorbei gleiten
Zwei Faltboote, darinnen
Zwei nackte junge Männer: Nebeneinander rudernd
Sprechen sie. Sprechend
Rudern sie nebeneinander.

(GW, 4:1013)

From this simple, quiet picture of two young men rowing and talking together, a favorite Brechtian message is drawn: cooperation and harmony produce peace and achieve results. The young men row as they talk, talk as they row. The words *rudern, sprechen,* and *nebeneinander* take on a general social and political significance, and acquire connotations of "make progress," "communicate and consult," and "cooperation" respectively. The effortless ease with which progress is achieved in this way is expressed in the word *gleiten*.

But it seems that only in such general images of an emblematic nature could Brecht successfully express the ideals of cooperation, dialogue, and productive discourse so dear to him. When he tries to offer answers to specific problems, real political and social crises, he adopts a posture which is alarmingly close to the schoolmasterly. In fact, whenever Brecht reverts to the direct address in order to promote positive action, the tone almost invariably fails. It becomes strident and forced, as in *Die Wahrheit einigt*:

> Freunde, ich wünschte, ihr wüßtet die Wahrheit und sagtet sie!
> Nicht wie fliehende müde Cäsaren: Morgen kommt Mehl!
> So wie Lenin: Morgen abend
> Sind wir verloren, wenn nicht . . .
> So wie es im Liedlein heißt:
> "Brüder, mit dieser Frage
> Will ich gleich beginnen:
> Hier aus unsrer schweren Lage
> Gibt es kein Entrinnen."
> Freunde, ein kräftiges Eingeständnis
> Und ein kräftiges WENN NICHT!
>
> (GW, 4:1011–12)

This is the worst poem in the *Buckower Elegien*. The exclamatory address, used so often in his directly propagandistic or politically exhortative poetry, was not Brecht's forte. Here what is presumably meant to be a kind of hearty seriousness comes across as unnatural. One is painfully aware of the poet's forced smile as he claps the "Freunde" on the back. No wonder he finds it difficult to hide his awkwardness in this jovial role: the "Freunde" are the same bleak party bureaucrats responsible for the "Kaderwelsch" and the hair-trigger reaction to popular disquiet dealt with so devastatingly elsewhere in the *Buckower Elegien*. Or are they perhaps the "sowjetische Freunde" of GDR parlance, those noticeably absent figures in Brecht's account of the 1953 uprising? That was the greatest taboo of all: the virtual Russian occupation of the GDR was a subject Brecht was not prepared to broach.

Whoever the "friends" are, Brecht's awkwardness with them comes out in the very syntax of the poem. It is disjointed and clumsy. The result is that the exhortation to positive thinking and cooperation sounds strident, almost shrill, and therefore unconvincing. This may also be due in part to the negative form in which the positive steps are advocated. Statements like "aus unserer schweren Lage / Gibt es kein Entrinnen" do not exactly inspire confidence, and the capitalized "WENN NICHT!" with which the poem ends sounds merely desperate, not constructive. It is a poem misconceived and gone wrong in its execution. The best thing about it is the title, expressing a favorite Brechtian notion. Though it may be a little over-idealistic, it is a pity a potentially rich and effective heading should be let down by what follows.

The four lines of verse quoted in *Die Wahrheit einigt* are by Alexander Tvardovski, and Brecht got to know them from the novel by W. Galaktinov and A. Agranovski, *Ein Strom wird zum Meer*, about a hydroelectric dam on the Volga. Perhaps Brecht should have kept his enthusiasm for this book out of his own writing. The other poem in the *Buckower Elegien* dealing directly with the Volga dam also adds nothing to the collection's value:

BEI DER LEKTÜRE EINES SOWJETISCHEN BUCHES

Die Wolga, lese ich, zu bezwingen
Wird keine leichte Aufgabe sein. Sie wird
Ihre Töchter zu Hilfe rufen, die Oka, Kama, Unscha, Wjetluga
Und ihre Enkelinnen, die Tschussowaja, die Wjatka.
Alle ihre Kräfte wird sie sammeln, mit den Wassern aus
    siebentausend Nebenflüssen
Wird sie sich zornerfüllt auf den Stalingrader Staudamm stürzen.
Dieses erfinderische Genie, mit dem teuflischen Spürsinn
Des Griechen Odysseus, wird alle Erdspalten ausnützen
Rechts ausbiegen, links vorbeigehn, unterm Boden
Sich verkriechen—aber, lese ich, die Sowjetmenschen
Die sie lieben, die sie besingen, haben sie
Neuerdings studiert und werden sie
Noch vor dem Jahre 1958
Bezwingen.
Und die schwarzen Gefilde der Kaspischen Niederung
Die dürren, die Stiefkinder
Werden es ihnen mit Brot vergüten.

(GW, 4:1014–15)

This is by no means the aberration that *Die Wahrheit einigt* represents, but it falls below the standard of the other poems in the *Buckower Elegien*. Perhaps in the cheerless summer of 1953, Brecht was encouraged by his reading of a book in which the positive achievements of the motherland of communism were described. And perhaps this poem is meant as a counterweight to the images of socialist breakdown and failure that mark these late poems. There seems to be no other reason for its inclusion among the Buckow elegies, where it is obtrusive.

The poem is successful enough, though not outstanding in any way, until the dash two-thirds of the way through the poem. There seems no need for the repetition of "lese ich," particularly since such parenthetical interpolations are often used as a signal for skepticism or disbelief. (Brecht is prone to this confusing use of such interpolations—"höre ich" is another.) And the lines "haben sie / Neuerdings studiert und werden sie / Noch vor dem Jahre 1958 / Bezwingen" are among the most lame ever written by Brecht. It was one of his powerful contributions to poetry to use simple, everyday, unadorned language in effective ways. But the language here sounds as if it comes from a schoolchild's geography essay. Brecht recovers the situation somewhat with the final three lines, but the damage has been done.

The direct approach seems to be successful only when Brecht is attacking, not when he seeks to make positive, affirmative points. His greater success with less direct, more oblique poetry is borne out by the other poems discussed above. Another example is *Eisen*:

Im Traum heute Nacht
Sah ich einen großen Sturm.
Ins Baugerüst griff er
Den Bauschragen riß er
Den eisernen, abwärts.
Doch was da aus Holz war
Bog sich und blieb.

(GW, 4:1012)

The general message of this is clear enough. As in the much earlier poem *Morgendliche Rede an den Baum Griehn* (from around 1920), in which the tree is praised for having survived, against the poet's expectations, a violent storm ("Und ich weiß jetzt: einzig durch Ihre unerbittliche / Nachgiebigkeit stehen Sie heute morgen noch gerade"), the value of flexibility is exemplified. A favorite Brechtian message once again, but one that, in the context of 1953, perhaps had special and personal significance. The poem can be read as a plea to the authorities, and to the rebellious workers, to give a little, bend a little, in order that they and the state of which they are citizens may survive. In this respect it may be that the title *Eisen* is an oblique reference to Stalin (the name means "steel") and Stalinist attitudes. Compared to the strident, overhearty appeal for cooperativeness in

Die Wahrheit einigt, Eisen makes its point about flexibility—a precondition of this cooperativeness—in a quiet yet effective way.

Eisen exemplifies the structure of many of the *Buckower Elegien*: from a described scene or action a meaning emerges that has a general as well as a specific level, the latter given in each case by the events of the summer of 1953. Even the spare little poem *Tannen*, on examination, shows this structure:

In der Frühe
Sind die Tannen kupfern.
So sah ich sie
Vor einem halben Jahrhundert
Vor zwei Weltkriegen
Mit jungen Augen.

(GW, 4:1012–13)

This is, in terms of language used, the simplest poem in the whole collection. But as one contemplates it, the very simple, minimal meaning expands, like concentric circles spreading from a stone dropped into a pool. Perhaps nowhere is Brecht closer to the haiku or to that simple, quiet Chinese poetry that so impressed him.[10] The basic theme, time passing, is established through the contrast of young and old eyes. Nature, in the form of the fir trees, remains constant, although the poet's attitude toward it may change. We recall the brash, nature-hating city dweller of *Vom armen B. B.*: "Gegen Morgen, in der grauen Frühe pissen die Tannen / Und ihr Ungeziefer, die Vögel, fängt an zu schrein." There the fir trees were viewed from the end of the night, as befits the dissolute young night owl of these early poems, not from the beginning of the day. It depends on one's point of view whether one sees the greyness of the dawn or the copper color of the trees as the rising sun catches them.

This subjectivity, the change in the way one looks at things, is brought home in *Tannen* by the lines: "Vor einem halben Jahrhundert / Vor zwei Weltkriegen / Mit jungen Augen." Not only has half a century gone by and the young eyes become old, but the events that have taken place in those five decades have altered the eyes too. These events are dominated by two world wars. We are reminded that Brecht's teenage years coincided with the first of these wars, and that the second, and the developments that led to it, fundamentally determined the life and work of the mature writer. The middle-aged eyes looking at the fir trees have seen a half century consisting largely of bloody strife and human suffering. The "so" in the third line is thus deceptive. On the one hand he does see the fir trees in the early morning light "in the same way"—in the sense that fir trees are fir trees and the sun's rays are sun's rays, they do not change. But on the other hand it is not in the same way as it was back when he was a boy, and cannot be, since living in the world, in history, changes vision and perception—and meaning.

All of this is conveyed by the little poem, and it is conveyed without sentimentality or pathos. There is no nostalgia for the innocence of childhood, no merely sentimental recollection. The then and now serve not to promote misty-eyed reminiscence but a quiet contemplation of what it means to live in the world in general and of what events the poet's life has been determined by in particular. It may be that there is a further feeling of sadness engendered, as with all evocations of the passing of time, by the notion of the inevitable end, of time running out. But *Tannen* seems to me to have very little of this. Its point is rather a dialectical one about constancy and change.

Beim Lesen des Horaz, on the other hand, does leave the reader with a sense of the poet's disappointment, or even mild despair:

Selbst die Sintflut
Dauerte nicht ewig.
Einmal verrannen
Die schwarzen Gewässer.
Freilich, wie wenige
Dauerten länger!

(GW, 4:1014)

This is also a poem about what the passage of time means, but in a different way from *Tannen*. *Tannen* is about the changes that living— and living through history—bring about in a person. *Beim Lesen des Horaz* is about the sad fact that man does not often live long enough to see the things he hopes for. The disappointment that accompanies this view is made greater by the opposite emotional movements embodied in the poem's two parts: the first four lines, and the last two. The first part is optimistic. In what is obviously a rejoinder to a remark of Horace about how long bad times go on,[11] Brecht points out that even such a catastrophe as the Flood finally came to an end: "Einmal verrannen / Die schwarzen Gewässer." Then, however, comes the pessimistic second part, which is all the more deflating for having been preceded by the consoling first four lines. Almost as an afterthought, suddenly it occurs to him that very few people (if indeed any) outlasted the flood, lived long enough to *see* the black waters receding.

At the general level, this is a dispirited and dispiriting view of man's life and hopes. The bad times, the difficult and crisis-ridden times, last too long for the individual. His hope of experiencing the receding of the flood is vain. As a specific reference to Brecht's own situation, it is likewise full of disappointment. The interpretation is difficult to avoid that Brecht here is admitting—more unreservedly than anywhere else—first that the situation in the GDR is bad ("schwarze Gewässer" is an emotive phrase) and second that he does not expect to live long enough to see things get better.

This makes *Beim Lesen des Horaz* the most negative poem in the *Buckower Elegien*. The bitterness of poems like *Die neue Mundart* and *Lebensmittel zum Zweck* has specific causes, and the possibility of improvement is at least left open. *Beim Lesen des Horaz* is both specific and general in its disillusionment, and offers no hope, even in the dimension of potentiality. There is a starkness about this poem that marks the low point for Brecht in these last years of his life. Perhaps most telling of all, the impatience that is to be felt and heard in other Buckow elegies is missing here. Impatience means that one feels change and improvement to be possible. Its absence in *Beim Lesen des Horaz*, the bleak acceptance of man's fate—and the fate of Bertolt Brecht, citizen of the GDR—is the final sign of resignation.

Resignation also figures in the poem that is the most difficult to interpret of all the Buckow elegies, the very first in the collection:

DER RADWECHSEL

Ich sitze am Straßenrand
Der Fahrer wechselt das Rad.
Ich bin nicht gern, wo ich herkomme.
Ich bin nicht gern, wo ich hinfahre.
Warum sehe ich den Radwechsel
Mit Ungeduld?

(GW, 4:1009)

The poem invites an interpretation that uncovers a meaning beneath the surface one. Not that this surface meaning, referring as it does to a common quirk of human behavior, is unimportant. It is true, at least of productive people, that any interruption of an activity, even when the activity is not important, is greeted with impatience, this being a general reaction to something not going according to plan, to time simply wasted.

Nevertheless, it is the *coded* meaning of the poem for which we look. Other Brecht poems of this kind, including others in this collection, lead us to search for such a meaning. The crucial lines are the central two. If we apply these to Brecht's life in general, or to the general situation in the GDR, we must read the second of these lines as an expression of wholesale disagreement with developments in the GDR. This is simply not plausible. All the evidence tells us that even where Brecht was worried by the shortcomings of the regime and of the new socialist state, he never doubted the overall direction and was careful not to allow his specific criticisms to be used as Western ammunition (cf. *Nicht so gemeint*). There is nothing that would make us believe that this poem represents the single exception.

It is difficult to see what other underlying *general* meaning we can give to that fourth line of the poem. An allusion to some purely private affair is possible but once again would be exceptional. There are several poems by Brecht that involve private allusions, but not in such a way as to obscure the central meaning of the poem. The personal allusion is in those cases merely an extra feature. The alternative is to read the poem in the specific context of the events of June 1953. I am not aware of any precise information about the genesis of the poem, but one can read the two central lines as an expression of Brecht's dilemma when confronted with the uprising. Torn between sympathy for the "berechtigte Unzufriedenheit"[12] of the workers and a profound fear that what was happening on the streets was the beginning of the counterrevolution, Brecht clearly did not like either the prospect of a return to the harsh conditions that helped produce 17 June, or the prospect of a popular revolt that could be exploited (and here Brecht's view was in line with that of the party leaders) for counterrevolutionary purposes by a mixture of petit bourgeois elements within the GDR and *provocateurs* from over the border. In the terms of the poem's imagery, the poet does not like the situation that existed prior to the uprising (which this situation caused); nor does he like the look of the new situation arising from the rebellion. But it is all too human to await with impatience what is to come, even if one is apprehensive about it.

If there is a personal political meaning to *Der Radwechsel*, this one is more plausible than the heavy-handed interpretation of (non-Marxist) Western critics, according to which the poem is a thinly veiled wholesale criticism of the GDR ("Ich bin nicht gern, wo ich hinfahre"). But my reading is also more plausible than the attempts by GDR critics like Schuhmann to generalize the situation described by the poem to such an extent that the impatience mentioned in the last line becomes simply the positive impatience of a man acutely conscious of the "Diskrepanz zwischen Erreichbarem und Erreichtem."[13]

If Western critics, as Schuhmann complains, tendentiously attach too one-sided a significance to Brecht's disquiet in this poem, he himself avoids a discussion of that crucial fourth line. To what does "wo ich hinfahre" refer?

Peter Paul Schwarz, although he has no part in that Western tendentiousness rightly criticized by Schuhmann, is not successful either in proposing a satisfactory reading of *Der Radwechsel*. Schwarz makes things difficult for himself by reading the line "Ich bin nicht gern, wo ich herkomme" as referring to Brecht's American exile. Given this sort of time scale, it is necessary to read the following, fourth line as referring to the GDR in general. Schwarz sees the problem here and seeks to extricate himself:

> Daß damit die Zukunftsperspektive eines humanen Sozialismus von Brecht keineswegs aufgegeben, sondern erst recht herausgestellt wird, verdeutlicht die überraschende Schlußfrage des Gedichts "Warum sehe ich den Radwechsel / Mit Ungeduld?", die der konkreten Situation des Radwechsels eine paradoxe gesellschaftliche Pointe abgewinnt: Denn obwohl sich die gesellschaftlichen Ziele des sozialistischen Systems noch keineswegs realisiert haben, Resignation also zu erwarten wäre, wird der in Ostdeutschland vollzogene Wechsel vom kapitalistischen zum sozialistischen Gesellschaftssystem von Brecht derart positiv gewertet, daß er ihn (aus der fiktiven Rückkehrperspektive des Gedichts) "mit Ungeduld" herbeigewünscht.[14]

Paradoxical is hardly the word for a turnaround from rejection of the perceived social and political goals of the GDR (in Schwarz's terms) to impatience to see them achieved: *illogical* would be more accurate. The real problem, however, lies with Schwarz's indentification of *Der Radwechsel* as a *Rückkehrgedicht*. Almost five years lay between Brecht's return to Berlin and the composition of this poem. The time for poems about coming home was long past. And all the other poems of the *Buckower Elegien* are about the present: the summer of 1953.

One is forced back to the reading outlined earlier, in which the third line refers to the situation existing *in the GDR up to 1953* and the fourth to the new situation arising in that year. My scanning of the criticism on this poem reveals an ironic ally in this supposition. In an extraordinary book,[15] Jürgen Link attempts an interpretation of Brecht's late poetry, including several of the *Buckower Elegien*, using a structuralist method of decoding the "symbols" in this poetry. Most of the results are as astounding as they are unconvincing. The epigraph, for example ("Ginge da ein Wind"), is deciphered as the "Literaturproduzent" Brecht needing a "Massenbewegung" ("Wind"), to create a "proletarisches Drama" ("Segel" = "Schiff"). "Stecken und Plane" stand for "unzugängliches literarisches Material." Amid the welter of "symbolic" references, however, Link occasionally hits on one that is illuminating. In this case he makes sense of *Der Radwechsel* by asking, to begin with, at what point in the history of the GDR the wheel change occurs. (This has of course less to do with structuralist symbol decoding than with sensible historical thinking.) Three answers suggest themselves: (1) Stalin's death (5 March 1953), (2) the proclamation of the "Neuer Kurs" (9 June), and (3) the uprising of 17 June. Link points out that in any case the three events are closely connected: "Der 'Neue Kurs' bedeutete einerseits eine partielle Revision des alten, unter Stalin verfolgten Kurses, andrerseits löste er indirekt die Ereignisse des 17. Juni aus."[16] Using Link's decoding, the wheel change = the announcement of the "Neuer Kurs"; the poem's third line (start of the journey) = "Alter Kurs" or Stalinism; and the fourth line (goal of the journey) = consequences of the "new course." Brecht dislikes equally the origin and the goal of the journey, but waits impatiently for the journey to continue to its goal: "Das 'Ziel' wird also in dialektischer Weise sowohl positiv wie negativ bewertet."[17] Whether Link is right in positing the proclamation of the "Neuer Kurs" as the watershed or whether—as I am inclined to think—the 17 June events are the key point in time, it really makes little difference. The important thing is that the events alluded to in the poem all take place within the GDR between 1949 and 1953 and that the wheel change represents a major turning point in the history of the German socialist state. My reason for preferring the 17 June is that *Radwechsel* suggests *Panne*, something going wrong that must be fixed. This seems to fit the *breakdown* of 17 June.

Link adds to the referential scope of the poem by equating the driver of the vehicle with the leadership of the GDR and the situation of the poet's sitting by the roadside with his political impotence. A further interpretation of the poem's ending is also offered: "Der heftige Wunsch, bald an ein nicht gewünschtes Ziel zu gelangen, läßt sich im Sinne der dialektischen Geschichtsauffassung verstehen: eine weitere negative Zwischenetappe ist offenbar für den weiteren Fortschritt nicht zu umgehen; schlimmer als alles wäre der Stillstand."[18]

This reading of *Der Radwechsel* is coherent within itself, does not leave unexplained anything within the poem, sensibly relates what the poem says to the situation in the GDR in 1953 as Brecht saw it, and fits with the other poems in the *Buckower Elegien* that refer to this situation. These poems include the deeply suspicious—almost paranoid—references to the petit bourgeois elements with their Nazi past that survive in the GDR (*Vor acht Jahren*); the depiction of institutions from Germany's past as maintaining their influence into the GDR present despite everything (*Heißer Tag, Gewohnheiten, noch immer*); and the poems criticizing the GDR leadership and bureaucracy for their actions before and during the 17 June crisis (*Die Lösung, Der Himmel dieses Sommers, Die neue Mundart, Lebensmittel zum Zweck, Die Kelle*), or reflecting Brecht's actions during that crisis (*Böser Morgen*).

In the context of these poems, *Der Radwechsel* functions as the integrating factor, a kind of taking stock of Brecht's reactions to 1953, but at the beginning rather than the end of the collection. (But given the uncertain status of the arrangement and order of the *Buckower Elegien*, this is perhaps of no consequence.) The poem expresses Brecht's dissatisfaction with the situation prior to the proclamation of the "Neuer Kurs" or the crisis of June 1953; the poet's onlooker status, his inability to influence this and later events ("Ich sitze am Straßenrand"); and his equal disquiet with what is to come from the "new course," or June 17. This little poem is thus at once an epigrammatic comment on the strange paradoxes of human behavior and an allegory of Brecht's experience of and response to events in the GDR in the summer of 1953.

Brecht's disappointment with what the events of 17 June had to his mind demonstrated—the party's loss of touch with the populace, the continued presence in many people of bourgeois, even fascist, tendencies, and the unstable and fragile nature of support for the communist state—is expressed clearly in the critical poems discussed above, whether they are critical of the retrograde elements in the GDR or of the leadership. And there is disappointment too in the more enigmatic poems among the *Buckower Elegien*, as *Beim Lesen des Horaz* shows. Sometimes there seems also to be hope, since disappointment for Brecht is followed by hope, by the insight into the *necessity* for hope. Perhaps there is a little of this hope in *Der Radwechsel*; perhaps the poet's impatience with delay has its roots in the hidden hope that "where I am going" may yet turn out to be a pleasant surprise. More than this, perhaps the word *Ungeduld* is to be read in the Marxist sense of *productive* impatience, and as a reference to that category of positive human thinking described by Ernst Bloch's "Prinzip Hoffnung."

The little epigraph that heads the collection also seems at first to demonstrate the importance Brecht attached to hope:

> Ginge da ein Wind
> Könnte ich ein Segel stellen.
> Wäre da kein Segel
> Machte ich eines aus Stecken und Plane.
>
> (GW, 4:1009)

The key to the poem is of course the subjunctive. The whole thing is hypothetical: if there *were*, I *would*. There is no wind, therefore a sail is useless, therefore it is pointless to think about making one. But the speculative *if*, with the hope that it embodies, expresses that irrepressibly creative, productive urge in man that Brecht valued so highly. Even sitting relaxed by the lake at Buckow, as we may picture the poet here, his idle thoughts incorporate this desire to act, to produce, to build.

The poem is unfinished in that its open end invites further *ifs*: If there are no sticks I could cut some from a tree; if there is no canvas I could use a bedsheet; if there is no bed I could . . . and so on ad infinitum, the way children, in whom the urge to build and create is so strong, play a game of chain invention.

But it *is* speculation when all is said and done. All remains in the realm of the hypothetical. Is there not resignation after all in this admission of potentiality, not achievement—of the possible, not the actual? A sign that Brecht at this stage of his life feels both hope and resignation is perhaps the wry smile we sense in the last poem of the Buckow elegies, *Bei der Lektüre eines spätgriechischen Dichters*:

> In den Tagen, als ihr Fall gewiß war—
> Auf den Mauern begann schon die Totenklage
> Richteten die Troer Stückchen grade, Stückchen
> In den dreifachen Holztoren, Stückchen.
> Und begannen Mut zu haben und gute Hoffnung.
>
> Auch die Troer also.
>
> (GW, 4:1016)

Even in a hopeless situation, purposeful activity has a comforting and cheering effect. Brecht's final line must be understood as an expression of sympathy from one who understands and shares the Trojans' compulsion to go on hopefully ordering their existence and attending to what is necessary—and at the same time as a knowing admission of the ultimate futility of such actions in some cases.

The framing of the Buckow elegies by these two short poems on the theme of man's need to hopefully construct is thus paradoxically the strongest indicator of the resignation of Brecht in his last years. It is the corollary of this need, namely the unfulfilled nature of hope (that makes hope necessary!), that produces the resignation. We need not read the imminent fall of Troy, in the final poem, as an indication of Brecht's fears for the survival of the GDR. The poem's emphasis is rather on the positive activity of work and its psychological results ("Mut" and "gute Hoffnung"). If there is a specific reference here it is probably to Brecht's own activities. Late in his life he had come to know disillusionment and resignation, but also the way one overcomes—has to overcome—these, namely through purposeful activity. Brecht is too skeptical and shrewdly intelligent, however, not to see the paradoxes in all this. Ultimately there is only the sadly ironic smile.

His disillusionment and resignation are probably related to the stage of life Brecht had reached as well as to the current situation in the GDR. Though it is this situation that keeps on cropping up, directly or indirectly, in the *Buckower Elegien*, it would be psychologically obtuse not to surmise that the political crisis of 1953 was a turning point in Brecht's life not just because of this crisis but because it came at a time when Brecht was vulnerable, starting to feel old and tired. There is a certain recognition of his own limitations, or of the limitations of his position. This certainly does not mean that Brecht gave up, withdrew, and became passive. His work in the three years left to him testifies to his activeness in the public sphere as well as in his own writing. It is a question merely of the unmistakable presence in his work, and nowhere more obviously than in the *Buckower Elegien*, of a tone of resignation and sadness. It is tempting to use the word *elegiac* to describe this tone. However, the term can be misleading. It is true that they are called the Buckow elegies. But the only other group of poems called *Elegien* by Brecht, the *Hollywood-Elegien* of 1942, are quite different poems, filled with a cold anger and disgust of which there is no trace in the later collection. The third poem in this small group is typical:

HOLLYWOOD-ELEGIEN

III
Die Stadt ist nach den Engeln genannt
Und man begegnet allenthalben Engeln.
Sie riechen nach Öl und tragen goldene Pessare
Und mit blauen Ringen um die Augen
Füttern sie allmorgendlich die Schreiber in ihren
    Schwimmpfühlen.

(GW, 4:849)

Calling such poems elegies can only have been bitter sarcasm. Compared with these expressions of revulsion with a false, exploitative, and ugly society, the Buckow poems certainly qualify much more readily for the title *elegies*. The word means, among other things, poems marked by personal emotion of an intense and usually painful kind. In Brecht's case the personal emotion is inextricably connected with the political events taking place around him. Even those feelings that we might call universal and general—resignation at not having achieved goals, disappointment at how slowly things change—are never expressed in a vacuum, as statements about the nature of man *tout court*. They are always linked to specific experience, and that for Brecht was ineluctably social and political. We might in fact view the *Buckower Elegien* as in part an attempt by Brecht to refashion the concept of elegy, in much the same way as the younger poet had refashioned the Moritat or the *Legende*, taking over the genre but adapting it, altering it so that it acquired a sociopolitical function. The purely subjective, personal emotion of the elegy becomes in Brecht's verse *personal-social*, the one sphere experienced through the other.

My discussion of the poems of the *Buckower Elegien* is intended to make clear how necessary it is to consider all the poems of the collection before making judgments and forming interpretative conclusions about any one poem. Though in some cases a poem's belonging to a set may not tell us much about it—some of the *Hauspostille* poems and some of the *Svendborger Gedichte* make perfectly good sense without their specific context—and though sometimes a poem's inclusion in a group tells us nothing beyond the obvious (the *Lesebuch für Städtebewohner*, for example), the possibility must not be overlooked that belonging to a set fundamentally shapes and directs a poem. In the case of the *Buckower Elegien* it is asking for trouble not to consider the individual poems as part of the collection. Each poem stands in an important and illuminating relationship—complementary or antithetical—with at least one other, and most in fact are members of a larger group. It is also impossible to consider these poems without the background of the events of 15 to 17 June 1953. There are four apparent exceptions to this: *Der Blumengarten, Der Rauch, Laute,* and *Die Musen*. They have not been discussed so far because they do not contribute to our understanding, except formally, of the other poems. But, as we shall see later, there is a sense in which even these poems shed important light on the total collection of which they are a part. Of the four, *Die Musen* presents the most difficult problem of interpretation.

Wenn der Eiserne sie prügelt
Singen die Musen lauter.
Aus gebläuten Augen
Himmeln sie ihn hündisch an.
Der Hintern zuckt vor Schmerz
Die Scham vor Begierde.

(*GW*, 4:1015–16)

This is in many ways the strangest poem in the whole collection. It does not seem to fit with any of the other types of poems in the *Buckower Elegien*, and the view of art expressed in it seems to bear little relationship to the gentle, distilled verse most often associated with this collection; but nor does it resemble the critical poems that make up such a large proportion of the *Buckower Elegien*.

Link takes "der Eiserne" to mean Stalin,[19] and despite the unconvincing nature of some of his other equations, this seems a likely reading. The "muses" are the obsequious hacks churning out prescribed art, existing in a masochistic relationship to the rigidly dogmatic cultural organs of the Stalinist state. The vivid and crass imagery of their subservience is perhaps an indication that Brecht's dislike of these party hacks had been heightened by the events of June 1953 to contempt. On the psychological level, it is tempting to speculate that Brecht was abreacting in this little poem his disquiet at these events and his strong feeling of guilt, feelings that he could not give rein to but had to sublimate or otherwise divert. So the aggression against the self (guilt about his failure to denounce publicly the Sozialistische Einheitspartei or the Russians) is directed outward at those writers even more supportive of the party and the system, the hacks who prostitute their meager talents in masochistic enjoyment of their contemptuous and brutal treatment.

The question raised toward the beginning of this chapter requires an answer: What are the reasons for the markedly more *direct* relationship in the *Buckower Elegien* between the poetry and the life experience of Bertolt Brecht? Though it is possible that this directness is merely a reflection of Brecht's age, of the feeling that the time for rhetorical tricks and playful subterfuge was past, I would argue that the crucial factor was the uniqueness, in Brecht's experience, of the crisis of 1953. The desperate seriousness of the situation, as he saw it, ruled out everything but earnestness. This was not a purely personal crisis that mental health required he cope with through a process of indirect transformation, as was the case with the city poems. And no kind of irony or rhetoric would have seemed in the least appropriate. The seriousness of the danger that Brecht perceived for the GDR and for the future of communism generally allowed nothing else but a forthright, direct response, devoid of masks. It was a far more immediate and proximate danger than the equally grave but less localized, less concentrated ones with which the exile had been confronted during the Third Reich. It is one thing to witness from afar the triumphant victories of fascism in 1940–41, and quite another to experience at close hand, on the streets of Berlin, the beginning—as Brecht saw it—of the counterrevolution that would destroy German communism and return the country to its Nazi past. In the one case, one could always hope that the next battle would see a victory for the forces of good, or feel that at least one was for the moment safe. But in the other case, there would be no next battle, only permanent disaster, and one would not be safe, one would have no future. Even after the danger had passed, there could be no rejoicing. Relief was mingled with deep depression at the thought of how easily the GDR population, or large parts of it, had succumbed, as Brecht saw it, to the superficial allure of the West with its seductive bright lights and glittering shop windows—and at how the gap between the masses and the leadership was not only large but had taken on the look of something endemic and systemic. The underlying pessimistic thought running through the *Buckower Elegien*—how long it takes for real change to take place, how slowly improvement occurs, how little can be achieved in such a long time—was something that, turned into poetry, permitted no authorial games. It is an indication of Brecht's defenselessness vis-à-vis the situation in 1953 that his poetry drops practically all veiling and masking. A clear sign of this is the almost total absence of overt relationships with his reader. When Brecht is in control, confident of his position and role as a writer, his relationship with his reader is easy, assured, and highly visible. Conversely, when doubt and self-doubt intrude—and in 1953 Brecht was not just frightened but above all forced into doubt about the whole GDR enterprise—the poet retreats into a more monologic and private mode.

But we should not allow the relatively low incidence in the Buckow elegies of open addresses to the reader to blind us to the fact that, like all poetry, these poems are engaged constantly in communication with the reader. The very presence of the *I* in the *Buckower Elegien*—and it is constantly present—means that we cannot escape the fact that self-projection goes on, that the poet attempts to suggest to (or force upon?) the reader a certain image of himself. When asserting the identity of the *I* in these poems with the historical Bertolt

Brecht, I referred to his known attitudes and actions regarding June 1953, and to the absence in the Buckow elegies of what I have called overt dissimulation (dissimulation that is deliberately transparent, where the reader is invited to see through the role-playing). But there are other kinds of dissimulation, and in any case we must not be deflected from the basic truth that all first-person poetry is necessarily involved in the projection of an image. One of the later Brecht's most famous self-images is that of the kindly, contemplative sage. Three of the *Buckower Elegien* give us Brecht in this role. The best known is *Der Rauch*:

> Das kleine Haus unter Bäumen am See.
> Vom Dach steigt Rauch.
> Fehlte er
> Wie trostlos dann wären
> Haus, Bäume und See.
>
> (GW, 4:1012)

Through the emblematic-epigrammatic form used so frequently by Brecht in this collection, the lesson or message emerges: nature without human signs and human constructions empty of life are worthless. It takes the smoke, evidence of the human element among the inanimate and the nonhuman, to make the little scene warm.

The same message is conveyed by *Laute*:

> Später, im Herbst
> Hausen in den Silberpappeln große Schwärme von Krähen
> Aber den ganzen Sommer durch höre ich
> Da die Gegend vogellos ist
> Nur Laute von Menschen rührend.
> Ich bin's zufrieden.
>
> (GW, 4:1014)

The Brecht who had called Buckow a "mean-minded nest of petit bourgeois" is seen here in a more friendly role. If given the choice between the sounds of nature or the sounds of human life, he will take the latter. Of course, the choice of "great swarms of crows" to represent nature may make this a rather poor contest, but I take Brecht's point seriously, not ironically. Both these little poems present Brecht as the *freundlicher Weise*, who assures us of his kindly disposition toward humankind. One would perhaps not want to take exception to this but for the fact that these poems appear in a collection whose central and urgent concern is the crisis of the summer of 1953. Far from being typical—an impression one could easily get from the literature on Brecht, in which these poems are discussed with disproportionate frequency—*Der Rauch* and *Laute* represent quite striking distractions from the main themes of the collection. These sagelike, contemplative pronouncements (and we can add *Rudern, Gespräche*) are apparently unpolitical, containing no reference to the disturbing time in which they were written. But this very absence ought to draw our critical attention to the function of such poems in Brecht's work in general and in the *Buckower Elegien* in particular. It was a favorite notion of Brecht himself that all of man's self-expression is political and ideological, even when (perhaps most of all when) it seems not to be. Are we not justified, as readers and critics, in asking questions about the significance of these little poems for Brecht's response to the one pressing, overwhelming political problem of the day? Is it not somewhat disingenuous, indeed escapist, in the summer of 1953, to express such fine sentiments, couched though they may be in verse of perfect simplicity?

Almost as if Brecht anticipated such critical questions, the second poem of the *Buckower Elegien* provides a kind of justification for the inclusion of gentle beauty in his work:

DER BLUMENGARTEN

Am See, tief zwischen Tann und Silberpappel
Beschirmt von Mauer und Gesträuch ein Garten
So weise angelegt mit monatlichen Blumen
Daß er vom März bis zum Oktober blüht.

Hier, in der Früh, nicht allzu häufig, sitz ich
und wünsche mir, auch ich mög allezeit
In den verschiedenen Wettern, guten, schlechten
Dies oder jenes Angenehme zeigen.

(GW, 4:1009)

In the midst of the familiar landscape of Brecht's country retreat—lake, fir tree and silver poplar—the flower garden provides the poet with an ideal image of his own work. It is to be arranged with such "wisdom" that even in "bad weather" it is able to provide the onlooker with—what? Pleasure in simple beauty? Distraction from the bad weather? Once again we might be driven to the objection that, in the context of the bad weather of 1953, such sentiments seem badly timed and out of place—so out of place, and so manifestly a substitute for the solution to problems, that one might speak of false consciousness. The author of *Schlechte Zeit für Lyrik*, after all, had rejected "die Begeisterung über den blühenden Apfelbaum" as the inspiration and subject matter for poetry in the dark days of 1939, and in *Ausschließlich wegen der zunehmenden Unordnung* had explicitly denounced as evasion poetry about the beauty of nature and the pleasures of life if it is written in times of pressing political urgency.

False consciousness, as I have argued, is also at the very heart of the key poem *Böser Morgen*. The image of misunderstood innocence projected so cleverly in that poem is an evasion. The display of bad conscience is, at least in part, calculated to gain the reader's sympathy and escape criticism. The confession suddenly turns out to be an artistic strategy whose purpose is defense and deflection. If *Der Blumengarten*, *Der Rauch*, and *Laute* offer images of simple beauty and an attitude of wise tranquility whose real motive is the avoidance of hard decisions, the motive in *Böser Morgen* is self-justification, made necessary by this same inability or refusal to confront the fundamental questions raised by the uprising of 1953: questions about the whole socialist enterprise, about the relationship of the leadership to the masses, about the role of the intelligentsia, and about Brecht's own role as the greatest German socialist writer.

6. Problems with His Readership: Brecht's Bad Poetry

Die Mühen der Gebirge liegen hinter uns
Vor uns liegen die Mühen der Ebenen.
—Brecht, *Wahrnehmung*

In the previous chapter it was pointed out that Brecht was more at home when exercising his critical and satirical powers than when presenting positive images and scenes to illustrate the excellence of communism in general or the GDR in particular. Of the *Buckower Elegien, Bei der Lektüre eines sowjetischen Buches* and especially *Die Wahrheit einigt* cannot fail to strike the unprejudiced reader as weak poems. Conversely, it is those poems that are severely critical, whether of the GDR regime or of parts of the GDR population, where the poet Brecht's gifts are best displayed. Poems like *Die neue Mundart* and *Die Lösung* in the one case, and *Vor acht Jahren* and *Heißer Tag* in the other, give ample evidence of the power, precision, and invention that made Brecht a major poet.

The same contrast between successful censure and unsuccessful eulogy can be seen elsewhere in Brecht's work from this period. The three poems, all from 1953, that precede the *Buckower Elegien* in the GW—*Nicht feststellbare Fehler der Kunstkommission, Das Amt für Literatur*, and *Nicht so gemeint*—are good examples of Brecht's ability to write incisive criticism as poetry. The first of these is a derisive comment on the use to which the practice of self-criticism is put in the GDR:

> Geladen zu einer Sitzung der Akademie der Künste
> Zollten die höchsten Beamten der Kunstkommission
> Dem schönen Brauch, sich einiger Fehler zu zeihen
> Ihren Tribut und murmelten, auch sie
> Zeihten sich einiger Fehler. Befragt
> Welcher Fehler, freilich konnten sie sich
> An bestimmte Fehler durchaus nicht erinnern. Alles, was
> Ihnen das Gremium vorwarf, war
> Gerade nicht ein Fehler gewesen, denn unterdrückt

Hatte die Kunstkommission nur Wertloses, eigentlich auch
Dies nicht unterdrückt, sondern nur nicht gefördert.
Trotz eifrigsten Nachdenkens
Konnten sie sich nicht bestimmter Fehler erinnern, jedoch
Bestanden sie heftig darauf
Fehler gemacht zu haben—wie es der Brauch ist.

(GW, 4:1007)

This is a densely and deftly written criticism of the pseudo–self-critics from the Kunstkommission, which had created much ill feeling through its philistine and authoritarian handling of the arts and in particular its suppression of good writing in favor of party-line but inferior work. Over and above its specific target, however, the poem attacks the abuse in the GDR generally of the Leninist principle of self-criticism, which of course is supposed to have an educative and productive function. "Dem schönen Brauch, sich einiger Fehler zu zeihen"—the sarcasm alerts us to the fact that Brecht is referring to a *perversion* of the practice of self-criticism. This sarcasm controls the tone of the whole poem and is marked by words and phrases such as *freilich, bestanden sie heftig darauf*, and *trotz eifrigsten Nachdenkens*; and by the clever phrasing (mimicking the speech of the pseudo-contrite bureaucrats) of "denn unterdrückt / Hatte die Kunstkommission nur Wertloses, eigentlich auch / Dies nicht unterdrückt, sondern nur nicht gefördert."

A similarly forthright attack, but using a kind of bland irony rather than sarcasm, is directed against the narrow philistinism and dogmatic rigidity of the GDR bureaucracy, in *Das Amt für Literatur*:

Das Amt für Literatur mißt bekanntlich den Verlagen
Der Republik das Papier zu, soundso viele Zentner
Des seltenen Materials für willkommene Werke.
Willkommen
Sind Werke mit Ideen
Die dem Amt für Literatur aus den Zeitungen bekannt sind.
Diese Gepflogenheit
Müßte bei der Art unserer Zeitungen
Zu großen Ersparnissen an Papier führen, wenn
Das Amt für Literatur für eine Idee unserer Zeitungen
Immer nur ein Buch zuließe. Leider
Läßt es so ziemlich alle Bücher in Druck gehn, die eine Idee
Der Zeitungen verarzten.
So daß

Für die Werke manches Meisters
Dann das Papier fehlt.

(GW, 4:1007–8)

Brecht is able to get off a volley at GDR newspapers as well as at his main target, the Literature Bureau that decides what constitutes a "welcome" work. As in *Nicht feststellbare Fehler*, the general issue of censorship, of who decides what is to be printed and read, is clearly visible in the background.

These two poems give us a Brecht who is willing to criticize negative aspects of the GDR in a vigorous way. They reflect his activity in 1953 on behalf of a less restrictive, less philistine cultural policy and his impatient desire to raise discussion about the arts above the rigid, uncomprehending dogmatism that characterized the GDR bureaucracy at this time. However, these criticisms are offset, as it were, by the poem that immediately follows, as a kind of corrective, in the GW:

NICHT SO GEMEINT

Als die Akademie der Künste von engstirnigen Behörden
Die Freiheit des künstlerischen Ausdrucks forderte
Gab es ein Au! und Gekreisch in ihrer näheren Umgebung
Aber alles überschallend
Kam ein betäubendes Beifallsgeklatsche
Von jenseits der Sektorengrenze.

Freiheit! erscholl es. Freiheit den Künstlern!
Freiheit rings herum! Freiheit für alle!
Freiheit den Ausbeutern! Freiheit den Kriegstreibern!
Freiheit den Ruhrkartellen! Freiheit den Hitlergenerälen!
Sachte, meine Lieben!

Dem Judaskuß für die Arbeiter
Folgt der Judaskuß für die Künstler.
Der Brandstifter, der die Benzinflasche schleppt
Nähert sich feixend
Der Akademie der Künste.

Aber nicht, um ihn zu umarmen, sondern
Ihm aus der schmutzigen Hand die Flasche zu schlagen
Forderten wir die Freiheit des Ellbogens.
Selbst die schmalsten Stirnen
In denen der Friede wohnt

Sind den Künsten willkommener als jener Kunstfreund
Der auch Freund der Kriegskunst ist.

(GW, 4:1008)

Though this was—surprisingly—not published until 1957, it clearly refers to the same events and debates in the GDR as the two preceding poems. Brecht vents his full aggressiveness on the reaction in West Germany to the attempts at reform in the GDR. Ever suspicious of the West's motives, and extremely sensitive to the possibility of having his work misused and turned against the GDR, Brecht lost no time in responding to the calls for freedom of speech and of the press that emanated from West Germany in the summer of 1953. With the "attempted subversion"—as Brecht saw it—of the GDR in June still fresh in his mind, he lashes out at the Western "freedom-mongers" in a fashion reminiscent of *Der anachronistische Zug*. (The echoes in the second stanza are quite strong.) Whatever one thinks of Brecht's reaction—a balanced view might accuse him of lack of differentiation and even paranoia—the poem is well written, with sure control over tempo, rhythm, and register. The hysterical shouts of the second stanza, mimicking the cries (as Brecht interpreted them) from over the border, are terminated abruptly by the calmly ironic "Sachte, meine Lieben!" Stanza three then introduces the dramatic image of the arsonist, out to start a conflagration in socialist Germany. This is very effective polemical writing, but it is unfortunate that it is followed by the lines "Dem Judaskuß für die Arbeiter / Folgt der Judaskuß für die Künstler." In his desire to discredit Western opinion Brecht apparently ignores the danger, for a German, of using names like Judas.

Nicht so gemeint is reminiscent of *Lebensmittel zum Zweck* with its bitter comment on the seductive attraction of the West for the GDR citizen. It makes it clear that Brecht sees all Western attempts to encourage a loosening up of the situation in the GDR—whether in the political sphere (17 June) or in the cultural sphere (the later cultural shake-up)—as attempts to bring the whole edifice down, not to promote improvement. This conviction explains the vehemence and anger of *Nicht so gemeint*, which culminates in the first lines of the final stanza.

The reader may well reject, in his turn, the lack of differentiation and the uncompromising hatred in Brecht's stance. But he is likely to be impressed by the poem on one level, its persuasiveness as rhetoric. The ending in particular, taking up the word *engstirnig* from the first line and using it to express the clear priority—philistine peace-lover rather than art-loving warmonger—is very effective. Logical argument would of course quickly expose the false alternatives, and unmask the progressions embodied in the second stanza as fallacious and sophistic. We are confronted here with the same problem presented by some of the *Buckower Elegien*, the contrast between artistic skill and political false consciousness. The problem, to which attention was directed in the previous chapter, involves basic questions about the function of art and its use or misuse.

But it is not with this problem that the present chapter concerns itself. The rhetorical and artistic skill of *Nicht so gemeint* contrasts with the rather crude nature of its political statement. There is another kind of Brecht poem in which political crudeness coincides with artistic crudeness. Here is a glaring example:

AN DIE STUDENTEN DER ARBEITER— UND BAUERNFAKULTÄT

1
Daß ihr hier sitzen könnt: so manche Schlacht
Wurd drum gewagt. Ihr mögt sie gern vergessen.
Nur wißt: hier haben andre schon gesessen
Die saßen über Menschen dann. Gebt acht!

2
Was immer ihr erforscht einst und erfindet
Euch wird nicht nützen, was ihr auch erkennt
So es euch nicht zu klugem Kampf verbindet
Und euch von allen Menschenfeinden trennt.

3
Vergeßt nicht: mancher euresgleichen stritt
Daß ihr hier sitzen könnt und nicht mehr sie.
Und nun vergrabt euch nicht und kämpfet mit
Und lernt das Lernen und verlernt es nie!

(GW, 4:1026–27)

Brecht in the role of finger-wagging schoolmaster. The embarrassment that we feel at this is such that we look around for explanations. Can he perhaps have been repaying a debt to the regime? Is the poem meant ironically? Neither of these offers a real escape. In answer to the first question: Writers stand by what they write, or fall by it. Here Brecht falls. As for the possibility of irony, there are no apparent signals, no markers to indicate to the reader, even one alert to such a possibility, that this is indeed a case of tongue in cheek, a deliberate send-up of that crudely didactic verse with its "belehrend" tone that was all too common in the officially sanctioned literature of the Aufbau period. We are forced to conclude, in the absence of such markers, that this poem, far from being a send-up, is unfortunately the real thing.

It is a hack's poem, its heavy moralizing ("Nur wißt: hier haben andre schon gesessen / Die saßen über Menschen dann. Gebt acht!") expressed in verse alternatively wooden or ringing with that hollow sound invariably produced by the headmaster's address to the departing students (the poem's final two lines). Echoes of earnest Schillerian classicism are heard in the second stanza. As for the poet's attitude, his tone of voice, what could have possessed someone with Brecht's sensitivity to adopt the cliché of the admonishing reminder to the younger generation of what they owe to their parents' generation? The full disaster of such a stance is on view here: the assumed moral superiority, the barely concealed aggression toward the younger generation, the emotional blackmail that asserts a debt only repayable by strict adherence to the parents' principles. No wonder the poem is stylistically so bad. Paraphrasing Heine, we might say "Dem Einschüchterer wird der gute Stil erschwert." It is difficult to write well if you know that what you are writing amounts to mere hectoring.

Brecht nevertheless tries to strike the right tone, and it is a tribute to his poetic skill that in other places he sometimes nearly succeeds:

> Panzereinheit, ich freue mich, dich schreibend
> Und für den Frieden werbend zu sehen
> Und ich freue mich, daß ihr schreibend
> Und für den Frieden werbend, gepanzert seid.
> (GW, 4:1028)

Brecht uses here a favorite device of his later poetry, the chiasmus. It is a neat structure making for a dense unity. Brecht makes good use of it in *Rudern, Gespräche*, for example:

> Es ist Abend. Vorbei gleiten
> Zwei Faltboote, darinnen
> Zwei nackte junge Männer: Nebeneinander rudernd
> Sprechen sie. Sprechend
> Rudern sie nebeneinander.
> (GW, 4:1013)

But here a quiet point is made by means of a very simple, calm vignette viewed from two angles. In the case of *Panzereinheit, ich freue mich* both the subject matter and the nature of the message are different, and the question arises whether, far from the form's reinforcing and imitating the message as in the Buckow poem, there is no gap in *Panzereinheit* between the sophisticated form and the one-dimensional, not to say naive, political statement. One need not be cynical to greet the picture of tank soldiers writing essays on peace (which they, naturally, are defending) with a certain amusement; nor need one possess a devious mind to be led by this poem to reflect on the various uses to which the word *Frieden* has been put. The use of a sophisticated structure to present such a vulnerable picture is likely to draw attention to the vulnerability.

This is true also of *Glückliche Begegnung*, likewise from the 1950s:

An den Junisonntagen im Junggehölz
Hören die Himbeersucher vom Dorfe
Lernende Frauen und Mädchen der Fachschule
Aus ihren Lehrbüchern laut Sätze lesen
Über Dialektik und Kinderpflege.

Von den Lehrbüchern aufblickend
Sehen die Schülerinnen die Dörfler
Von den Sträuchern die Beeren lesen.

(GW, 4:1000)

Once again Brecht uses his mirroring structure, and once again we must ask whether the very sophistication of the structure merely draws attention to the dubiousness of the message. The rosy picture of total harmony presented by the poem: village and school, theory and praxis, *Kopfarbeit* and *Handarbeit*, the fruits of Marxist theory and the fruits of the raspberry canes—is a veritable socialist cliché. But we need not even adopt a skeptical attitude to feel acutely the point at which the poem nosedives into the unintentionally comical. It is in the fourth and fifth lines, in which we are confronted with the picture of the girls reading out loud sentences about "dialectics and child care." Brecht might as well have said "Dialektik und Rübenbau"—the comic incongruity could hardly have been greater. Brecht's desire to avoid "hierarchical thinking" and his eagerness to take up an egalitarian stance (child-care nurses are as important as economists or engineers) has landed him with a juxtaposition of words that is sadly comic.

Brecht makes this gaffe, I suggest, because he is trying too hard. Like the lady who doth protest too much he overdoes the socialist utopia and immediately strikes false notes. Whether this going too far is the result of allowing ideology to carry him away or whether he rather creates in his poem something in which he would like to believe, but at heart does not, is not very important. Either way, the false note betrays the poet who is false to himself—whether to his intelligence or his integrity matters little. The harmonious picture of *Rudern, Gespräche* works because it is not presented within an ideological framework: its positive image is accompanied by no specific political message, its structure is not closed. In *Glückliche Begegnung* the ideological framework is given precisely by that fatal fifth line: "Über Dialektik und Kinderpflege." The political message about the "happy encounter" between the simple villagers and the trained specialists might have survived were it not for this line and to a lesser extent the preceding one with its unpleasant evocation of rote learning and mechanical repetition as pedagogical methods.

It is not the political or ideological nature of such poetry that proves its undoing. I am not advancing here the by now discredited view that politics sullies art. On the contrary, most of Brecht's good work is explicitly political. What is being asserted here is that Brecht is incapable of presenting a convincing positive picture of socialism achieved or in the process of being established. Earlier, in the 1930s, in exile, his art had a different function. It is aggressive and critical; it is either in an attacking mode (assaults on fascism, for example) or is borne along by a fighting sense of urgency. In both cases Brecht is writing, arguing, and persuading from a minority, underdog position. Once he goes to East Berlin, this is not true any longer. Now he is with the majority, his function is no longer to urge the fighters forward to the goal glowing dimly on the horizon but to support a status quo, an established order with whose general goals he is in accord. Formerly his critical, aggressive talents could be employed in an unproblematic way in attacking fascism and capitalism. Now these talents must be used sparingly, at least where criticism of the new German socialist state is concerned. And for every carefully couched criticism leveled at the GDR, there must be a tirade against the West. It is likely that some of the passion and violence of emotion that we feel in poems like *Nicht so gemeint* is transferred aggression: unable to vent fully his dissatisfaction and frustration at events and persons in the GDR, Brecht is all the more savage toward the enemy over the border.

It is in the eulogistic poems after 1948 that the real trouble lies. Whereas during the exile years even the most single-minded propagandistic poems have a genuine enthusiasm, an élan, the later poems praising the achievements of socialism have a hollow ring. The difference is clearly discernible if one sets one of the exile poems against a GDR piece. Even the euphoric *Inbesitznahme der großen Metro durch die Moskauer Arbeiterschaft am 27. April 1935*, for all its rosy hues and naivety, does not grate the way later eulogies do:

> Wir hörten: 80 000 Arbeiter
> Haben die Metro gebaut, viele noch nach der täglichen Arbeit
> Oft die Nächte durch. Während dieses Jahres
> Hatte man immer junge Männer und Mädchen
> Lachend aus den Stollen klettern sehen, ihre Arbeitsanzüge
> Die lehmigen, schweißdurchnäßten, stolz vorweisend.
> Alle Schwierigkeiten—
> Unterirdische Flüsse, Druck der Hochhäuser
> Nachgebende Erdmassen—wurden besiegt.
> . . . .
> Als nun die Bahn gebaut war nach den vollkommensten
>   Mustern
> Und die Besitzer kamen, sie zu besichtigen und
> Auf ihr zu fahren, da waren es diejenigen
> Die sie gebaut hatten.
> Es waren da Tausende, die herumgingen
> Die riesigen Hallen besichtigend, und in den Zügen
> Fuhren große Massen vorbei, die Gesichter—
> Männer, Frauen und Kinder, auch Greise—
> Den Stationen zugewandt, strahlend wie im Theater, denn
>   die Stationen
> Waren verschieden gebaut, aus verschiedenen Steinen
> In verschiedener Bauart, auch das Licht
> Kam aus immer anderer Quelle.
> . . . .
> . . . . Und all dies
> War in einem einzigen Jahr gebaut worden und von so
>   vielen Bauleuten
> Wie keine andere Bahn der Welt. Und keine
> Andere Bahn der Welt hatte je so viele Besitzer.
>
> Denn es sah der wunderbare Bau
> Was keiner seiner Vorgänger in vielen Städten vieler Zeiten
> Jemals gesehen hatte: als Bauherren die Bauleute!
> Wo wäre dies je vorgekommen, daß die Frucht der Arbeit
> Denen zufiel, die da gearbeitet hatten? Wo jemals

Wurden die nicht vertrieben aus dem Bau
Die ihn errichtet hatten?
Als wir sie fahren sahen in ihren Wagen
Den Werken ihrer Hände, wußten wir:
Dies ist das große Bild, das die Klassiker einstmals
Erschüttert voraussahen.

(GW, 4:673–75)

This is arguably the most effusive piece of propaganda from the poetry of the 1930s. The result of Brecht's witnessing the opening of the Moscow underground during his visit in 1935, the poem glows with enthusiasm. We may reflect on what Brecht had to forget—at least temporarily—in order to be able to write this. It was not, as Völker asserts, "die Ausschmückung der Stationen mit Marmor und edlen Hölzern, den Ballsaalcharakter und die Protzsuche . . . , die seinem nüchternen ästhetischen Empfinden und seinen klaren künstlerischen Auffassungen widersprachen."[1] More important than any aesthetic quibbles Brecht might have had with the metro's interior decoration should have been the fact that, precisely at this time, evidence of persecution in the Soviet Union was mounting. Kirov had been assassinated a few months before and the trials of Zinoviev and his circle, and of the Leningrad NKVD leadership—the first of the purge trials—had taken place in January 1935. Could Brecht have been unaware of the often arbitrary repressiveness of a regime that two years later was to send numerous friends (Sergei Tretiakoff, Carola Neher, Ernst Ottwalt) to camps where they perished? If Brecht *was* worried about events such as these in the Soviet Union, his description of the opening of the Moscow metro shows no sign of it. The idea that moves like a central thread through the poem—that for the first time in history the builders are the owners—inspires an enthusiasm that, as it were, buoys up the text above doubt. We may wish to criticize Brecht for wearing blinkers, or for inflating a mundane situation to one of world historical import. That the workers, not the dignitaries, are the first to ride in the subway does not in itself mean much beyond the symbolic level. And in what sense that is important are the workers the "Bauherren" of the metro? *But the poem does not ring false*. There is nothing in it that strikes the jarring note which betrays to us the fact that the poet is not happy in his skin. Similarly in the earlier, programmatic propaganda poems, such as the *Lieder und Chöre* from *Die Mutter* and *Die Maßnahme*, though one might raise general questions about the level of such propaganda as poetry, one can find little to embarrass a major poet of Brecht's political persuasion. To illustrate, here is one of the best-known *Maßnahme* poems:

WER ABER IST DIE PARTEI?

Wer aber ist die Partei?
Sitzt sie in einem Haus mit Telefonen?
Sind ihre Gedanken geheim, ihre Entschlüsse unbekannt?
Wer ist sie?

Wir sind sie.
Du und ich und ihr—wir alle.
In deinem Anzug steckt sie, Genosse, und denkt in deinem
    Kopf.
Wo ich wohne, ist ihr Haus, und wo du angegriffen wirst,
    da kämpft sie.

Zeige uns den Weg, den wir gehen sollen, und wir
Werden ihn gehen wie du, aber
Gehe nicht ohne uns den richtigen Weg
Ohne uns ist er
Der falscheste.
Trenne dich nicht von uns!
Wir können irren, und du kannst recht haben, also
Trenne dich nicht von uns!

Daß der kurze Weg besser ist als der lange, das leugnet keiner
Aber wenn ihn einer weiß
Und vermag ihn uns nicht zu zeigen, was nützt uns seine
    Weisheit?
Sei bei uns weise!
Trenne dich nicht von uns!

(GW, 1:656)

As with *Inbesitznahme der großen Metro*, it is what is *not* being said here that worries us. In the latter poem no mention is made of those other aspects of life in the Soviet Union in the 1930s that not only contrast with the joyful picture presented by Brecht but undermine its legitimacy. In *Wer aber ist die Partei?* we have a case of the begged question. The poet argues eloquently that the Party has no existence beyond that of its individual members. It exists through and in them. But every body must have a head to direct it, and every organization must be led. Who leads and directs the Party? That question has been quite simply one of the most crucial and vexed since, at the latest, 1917. One begs it at one's peril. And yet once again the poem seems to ride confidently and eloquently, even persuasively, above such severe doubt. Though we may want to argue with the poem's statements, we do not feel that the way in which they are put betrays the poet's bad faith. The poem as poem does not cause us to feel embarrassment or contempt. The sure treatment of his theme, the rightness of the calmly yet insistently persuasive tone, the cleverly varied structure with its repetitions, and the familiar effectiveness of the line divisions—all this suggests to us a poet who is not only in control but completely in harmony with himself. There is no sign of the stridency, false emotion, awkward address, and bad phrasing that characterize the GDR poems praising or explaining the socialist way.

Practically all the post-1948 poems of prosocialist propaganda are, in fact, painful; very few of the earlier poems in a similar vein are. What might be the reasons for this marked discrepancy? It is unlikely that the cause was a lessening of Brecht's commitment to communism. Though his experiences in the GDR, particularly during 1953, undoubtedly produced disappointment and disillusionment, Brecht did not waver in his support for communism and for the German communist state. On the contrary, his response to June 1953 was one of shocked dismay swiftly followed by an agitated determination that communist rule and order should be rigorously maintained. The problem was rather his inability to carry over, in his work, the earlier uncomplicated advocacy of the socialist way into the GDR. It was one thing to paint, during the years of exile, a picture of a future better world, another to maintain one's revolutionary élan while observing at first hand the actual development of this better world, a development that was often problematic. For Brecht the difficulties of the plain proved to be greater than the difficulties of the mountains.

The awkwardness and falseness that mar the later procommunist poems are frequently traceable to a misconceived relationship between author and reader. We can focus this problem clearly if we ask the dual question: For whom are these poems written, and to whom are they addressed? With a poem like *Panzereinheit*, the answer might seem obvious enough:

> Panzereinheit, ich freue mich, dich schreibend
> Und für den Frieden werbend zu sehen
> Und ich freue mich, daß ihr schreibend
> Und für den Frieden werbend, gepanzert seid.
>
> (GW, 4:1028)

The poet addresses the members of the tank unit; it is for them that the poem is written. But *is* it? It is not a private communication, but a text included, and always intended to be included, in a collection of poetry. (Elisabeth Hauptmann reports, in the notes to GW, 4, that it was presumably destined for the planned *Friedensfibel*.) It is thus directed at the reader, any reader of Brecht's poetry. Hauptmann tells us that Brecht wrote the four-liner to go with a photograph he had found in the magazine *Neues China*, bearing the caption: "Die Besatzungen einer Panzereinheit der chinesischen Volksbefreiungsarmee unterschreiben den Appell des Weltfriedensrates zur Ächtung des Atomkrieges."[2] The poem is thus "addressed" to some faces on a photograph, which makes it clear that this apparent addressee is merely the occasion, the excuse, for a little poem aimed at Brecht's reading public.

But Brecht is unclear about whom he is actually addressing—tank troops or readers of his poetry—or rather, about the *difference* between a quasi-dramatic address to certain personages (within the framework of a poem) and the address that this poem constitutes. The situation would be somewhat different, but no better, if this text appeared, as seems to have been intended, underneath the photograph along with other photographs and their texts. Then the relationship of poet to addressee would be clearer. We, the real addressees, would see the communication between poet and the tank troops as the text we are intended to receive. But the real problem would remain, namely the problem of the poem's naivety. It is a problem no matter whom Brecht had in mind as the actual target for the *Friedensfibel*. If his envisaged reader was the "ordinary person," the naivety is condescension: one kind of poetry for the simpleminded, another for the sophisticates. If he considered, more realistically, that these texts would be read by the kind of people who normally read Brecht poems, of whatever kind, the naivety is simply misplaced, or erects a class barrier, since the sophisticates, in *their* turn, take such texts as not meant for them but for the "simple man."

This, it might be said, surely reflects a no-win situation for Brecht: if he wants to actually write for the common man he must write simply, must use picture books with simple captions. This means that a sophisticated audience reading such material (and he himself) are embarrassingly reminded of the real difference separating them from the common herd, and of the difficulties such a relationship involves for a Marxist. There may no longer be one law for the rich and another for the poor, but there is one poetry for the sophisticated and another for the simple.

Problems with His Readership 171

A certain kind of critic would triumphantly point to this dilemma as proof that good art and propaganda do not mix. But I do not think that this is the case. It is not so that propaganda and good art are mutually exclusive, or that poetry directed at a wider audience must fall into a hole located between the sophisticate and the common man. One can cite many examples from Brecht's own work to support this. The most appropriate is the *Kriegsfibel*, a collection of photographs with verse captions of precisely the same kind as the planned but barely begun *Friedensfibel*. The sixty-nine four-liners written during the war years contain not one single example of the weaknesses and false notes that attract our uncomfortable attention in *Panzereinheit* or *An die Studenten der Arbeiter*. (The three quatrains that constitute the latter were also intended for the *Friedensfibel*.) Occasionally, indeed, the *Kriegsfibel* contains very good poetry. Beneath a photograph of factory workers maneuvering huge sheets of metal are the following lines:

2

"Was macht ihr, Brüder?"—"Einen Eisenwagen."
"Und was aus diesen Platten dicht daneben?"
"Geschosse, die durch Eisenwände schlagen."
"Und warum all das, Brüder?"—"Um zu leben."

(GW, 4:1035)

And a photograph of a blind German soldier in a Russian military hospital prompts the comment:

56

Vor Moskau, Mensch, gabst du dein Augenlicht.
O blinder Mensch, jetzt wirst du es verstehn.
Der Irreführer kriegte Moskau nicht.
Hätt er's gekriegt, hättst du es nicht gesehn.

(GW, 4:1045)

It is clear from the *Kriegsfibel* that it is not the attempt to write readily graspable verse—pictorially buttressed, for a broad readership that includes both intellectuals and ordinary people—that fails. It is rather the attempt, in Brecht's changed circumstances after 1948, to write such verse *for a new public*: the citizens of the new German socialist state. The new public was a real public, the kind he had not had since 1933. In exile Brecht, like all his writer colleagues, had no public in the normal sense. Their works were read by a very limited group. From 1933 to 1946 or so Brecht wrote in effect for fellow exiles, which meant in the main fellow writers and intellectuals at the middle and left of the political spectrum, united in their opposition to fascism. These were the people who actually read him. Of course, Brecht was, in a more important sense, writing not for them exclusively or even principally, but for a broad public or for posterity—or at least convinced himself that he was. It is the conviction that counted, that gave Brecht the power and stamina to create major works—for a public that did not, in any immediate sense, exist. When it came to exist, it was the public of the GDR, a public he could hear and observe and contemplate—and be unsettled by.

There were two aspects to this uncertainty. One was Brecht's suspicion of large elements of the GDR population, such as emerges in poems like *Vor acht Jahren* ("Der Postbote hat einen zu aufrechten Gang. / Und was war der Elektriker?") and in his characterization of Buckow as "ein mißgünstiges Kleinbürgernest." Clearly Brecht was not writing for these people, although he might have been indirectly writing *at* them in poems like *Nicht so gemeint*, directed in the first instance at the West but aimed perhaps by extension at those elements in the GDR with pro-West views. Was he then writing only for the faithful, the already converted supporters of the peasants' and workers' state? The problems here are obvious. Preaching to the converted is notoriously unproductive. Perhaps, though, he was preaching to a generation that would read him as part of its schooling. In the new German socialist state, Bertolt Brecht was bound to become one of the most anthologized poets. His verse would sooner or later be obligatory for schools, whether these were day schools for the young or night schools for the workers. But this posed the problem referred to above: the problem of the tone and posture to be adopted when addressing the young and the uneducated. Brecht the "Volksdichter" of the *Kriegsfibel* had been successful and convincing, but Brecht the "Staatsdichter" in East Berlin was not.

Whether Brecht was aware of this aspect of his new situation after 1948 or not, there are signs of dismay in his private or semiprivate remarks about the reception and function of his work in the GDR. Perhaps he had expected to find, after fourteen years in the wilderness, some kind of ideal public, in a new Germany that incorporated his ideas and ideals. He was sorely disappointed, as occasional comments like the following indicate: "unsere aufführungen in berlin haben fast kein echo mehr. in der presse erscheinen kritiken monate nach der erstaufführung, und es steht nichts drin, außer ein paar kümmerlichen soziologischen analysen. das publikum ist das kleinbürgerpublikum der volksbühne, arbeiter machen da kaum 7 prozent aus."³ Brecht goes on to console himself with the thought that all will be well if the didactic function of his theater techniques is perceived. But it is a despairing hope rather than a confident expectation, and the tone of the diary entry remains one of discouragement and disillusionment.

The gap between Brecht's expectations regarding his new public and the actuality is brutally spelled out by Hans Mayer:

> Wie aber, wenn das neue Publikum der Arbeiter ausblieb und am Schiffbauerdamm plötzlich im Zuschauerraum jene Leute aus der westlichen Welt saßen, die aus Überdruß an den letzten Moden des bürgerlichen Reiztheaters gekommen waren, den Reizen eines reizlos didaktischen Theaters der Gesellschaftsveränderung sich auszusetzen. Daß Brecht mit seiner Theaterarbeit die Glückserwartungen der Berliner Arbeiter enttäuschen mußte, die immer noch gewohnt waren, einen Theaterabend zu identifizieren mit hergebrachten Spielweisen bürgerlicher Freizeitgestaltung, war unverkennbar. Er konnte sich nicht mit dem Einwand zufrieden geben: dergleichen sei unvermeidlich in einer Übergangszeit, da seine Zuschauer immer noch das gesellschaftliche Produkt der faschistischen Aera repräsentierten. Es kamen aber seit 1950 auch junge Arbeiter zum Schiffbauerdamm, die keine Hypothek des Dritten Reiches mitbrachten; allein sie reagierten gleichfalls befremdet, und wechselten lieber hinüber ins Metropoltheater, wo man die konzentrierte Verlogenheit der späten Wiener Operette bewundern durfte.⁴

Mayer rightly describes Brecht's expectations with regard to his GDR public as unrealistic: "Gewiß erwartete Brecht alles von den neuen Theaterbesuchern, die er sich, nach Absolvierung der marxistischen Lehre, nur als Mitglieder einer sozialistischen Gesellschaft vorstellen mochte."⁵

It may be that the disappointment of these expectations made Brecht, for the first time, uncertain about his relationship to his public—or drew his attention for the first time to the realities of his role as "poet for the people." Earlier there had been a confident certainty about this role. It is expressed in forthright fashion in the poem *Die Literatur wird durchforscht werden*:

I

Die auf die goldenen Stühle gesetzt sind, zu schreiben
Werden gefragt werden nach denen, die
Ihnen die Röcke webten.

Nicht nach ihren erhabenen Gedanken
Werden ihre Bücher durchforscht werden, sondern
Irgendein beiläufiger Satz, der schließen läßt
Auf eine Eigenheit derer, die Röcke webten
Wird mit Interesse gelesen werden, denn hier mag es sich um Züge
Der berühmten Ahnen handeln.

Ganze Literaturen
In erlesenen Ausdrücken verfaßt
Werden durchsucht werden nach Anzeichen
Daß da auch Aufrührer gelebt haben, wo Unterdrückung war.
Flehentliche Anrufe überirdischer Wesen
Werden beweisen, daß da Irdische über Irdischen gesessen sind.
Köstliche Musik der Worte wird nur berichten
Daß da für viele kein Essen war.

II

Aber in jener Zeit werden gepriesen werden
Die auf dem nackten Boden saßen, zu schreiben
Die unter den Niedrigen saßen
Die bei den Kämpfern saßen.
Die von den Leiden der Niedrigen berichteten
Die von den Taten der Kämpfer berichteten
Kunstvoll. In der edlen Sprache
Vordem reserviert
Der Verherrlichung der Könige.

Ihre Beschreibungen der Mißstände und ihre Aufrufe
Werden noch den Daumenabdruck
Der Niedrigen tragen. Denn diesen
Wurden sie übermittelt, diese
Trugen sie weiter unter dem durchschwitzten Hemd
Durch die Kordone der Polizisten
Zu ihresgleichen.

Ja, es wird eine Zeit geben, wo
Diese Klugen und Freundlichen
Zornigen und Hoffnungsvollen
Die auf dem nackten Boden saßen, zu schreiben
Die umringt waren von Niedrigen und Kämpfern
Öffentlich gepriesen werden.

(GW, 4:740–41)

The ideological justification of art is clearly expressed here: in that time still to come writers will be judged according to their political and class sympathies. "Noble language" and "exquisite expressions" will count only if they have been deployed in the service of the "Niedrigen." We are in no doubt where Brecht stands, or rather sits: "auf dem nackten Boden," "unter den Niedrigen," "bei den Kämpfern." In 1939 in exile, when this poem was written, there was no problem regarding Brecht's self-understanding. He was on the side of the underdogs, the oppressed and exploited, and fought on their behalf—as a writer. Of course, the metaphor that presented him sitting "on the bare floor" "among the humble people" was just that: a metaphor. In reality, Brecht lived and wrote ("fought") in comfortable circumstances, with spacious working facilities in households geared entirely to his writing and containing, among other things, a live-in editorial assistant. This discrepancy between the actually and the metaphorically true, which was of little importance in the years of exile, took on a different look after 1948, when Brecht found himself a member of a privileged group. His relationship to the "humble" suddenly became problematic. It was one thing to identify with an abstract proletariat to which, because it was abstract, one could address one's poetry. It was another thing altogether to confront a real proletariat, and not as a refugee occupying bare floorboards but as—willy-nilly—a privileged member of an elite, with considerable influence and a country house outside Berlin. The poet who had been able to address a fictionalized public of "Niedrigen"—often brilliantly—during the exile years now found himself confronted by a real public, *to whom he did not know how to talk*.

This problem is not long in emerging after Brecht's return to Germany. Practically the first poem directed at his new audience, the *Aufbaulied* of 1948, already manifests the awkwardness, the flatness, the forced enthusiasm, the off-target phrases, that characterize the bad poems discussed above:

1
Keiner plagt sich gerne, doch wir wissen:
Grau ist's immer, wenn ein Morgen naht
Und trotz Hunger, Kält und Finsternissen
Stehn zum Handanlegen wir parat.
   Fort mit den Trümmern
   Und was Neues hingebaut!
   Um uns selber müssen wir uns selber kümmern
   Und heraus gegen uns, wer sich traut!

2
Jeder sitzt mal gerne unterm Dache
Drum ist aufbaun gar kein schlechter Rat.
Aber es muß sein in eigner Sache
Und so baun wir erst 'nen neuen Staat.
   Fort mit den Trümmern
   Und was Neues hingebaut!
   Um uns selber müssen wir uns selber kümmern
   Und heraus gegen uns, wer sich traut!

3
Und das Schieberpack, das uns verblieben
Das nach Freiheit jammert früh und spat
Und die Herren, die die Schieber schieben
Schieben wir per Schub aus unserm Staat.
   Fort mit den Trümmern
   Und was Neues hingebaut!
   Um uns selber müssen wir uns selber kümmern
   Und heraus gegen uns, wer sich traut!

4
Denn das Haus ist hin, doch nicht die Wanzen
Junker, Unternehmer, Potentat.
Schaufeln her, Mensch, schaufeln wir den ganzen
Klumpatsch heiter jetzt aus unserm Staat.
   Fort mit den Trümmern
   Und was Neues hingebaut!
   Um uns selber müssen wir uns selber kümmern
   Und heraus gegen uns, wer sich traut!

5
Besser als gerührt sein, ist: sich rühren
Denn kein Führer führt aus dem Salat!
Selber werden wir uns endlich führen:
Weg der alte, her der neue Staat!
   Fort mit den Trümmern
   Und was Neues hingebaut!
   Um uns selber müssen wir uns selber kümmern
   Und heraus gegen uns, wer sich traut!

(GW, 4:955–56)

A poem intended to be bursting with energy and enthusiasm bursts instead with clichés ("Grau ist's immer, wenn ein Morgen naht"), awkward syntax and vocabulary ("Stehn zum Handanlegen wir parat"), and flat lines ("Drum ist aufbaun gar kein schlechter Rat"), not to speak of the childish final line of the refrain. The only moderately good lines are those in which the enthusiasm takes the form of aggression against the class enemy, as in stanza 4. This bears out the point made in my discussion of the *Buckower Elegien*, that there is a fairly precise correlation between aggressively critical poems and literary value, and conversely between positive—that is, exhortative or eulogistic—poems about the GDR and literary worthlessness.

The major point made earlier in the present chapter about the discrepancy between pre-1948 and post-1948 socialist poems can also be supported here by a comparison between the *Aufbaulied* and the poem that immediately follows it in the *GW*, the *Zukunftslied*. The latter was also written in 1948, but despite its title it is essentially a poem that looks *back*, not forward:

ZUKUNFTSLIED

1
Und es waren mächtge Zaren einst im weiten Russenreich.
Und man sah sie niedertreten die Muschkoten und Proleten
Und sie speisten, in Pasteten, alle Hähne, die drum krähten
Und die Guten sah man bluten, und den Zaren war es gleich.
    Aber eines Tages war das nicht mehr so
    Und zu Ende waren tausend Jahre Not.
    Aus der Jammer: Über der Getreidekammer hob sich hoh
    Eine wunderbare Fahne, die war rot.

2
Und es saßen große Herren einst in Polen, reich und stolz.
Und sie führten große Kriege in den Panzern mit Motoren
Und es wurden keine Siege, sondern Polen war verloren
Und der Bauer zog den Pflug, und dieser Pflug, der war aus Holz.
    Aber eines Tages war das nicht mehr so
    Und zu Ende waren tausend Jahre Not.
    Aus der Jammer: Über der Getreidekammer hob sich hoh
    Eine wunderbare Fahne, die war rot.

3
Und es hatten fette Händler fern in China einst ein Heer.
Und so sah man faul die Satten, und die Hungrigen sah man fronen
Vier mal hundert Millionen ausgesaugt von tausend Ratten
Denn die fetten Händler hatten fette Freunde überm Meer.
    Aber eines Tages war das nicht mehr so

> Und zu Ende waren tausend Jahre Not.
> Aus der Jammer: Über der Getreidekammer hob sich hoh
> Eine wunderbare Fahne, die war rot.
>
> 4
> Als wir zogen gegen Osten, ach, besiegt von unsern Herrn
> Die uns gegen Brüder warben, haben die mit Tank und Wagen
> Uns im Kaukasus geschlagen; und es darben, die nicht starben
> Und schon wollen neue Herrn uns in neue Kriege zerrn.
> Aber eines Tages war das nicht mehr so
> Und zu Ende waren tausend Jahre Not.
> Aus der Jammer: Über der Getreidekammer hob sich hoh
> Eine wunderbare Fahne, die war rot.
>
> (GW, 4:956–57)

The title is a misnomer. Far from presenting a future perspective, the poem talks about what was and has now ceased to be; and it draws its emotional and rhetorical force not simply from the satisfaction embodied in the refrain but even more from the denunciation of the various bogeymen in the four stanzas. Once again it is plain: Brecht is most at home when he is occupying an attacking, critical position and, conversely, at his weakest when it comes to producing works of enthusiasm and praise directed at a GDR audience of which he is unsure. Even a poem with the title "Song of the future" turns into a denunciation of the enemies of the past who, the poem itself makes clear, *are already defeated*. In the terms of Brecht's own poem *Wahrnehmung*, he would rather look back at those mountains whence he has come than look forward at the plain stretching before him.

There is one further indication that Brecht's problem in addressing his new public after 1948 in positive terms is a problem precisely of his relationship to this new public: namely, the moment the address becomes stylized, the moment the voice in the poem falls into a rhetorically defined role, Brecht's difficulties recede. It is as if the more "verfremdet" the poet Brecht's address to his public is, the more comfortable he feels. By adopting the "alienating" stylization, he can speak directly and yet indirectly, like the actor who, addressing an audience, nevertheless does not make eye contact with them. The poem *An meine Landsleute*, written, like the two poems just discussed, in the early GDR years (in 1949), is an example of this "alienating" stylization:

> Ihr, die ihr überlebtet in gestorbenen Städten
> Habt doch nun endlich mit euch selbst Erbarmen!

Zieht nun in neue Kriege nicht, ihr Armen
Als ob die alten nicht gelangt hätten:
Ich bitt euch, habet mit euch selbst Erbarmen!

Ihr Männer, greift zur Kelle, nicht zum Messer!
Ihr säßet unter Dächern schließlich jetzt
Hättet ihr auf das Messer nicht gesetzt
Und unter Dächern sitzt es sich doch besser.
Ich bitt euch, greift zur Kelle, nicht zum Messer!

Ihr Kinder, daß sie euch mit Krieg verschonen
Müßt ihr um Einsicht eure Eltern bitten.
Sagt laut, ihr wollt nicht in Ruinen wohnen
Und nicht das leiden, was sie selber litten:
Ihr Kinder, daß sie euch mit Krieg verschonen!

Ihr Mütter, da es euch anheimgegeben
Den Krieg zu dulden oder nicht zu dulden
Ich bitt euch, lasset eure Kinder leben!
Daß sie euch die Geburt und nicht den Tod dann schulden:
Ihr Mütter, lasset eure Kinder leben!

(GW, 4:965)

The reader of Brecht will identify one device of alienation in the first line. He will recall that other famous beginning, "Ihr, die ihr auftauchen werdet aus der Flut," and then no doubt see also the similarity of the present title to that of the earlier poem, *An die Nachgeborenen*. And since all quotation (including self-quotation) is in Brecht's own terms "Verfremdung," the alienating effect is immediately present. It is further strengthened by the stylized biblical language ("Ich bitt euch, habet mit euch selbst Erbarmen!") recurring at the end of each stanza and by the repetitive structure of the poem: "Ihr Männer, Ihr Kinder, Ihr Mütter"; "Ich bitt euch" repeated together with the injunctions "habet mit euch selbst Erbarmen!" and "greift zur Kelle, nicht zum Messer!"; and the like.

Though it is certainly not one of Brecht's best poems, this highly structured and stylized poem works because it avoids the problem of the direct and specific address that proves to be Brecht's undoing in other places.[6] It is strange that Brecht, the vastly experienced and perceptive man of the theater, seems to forget here that the direct, unreflected address to a real public in a poem does not work. In terms of the analogy used above, a good actor addressing his audience, even when fixing an individual spectator at close range, does not make eye contact but focuses on a point somewhere else, aware that his words are not a private communication from himself to a specific individual, or even to a body of specific individuals, but a text addressed to the *audience*, a nonindividuated and in an important sense even abstract body. The times when Brecht does forget or disregard this fundamental truth about artistic communication are precisely those occasions when, as he writes, he sees before him, too naively as it were, his actual public after 1948. On these occasions the artistic miscalculation is compounded—perhaps caused—by Brecht's (mis)apprehensions about this public and the difficulties he has in relating to it.

It is a strange fact that Brecht's confidence in Marxism, in his own mission as a Marxist writer, and in the communist enterprise itself survived the years of Stalin's purges, executions, and terror only to founder somewhat when he was confronted by a German communist state in its infancy. In the 1930s and 1940s Brecht retained his faith—in turn obstinately, blindly, and willfully—in the communist way and in the USSR as the communist motherland, while millions of people died during the collectivization of agriculture and Stalin's police killed millions more. David Pike's devastating account[7] tells us what this entailed in the way of contortions and obtuseness on Brecht's part. Even when he himself was exposed to savage attacks from hostile factions among German left-wing emigrés and their Russian friends, Brecht barely wavered, and every doubt expressed in the *Arbeitsjournal* or in *Me-ti* is quickly followed by a rationalization or justification, often masquerading as "dialectical thinking." But when he went in 1948 to East Berlin, capital of a (much less savage and repressive) new German communist state, the writer Brecht found that he did not know how to address his countrymen and comrades. Though the master still produced, in the private vein, verses of simple elegance and unobtrusive originality—in love poems and poems of quiet reflection—he was unable to show anything but awkwardness in his direct appeals to his public.

7. *Exegi monumentum*:
The Poet's Fame

The poet Brecht was fond of valedictions. Fascinated from his early days by François Villon's *Testament*, he kept producing his own farewells to the world and his contemporaries. Some of his most famous poems are of this kind, including the two that seem to layman and expert alike to represent the essence of Brecht: *Vom armen B. B.* ("Wir wissen, daß wir Vorläufige sind / Und nach uns wird kommen: nichts Nennenswertes") and *An die Nachgeborenen*. Included among the last poems in the GW is a briefer farewell, this time in the form of a rather two-faced directive concerning his grave:

> Ich benötige keinen Grabstein, aber
> Wenn ihr einen für mich benötigt
> Wünschte ich, es stünde darauf:
> Er hat Vorschläge gemacht. Wir
> Haben sie angenommen.
> Durch eine solche Inschrift wären
> Wir alle geehrt.
>
> (GW, 4:1029)

The poem refers to Horace's ode *Exegi monumentum aere perennius* (the final ode of Book 3), in which the Roman writer proudly asserts the permanence of his literary achievement: "I have raised up a monument more lasting than bronze." Brecht's poem seems on the face of it to be a modest waving aside of such ambitions. But of course it is not, as Hans Mayer, putting his finger on the blatant dissemblance, observes: "Obenhin nimmt sich das als pure Bescheidenheit aus. Es ist überaus stolz. Brecht schreibt der Nachwelt vor, wie sie ihn zu verstehen habe; nimmt sogar das Urteil der Nachwelt vorweg, diktiert es ihr recht eigentlich in die Feder oder ins Instrumentarium des Steinmetzen."[1] Walter Hinck has taken Brecht to task for writing such an "unbrechtisch" piece: "Hätte der Wunsch gelautet: prüft meine Vorschläge, achtet sie und ändert sie deshalb ab— der Brecht-Leser hätte sich in diesem Gedicht heimischer gefühlt. Und wenn sich etwa die Vorschläge auf nichts anderes beziehen als auf eine Methode, eben die dialektische Methode Brechts? Auch dann bleibt eine Spur von Selbstgerechtigkeit in der Haltung des

Weisen."[2] Hinck then attempts a partial rescue of the poem by suggesting the possibility of a more complex—and more Marxist—meaning of the gravestone inscription: "Vorschläge annehmen" can be interpreted as "weiterbauen, das Werk weiterdenken, Vorschläge prüfen und ausführen, angedeutete Möglichkeiten realisieren, das künstlerische Werk vervollständigen in die Lebenswirklichkeit hinein."[3] Despite this possibility, however, Hinck comes to the conclusion that in the final analysis there is a contradiction in this poem: "Es ist der Widerspruch zwischen dem verborgenen Dogmatiker—man denke auch an die grandiose Einseitigkeit der Theatertheorie—und den Dialektiker Brecht."[4]

The case made out by Hinck in his brief article gives plenty of support for this judgment, which might profitably be extended as a critical approach to other areas of Brecht's work. Hinck, however, goes on to mention another poem concerned with Brecht's posthumous reputation, *Warum soll mein Name genannt werden?*, which he presents as an example of the more modest, more decently socialist (more "brechtisch"?) attitude toward the poet's remembrance by future generations.

1
Einst dachte ich: in fernen Zeiten
Wenn die Häuser zerfallen sind, in denen ich wohne
Und die Schiffe verfault, auf denen ich fuhr
Wird mein Name noch genannt werden
Mit andren.

2
Weil ich das Nützliche rühmte, das
Zu meinen Zeiten für unedel galt
Weil ich die Religionen bekämpfte
Weil ich gegen die Unterdrückung kämpfte oder
Aus einem andren Grund.

3
Weil ich für die Menschen war und
Ihnen alles überantwortete, sie so ehrend
Weil ich Verse schrieb und die Sprache bereicherte
Weil ich praktisches Verhalten lehrte oder
Aus irgendeinem andren Grund.

4
Deshalb meinte ich, wird mein Name noch genannt
Werden, auf einem Stein

Wird mein Name stehen, aus den Büchern
Wird er in die neuen Bücher abgedruckt werden.

5
Aber heute
Bin ich einverstanden, daß er vergessen wird.
Warum
Soll man nach dem Bäcker fragen, wenn genügend Brot da ist?
Warum
Soll der Schnee gerühmt werden, der geschmolzen ist
Wenn neue Schneefälle bevorstehen?
Warum
Soll es eine Vergangenheit geben, wenn es eine
Zukunft gibt?

6
Warum
Soll mein Name genannt werden?

(GW, 4:561–62)

It is true that, at first glance, this seems to be a clear renunciation by the poet of his claim to fame, even a rejection of remembrance by a future generation that, inhabiting a better world, will have no need of the work of a poet battling with the conflicts and problems of a "dark age." The poem's argument is of the "once . . . but now" type. Beginning with what is obviously the first half of a statement ("Einst dachte ich . . . "), the poet makes the reader wait four stanzas for the other half ("Aber heute bin ich einverstanden . . . "). But, through a typically Brechtian ploy (discussed in chapter 4), by the time this second half (containing the true message, as we expect) actually comes, we are not so prepared to accept it, since its statement—relinquishment of fame—does not sit at all well with the very positive and persuasive contents of the first half. To express this movement in terms of rhetoric (for this is what it is): the "Einst dachte ich" with which the poem begins prepares the reader to reject or at least see the weakness of what follows. What follows, however, must seem wholly reasonable and admirable. Indeed the terms are the most positive of which Brecht is capable: "das Nützliche rühmen," "gegen die Unterdrückung kämpfen," "praktisches Verhalten lehren."

What can possibly be said against the poet's being remembered "in fernen Zeiten" for such positive achievements? One answer, as Hans Mayer points out, is the Leninist one that the dialectical process involves cancellation: "Zum Leninismus gehört, weil er Dialektik be-deutet, auch die 'Aufhebung' als Annullierung. 'Wird das klassenlose Ziel erreicht sein', meint Bloch, 'so wird man aus Stücken dieser Art nicht mehr so viel zu lernen haben'. . . . Mit solcher Einschränkung wäre auch der späte Brecht als Dialektiker einverstanden gewesen."[5] But just how far Brecht *is* "einverstanden," at any time in his life, is problematic. To the extent that this agreement with the Leninist principle and therefore with his being forgotten is countered by a defiantly maintained pride in his achievements and even a reasonable certainty of their enduring, these achievements *will* ensure for him a "place in history." The theoretical acceptance of the dialectical process is one thing; Brecht's considerable self-esteem, his confidence in the enduring importance of his work, is another.

Besides the unexpectedly convincing nature of what follows "Einst dachte ich," one other feature of the poem strongly supports this reading. The questions in stanza 5 ("Warum / Soll man nach dem Bäcker fragen," etc.), though superficially in support of the principle of "Aufhebung," are in fact equally supportive of the opposite, since one can think—and a good Marxist-Leninist can also think—of perfectly satisfactory answers to each. In particular the final question, "Warum / Soll es eine Vergangenheit geben, wenn es eine / Zukunft gibt?" cannot be answered in a simple negative way, as Brecht very well knew. The dialectic, after all, involves the *overcoming* of the past, not its obliteration. One does not need Marx's dictum about the dangers of disregarding history to see the weakness of these "rhetorical" questions and therefore of the argument. It is, I suggest, an intentional weakness, designed to cast doubt on the rightness of the poet's "agreement" that his name be forgotten. Brecht is up to his old trick of inviting the reader to demur. The apparently rhetorical questions (i.e., ones requiring no answer) are in fact real questions, stimulating thought and inviting response. Likewise with the two brief lines that end the poem as stanza 6: the question, on the face of it purely rhetorical, in fact demands a response, forces the reader to think. Far from setting the seal on a clear and convincing argument, these lines (which repeat the title) have the effect of throwing the poem open once more. It is a characteristic and finely handled Brechtian technique, reminiscent of the end of *Ausschließlich wegen der zunehmenden Unordnung*:

> Ausschließlich wegen der zunehmenden Unordnung
> In unseren Städten des Klassenkampfs
> Haben etliche von uns in diesen Jahren beschlossen
> Nicht mehr zu reden von Hafenstädten, Schnee auf den
>   Dächern, Frauen

Geruch reifer Äpfel im Keller, Empfindungen des Fleisches
All dem, was den Menschen rund macht und menschlich
Sondern zu reden nur mehr von der Unordnung
Also einseitig zu werden, dürr, verstrickt in die Geschäfte
Der Politik und das trockene "unwürdige" Vokabular
Der dialektischen Ökonomie
Damit nicht dieses furchtbare gedrängte Zusammensein
Von Schneefällen (sie sind nicht nur kalt, wir wissen's)
Ausbeutung, verlocktem Fleisch und Klassenjustiz eine Billigung
So vielseitiger Welt in uns erzeuge, Lust an
Den Widersprüchen solch blutigen Lebens
Ihr versteht.

(GW, 4:519)

The reader, likely to be overwhelmed by this dense poem consisting of a single, practically unpunctuated sentence, is sent back to read it again by the final "Ihr versteht"; not sure that he *does* fully understand, he goes back to the beginning. At the end of *Warum soll mein Name* too we are in effect directed to reread the poem, and that means rereading the poet's achievements, this time consciously setting them against his "agreement" to be forgotten.

What emerges from all this is a statement that is, at the very least, ambiguous, declaring on one level the poet's acceptance of the inevitable relativizing of the present as it becomes part of a "Vergangenheit" and on another level his proud wish, and even confident expectation, that he will be remembered and held in esteem even "in fernen Zeiten," that his contributions to his time will not be forgotten by future generations, but will remain useful and instructive. There is no resolution offered to this antinomy, either in this particular poem or in Brecht's work in general. The final question, the title question, remains therefore an open one.

Like Walter Hinck, Carl Pietzcker makes the mistake of taking the utterances in *Warum soll mein Name* at face value, accepting the surface text as Brecht's straightforward, not-to-be-doubted statement to us. In his comments on the poem, Pietzcker then compounds this error by linking its message, as he understands it, to Brecht's psychological problems, as he understands *them*. *Warum soll mein Name* is discussed together with another poem, *Lob der Vergeßlichkeit*, in the context of the younger Brecht's alleged nihilistic longing for oblivion: "In das Lob einer Vergeßlichkeit . . . geht die geheime und nicht ganz abgearbeitete frühe Sehnsucht nach dem Erlöschen der Realität ein," and "späte Reste der frühen Sehnsucht nach dem Erlöschen des Subjekts sind in das Gedicht eingegangen."[6] These traces,

Pietzcker goes on, are still more clearly to be seen in *Warum soll mein Name*: "Das 'dichtende Ich' wünscht insgeheim, vergessen zu werden; es wendet sich, in der Negation noch an den bürgerlichen Individualismus gebunden, gegen den eigenen Ruhm und ist nicht imstande, sein Weiterleben im Gedächtnis aus anderer denn aus gegenindividualistischer Perspektive zu betrachten."[7] This is a good example of the kind of interpretive practice that is encountered so often in Brecht criticism and that has been taken to task on other occasions in this book. On the basis of a reading of a text that neglects its communicative strategies and rhetorical structures, inferences are drawn about the writer's psychobiography. The psychobiography thus constructed is then used as a basis for further interpretations, and so on, to and fro, in a two-way process where each pole, biography and interpretation, is used to prop up the other but where both poles are, from the outset, unreliable.

The two contradictory attitudes side by side (or one behind the other) in *Warum soll mein Name*—belief in the Leninist principle of "Aufhebung," according to which today's achievements are tomorrow's footnotes, and a conviction nonetheless about one's immortality as a writer—can each be found on their own elsewhere in Brecht's work. The certainty of, and a grim satisfaction in, the inexorably obliterating effect of time and the rapid forgetfulness of those who follow us can be expressed with devastating clarity:

BEI DER NACHRICHT VON DER ERKRANKUNG EINES MÄCHTIGEN STAATSMANNS

Wenn der unentbehrliche Mann die Stirn runzelt
Wanken zwei Weltreiche.
Wenn der unentbehrliche Mann stirbt
Schaut die Welt sich um wie eine Mutter, die keine Milch für ihr Kind hat.
Wenn der unentbehrliche Mann eine Woche nach seinem Tod zurückkehrte
Fände man im ganzen Reich für ihn nicht mehr die Stelle eines Portiers.

(GW, 4:881)

This is one perspective on the fate of the famous. *Ich benötige keinen Grabstein* presents quite a different one. What makes *Warum soll mein Name* a more complex poem is the coexistence of these two perspectives in a way that, contrary to initial expectations, tips the balance firmly in favor of the second perspective. This happens again, though much more obviously, in another poem on the subject of Brecht's reception and effect:

DER SCHÖNE TAG, WENN ICH NUTZLOS GEWORDEN BIN

Das ist ein fröhlicher Tag, an dem es heißt:
Legt die Waffen weg, sie sind nicht mehr nötig!
Das waren gute Jahre, nach denen
Die Waffen aus den Schuppen gezogen werden, und es zeigt sich:
Sie sind rostig.

Freilich wünschte ich, daß mich der letzte erst weglegt
Der von den Hunden gebissen wurde.

(GW, 4:1028)

As in *Warum soll mein Name* the poet looks forward to a future when the struggles of the present will be forgotten and when his work will no longer be needed. And as in *Warum soll mein Name* this turns out to be only half of the matter. The other half—Brecht's desire *not* to be forgotten and cast aside—is more overtly expressed in the later poem. *Der schöne Tag* has a sting in its tail, announced typically by a pause before the final two lines and the word—always ominous in Brecht's work—*freilich*. For who can be sure that he is the last to be "von den Hunden gebissen"? Better to play safe and keep on reading Brecht, even if you are one of the "Nachgeborenen" living in a better world.

Here the ironic last two lines bring out into the open Brecht's wish not to be forgotten, not to be "laid aside" by a future generation that might prematurely think of itself as having achieved the utopian goal. The implications here are numerous (they involve the vexed question of Brecht's actual attitude to the utopia), but we should note that the irony here is also self-irony. The poet is only too conscious of the personal motives for his warning. The characteristic sly smile not only signals the clever joke at the expense of the "Nachgeborenen" but reflects self-knowledge, knowledge of human vanity.

Though the obviousness of this ironic ending of *Der schöne Tag* sets it apart, it by no means follows that irony is entirely absent from the other poems discussed so far. The very rhetorical structure I have suggested for *Warum soll mein Name*—the real argument underlying the apparent—is ironic in type. Surreptitiously, so to speak, the poet manages to convey alongside the surface message of the poem at least as strongly the opposite message. And there is more than a hint of irony in the first two lines of *Ich benötige keinen Grabstein*. They are too strongly reminiscent of countless jokes of the type, "I really don't want a drink. However, if you insist, I'll have a glass of Dom Perignon 1908." And the final two lines are pure Groucho Marx: "Madam, your perspicacity and taste do you credit" (to a lady who has just entrusted her business affairs to him). These humorous undercurrents convey to the reader being so openly addressed that the poet is well aware of the irony involved in the request, "I don't need a monument, but if you want to erect one for me, make sure you write on it how humble I was."

To avoid misunderstandings: this is not the kind of irony that is designed utterly to destroy or negate. It is subtle and two-faced, since it allows the earnestness of what is ironically illuminated to persist. The seriousness of the statements in *Ich benötige keinen Grabstein, Warum soll mein Name*, and the first part of *Der schöne Tag* is not at issue, merely their status as *only* serious, as unambiguous. There can be no doubt that Brecht was in earnest about both the necessity and the intrinsic value of the cooperative effect described in the gravestone inscription; or that he seriously believed and accepted the Leninist principle of "Aufhebung" spelled out in *Warum soll mein Name*; or, for that matter, that he truly wished for a world in which "der Mensch dem Menschen ein Helfer ist." But the poet who writes about these things also possesses, as numerous contemporaries attest, a considerable "Selbstbewußtsein," and finds that this brings him into certain paradoxical and ambiguous situations: "Aufhebung," yes, but how does he feel when he reflects that this may imply the "cancellation" of *his* work also? Cooperation through proposal and discussion, yes, but certain proposals are worth more than others—discussions need leaders (they need not *appear* to lead); and was he not (our self-conscious poet reflecting on all this) "right," as the early draft of *Ich benötige keinen Grabstein* asserts? There he had written:

ich benötige keinen grabstein wenn
ihr keines benötigt
sonst wünschte ich es stehe darauf:
ich habe recht gehabt. dennoch
habe ich gesiegt. zwei
unzertrennliche sätze.[8]

Since he is intelligent, and cannot resist the subtlety of the paradox, the poet caught up in these ambivalences and ambiguities makes something of them: he utilizes them creatively, artistically, in his work. There both receive their due, the earnest beliefs and their ironic comment or illumination, in a paradoxical process that can *only* be rendered by irony. Nothing else can bridge the gap between the contraries of modest acceptance of the obliteration of his name and work on the one hand and proud self-assertion on the other. And of course irony does not *really* bridge them either, does not overcome the contradiction, does not offer a logical solution. It is an intellectual and literary device, expressing the author's knowledge of the contradiction and of the frailty of his own position. Such irony retains the poet's serious commitment (and the good conscience that goes with it) while at the same time indulging his healthy self-assurance and proud individuality. This kind of irony is used to let the critical, skeptical, or simply intelligent reader know, in an aside as it were, that he, the poet Brecht, is of course aware of the contradiction. It is the literary expression, we might say, of Brecht's much mentioned "verschmitztes Lächeln."

It should be made clear that we are not talking here of reconciliation or of resolution on a higher level. We are not helped by simple recourse to the dialectic, that cure-all in the hands of many Marxist critics confronted with unfortunate contradictions in a writer whose function as a Marxist classic must be preserved at all costs. What must not be cannot be, and so the contradictions are conjured away, turned—with some juggling—into that kind of "productive discord" that leads to a higher truth. Far from it, in this case: the discord, the unresolved and unresolvable contradiction, is itself the truth. Irony is the means of making this truth artistically transmissible and intellectually acceptable.

The comments offered above would amount at best to a rather academic alternative reading, were it not for the fact that these poems are central to an understanding of Brecht's self-perception and self-projection. Each of the texts discussed in this chapter is concerned with Brecht's role, his identity and his status as a writer, and the effect his work has and will have. We have seen on repeated occasions in previous chapters that this is a favorite topic in Brecht's poetry about himself. When he talks about himself, in poems as different as *Schlechte Zeit für Lyrik, Ausschließlich wegen der zunehmenden Unordnung, An die Nachgeborenen, Verjagt mit gutem Grund, Die Auswanderung der Dichter*, as well as the poems discussed in this chapter, he talks always in a *self-defining* way. It is not, of course, the kind of self-definition that is lyrical self-exploration in the traditional sense, especially not in the German tradition of *Innerlichkeit*. If we say that Brecht had problems with his identity, then we cannot mean the kind of turgidly metaphysical, ontological, or existential problems experienced, in ethereal isolation and with lyrical agony, by the Hofmannsthals and Rilkes and Benns. We mean rather problems of role, problems arising from the contradictory relationship between the personal and the public self, between the need for self-expression and the demands of social and political obligation. These problems, I have argued, existed in far greater measure than the critical literature on Brecht usually allows. The poems discussed above are merely the tip of an iceberg that comprises not only the first-person poetry in toto but also the *Tui* complex, the *Keunergeschichten*, the *Flüchtlingsgespräche*, *Galilei*, and the *Arbeitsjournal*.

The contradictions emerge most clearly where the poet Brecht presents himself to his present and future readers, where he portrays himself and permits himself to speculate about how he might be seen by others, now and in the future. This question, the question of his present and posthumous fame is, for a Marxist writer, a difficult one—ideologically touchy, and personally embarrassing. Brecht himself varies in the way he handles the subject. There is his inclusion of his own name among those of the great writers in *Die Auswanderung der Dichter*.

> Homer hatte kein Heim
> Und Dante mußte das seine verlassen.
> Li-Po und Tu-Fu irrten durch Bürgerkriege
> Die 30 Millionen Menschen verschlangen
> Dem Euripides drohte man mit Prozessen
> Und dem sterbenden Shakespeare hielt man den Mund zu.
> Den François Villon suchte nicht nur die Muse
> Sondern auch die Polizei.
> "Der Geliebte" genannt
> Ging Lukrez in die Verbannung
> So Heine, und so auch floh
> Brecht unter das dänische Strohdach.
>
> (GW, 4:495)

No irony here, apparently, although the audacity of Brecht's self-assessment makes one look for it. His presence in such exalted company is simply taken for granted. But then it is taken for granted also in the three previously discussed poems that I have suggested must all be read as partly ironic and partly serious (*Ich benötige keinen Grabstein, Warum soll mein Name genannt werden?* and *Der schöne Tag, wenn ich nutzlos geworden bin*). These poems form part of the material that we might label "Brecht als Klassiker." The unspoken assumption behind all three is that the poet has achieved the kind of status that causes his fellows to think of appropriate stone memorials for him, that makes it likely that his name will live on long after he is dead, and that leads people in troubled times to reach for the volume that bears his name. Brecht, by the very act of modestly rejecting these signs of fame, implicitly affirms his status as a classic. After all, were this status not clear, he would have no cause to write the poems in the first place.

He began writing them, these devious disclaimers that in reality stake a claim to fame, at a remarkably early age. *Ich benötige keinen Grabstein*, though it is included in the last poems of the *GW*, dates back to around 1933, to a time in other words when Brecht was in his midthirties. Great writers tend to know quite early that they are destined for fame. This is not an idle comment. If we set aside the tortured self-doubters (Kafka, for example), we can say that part of being an important writer is knowing that one is important. Brecht's image, carefully cultivated, as the modest sage in no way prevents him from aspiring, in his wry way, to eternal renown (among other things as a modest sage). The self-effacing exhortations to his readers to question, not to accept teachings (including his) too readily, are made from a position of strength and authority. Sometimes Brecht lets us know, through irony, that he is aware of the covert arrogance of his stance. Walter Hinck's criticism of *Ich benötige keinen Grabstein* as "unbrechtisch" is valid only if one takes the poem at face value. This, I have suggested, both overlooks the ironic dimension of the text and begs questions about what *is* typically "brechtisch." Brecht's gravestone directions are, on the contrary, very Brechtian, precisely because they constitute an example among many in the first-person poetry of apparent modesty that masks a proud self-assertiveness, which in turn is informed by an irony that gently mocks poet and reader alike. In this sense the gravestone inscription of the poem, "Er hat Vorschläge gemacht. Wir / Haben sie angenommen," is the *most* typically Brechtian touch of all.

It is well known that Brecht's actual gravestone, in the Dorotheen-Friedhof next to his Berlin house, is a simple irregular stone, a small boulder on which is written, unadorned, his name. In its way this too is a Brechtian touch, a masterpiece of calculated understatement, expressing a variety of his favorite teachings: that greatness is simple, that stark unadornment is more effective than splendor and ornament, and that true pathos is achieved through underplaying. Brecht went to considerable pains to obtain *his* spot in the overcrowded cemetery onto which his study window looked. He had picked the place out in advance. It is just a few meters away, diagonally opposite, from Hegel's grave. It is in the nature of *Klassiker* to seek out their own kind. If this final act, so to speak, demonstrates the staging instincts of the man of the theater, the plain inscription "Bertolt Brecht" on the irregular natural stone is the last message to his readers from a poet who from his early days was acutely aware of his relationship to his public. This final communication is marked by that same mixture of self-revelation and self-concealment initially described in the introduction to this book and met with so often in Brecht's poetry. To the end Brecht was intent upon projecting an image of himself at once decently humble (untrue) and guileless in his art (also untrue). The mixture is successfully calculated to produce in his reader fondness for the poet and admiration for his art. The properly skeptical critic may sometimes wonder whether the former feeling is justified, but he will hardly withhold the latter.

Notes

Introduction

1. Brecht, *Gesammelte Werke in acht Bänden*, 8:385–91, 391–92 respectively. All subsequent references to Brecht's work will be to this edition, using the abbreviation *GW* followed by the volume and page numbers.
2. *GW*, 8:56.
3. Kreuzer, "Zur Periodisierung der 'modernen' deutschen Literatur," 500–529, esp. 506–10.
4. Wellek, "Genre Theory, The Lyric, and 'Erlebnis,'" 408. See also Gadamer, *Wahrheit und Methode*, 52–60.
5. Spinner, *Zur Struktur des lyrischen Ich*, 14–15.
6. Killy, *Elemente der Lyrik*, 4.
7. See for example Staiger (*Goethe*, vol. 1) on the Italian journey (545–46), Werther (152–53), and Gretchen (239–41).
8. Frisch, "Der Autor und das Theater," 5:342.
9. Esslin, Review of Knopf's *Bertolt Brecht*, 185.
10. Ibid., 186.
11. Steinweg, *Das Lehrstück*.
12. Esslin, Review of Knopf's *Bertolt Brecht*, 187.
13. Bay, Review of Schwarz's *Brechts frühe Lyrik, 1914–1922*, 168.
14. Ibid.
15. Zimmerman, "Die Last der Lehre," 101–7.
16. Pietzcker, *Die Lyrik des jungen Brecht*, 114–15.
17. Ibid., 115.
18. Ibid., 118.
19. Schuhmann, *Der Lyriker Bertolt Brecht, 1913–1933*.
20. Schwarz, *Brechts frühe Lyrik, 1914–1922*.
21. Pietzcker, *Die Lyrik des jungen Brecht*.
22. Schwarz, *Lyrik und Zeitgeschichte*.
23. This is the most recent German publication on Brecht's poetry.
24. Mennemeier attempts in a single footnote (217–18) to present a general view, but this remains, inevitably, sketchy and speculative. His characterization of Brecht's poetry as "ein mehr und mehr seiner selbst bewußt werdendes künstlerisches Streben . . . , zwischen Nicht-Einheit und Einheit als 'idealen' Extremen des Schaffens zu vermitteln" (217) is interesting, but is only one of many possible perspectives.

Chapter 1

1. Pietzcker, "Von der Kindesmörderin Marie Farrar," 185.
2. Ibid.
3. Ibid.
4. Wilson, "Readers in Texts," 848–63.
5. Ibid., 848.
6. Ibid.
7. Terminology varies: Iser uses "impliziter Leser" in analogy with Wayne Booth's "implied author"; Wolff prefers "intendierter Leser." "Leserrolle" is used to denote the role created for the implied reader by the text, the role he is required to adopt. "Leserfiktion" is then the fictional (characterized) reader. Iser attempts to make a distinction between "intendierter Leser" and "impliziter Leser," seeing the former as a historical/sociological category and the latter as an ahistorical text-structure. (See Iser, *Der Akt des Lesens*.) But as Wilson shows ("Readers in Texts," 851–52), this distinction is fallacious.
8. Wilson, "Readers in Texts," 858.
9. Ibid., 852. See also Maurer, "Formen des Lesens," 472–98.
10. Nelson, "The Fictive Reader and Literary Self-Reflexiveness," 182–83. See also Wilson, "Readers in Texts," 858.
11. The spelling and order of the names vary in the literature on Brecht. I have adopted the version used by Dietmar Grieser, who interviewed the woman concerned. (Grieser, "Bertolt Brecht 80 Jahre," 5–15).

Chapter 2

1. Esslin, *Brecht: A Choice of Evils*, 151.
2. Ibid., 150–51.
3. In such accounts the transition is often presented as taking place via a behaviorist phase. See Knopf, *Bertolt Brecht*, 80–90. Knopf's own position here, though also Marxist, is critical and skeptical.
4. Schuhmann, *Der Lyriker Bertolt Brecht, 1913–1933*.
5. See Esslin, *Brecht: A Choice of Evils*, 12–30; even comparatively recent biographies such as Schumacher and Schumacher's *Leben Brechts* take over this view.
6. Schuhmann, *Der Lyriker Bertolt Brecht, 1913–1933*, 152.
7. Schwarz, *Brechts frühe Lyrik, 1914–1922*, 105.
8. Pietzcker, *Die Lyrik des jungen Brecht*, 13.
9. The terminology is that of Schwarz (*Brechts frühe Lyrik*, 135), but it exactly describes what Pietzcker is attempting.
10. Pietzcker, *Die Lyrik des jungen Brecht*, 28.
11. Ibid., 28.
12. Ibid., 117.

13. Ibid., 118.
14. Morley, "Two Brecht Poems," 5–25.
15. Willett and Manheim, *Bertolt Brecht: Poems, 1913–1956*, 524.
16. Lehmann and Lethen, *Bertolt Brechts 'Hauspostille,'* 146–72.
17. Pietzcker, *Die Lyrik des jungen Brecht*, 76–154.
18. See esp. Schuhmann, *Der Lyriker Bertolt Brecht, 1913–1933*, 44, and Schwarz, *Brechts frühe Lyrik, 1914–1922*, 196; also Thomson, "Sachlichkeit und Pathos," 183–205, and Sokel, "Brecht und der Expressionismus," 47–74.
19. See esp. 44–49.
20. For the influence of Villon, Rimbaud, and Kipling on Brecht, see Mennemeier, *Bertolt Brechts Lyrik*, 25–38, and Lyon, *Bertolt Brecht and Rudyard Kipling*.
21. Pietzcker, *Die Lyrik des jungen Brecht*, 204.
22. Schwarz, *Brechts frühe Lyrik, 1914–1922*, 159–60.
23. Blume, "Das ertrunkene Mädchen," 108–19.
24. Schwarz, *Brechts frühe Lyrik, 1914–1922*, 175.
25. Ibid., 159–60.
26. Pietzcker, *Die Lyrik des jungen Brecht*, 117. My translation.
27. Trilling, *Sincerity and Authenticity*.
28. Frisch and Obermeier, *Brecht in Augsburg*, present a range of material comprising both contemporary comment and reminiscence. For further sources see Völker, *Bertolt Brecht: Eine Biographie*, chaps. 2 and 3.
29. Münsterer, *Bert Brecht: Erinnerungen*, 116–17. The poem referred to is presumably "Vom Klettern in Bäumen." This, "Vom Schwimmen in Seen und Flüssen," and some other planned poems were to be called *Evangelien*, in line with the general parodistic nomenclature of the *Hauspostille*.
30. Frisch and Obermeier, *Brecht in Augsburg*, 110–11. Harrer is speaking of the years 1917–18.
31. Mayer, *Brecht und die Tradition*, 22.
32. Schwarz, *Brechts frühe Lyrik, 1914–1922*, 135.

Chapter 3

1. Seliger, *Das Amerikabild Bertolt Brechts*, 28.
2. Schuhmann, *Der Lyriker Bertolt Brecht, 1913–1933*, 149–77.
3. Hauptmann, "Notizen über Brechts Arbeit 1926," 243. Cf. Brecht's *Tagebuch* entry for 3 December 1921: "Gern möchte ich die 'Johanna' jetzt schreiben, um dann die Hände für die Trilogie 'Asphaltdschungel' freizuhaben" (177).
4. See *GW*, 8:429–30.
5. A German translation of Jensen's novel *Hjulet* (The wheel) appeared in 1921. Its influence on *Im Dickicht der Städte* is unmistakable.
6. Völker, *Bertolt Brecht: Eine Biographie*, 99. The first quotation is from Benjamin, *Versuche über Brecht*, 68; the second from Marieluise Fleisser, "Zu

Brecht," *Materialien zum Leben und Schreiben der Marieluise Fleisser*, cited by Völker, 923.

7. Völker, *Bertolt Brecht: Eine Biographie*, 100.
8. Ibid., 110–13.
9. Ibid., 106–7.
10. Ibid., 105.
11. Ibid., 65.
12. Brecht, *Aufzeichnungen*, 213 (ca. 1930).
13. Schumacher and Schumacher, *Leben Brechts*, 42.
14. Ibid.
15. The original version (BBA 436/25–28) contains only one stanza that might convey something of Brecht's real suffering:

> Denn ich spiele mitunter in viel Gesichtern (sic) Gitarre
> und verstehe mich nicht gut und bin leidlich allein.
> Die fressen die rohen Wörter. Es sind andere Tiere.
> Ich aber liege und spüre im Rücken noch einen Stein.

Against this one has to set the original beginning of stanza 2, with its casual assertion of city experience:

> In der Asphaltstadt bin ich daheim. Seit vielen Jahren
> Städte
> lebe ich dort [!] als ein Mann, der die T̶s̶chungel kennt.

16. Bronnen, *Tage mit Bertolt Brecht*, 34–38.
17. Willett and Manheim, *Bertolt Brecht: Poems, 1913–1956*, 534.
18. Brecht, *Tagebuch*, 180.
19. Ibid.

Chapter 4

1. This point is made by Jürgen Becker in a poem entitled "Gute Zeiten, nicht nur für Lyrik," 64–66.
2. Willett and Manheim, *Bertolt Brecht: Poems, 1913–1956* has "insolent," 331.
3. Brecht, *Arbeitsjournal*, 1:171.
4. Willett and Manheim, *Bertolt Brecht: Poems, 1913–1956*, 573–74, give the known and probable circumstances of the genesis and publication of the three parts.
5. "Das Göttliche," 147.

Chapter 5

1. Seidel, "Vom Kaderwelsch," 1087–90.
2. Sonderband Bertolt Brecht II; see Knopf, *Brecht Handbuch*, 191–204, for a more balanced overview of the *Buckower Elegien*, though not for his recommendation of Dieter Thiele's account of them in the latter's *Bertolt Brecht: Selbstverständnis*, 68–116, a book that is motivated by the transparent desire to remove all traces of the problematical from Brecht's view of the intellectuals, of himself as an intellectual, and of his relationship to the "masses."
3. Völker, *Bertolt Brecht: Eine Biographie*, 393–96, gives a brief summary of the events of 15–17 June. See also Wekwerth, "Brief an einen westdeutschen Journalisten," 189. Brown, "Brecht and the 17th of June, 1953," gives a fairly full and balanced account of the crisis and Brecht's reaction to it. See also Pachter, "Brecht's Personal Politics," and Hayman, *Brecht: A Biography*, 366–73.
4. Freie Wahlen.

Es ist der älteste Trick der Bourgeoisie, den Wähler frei seine Unfreiheit wählen zu lassen, indem man ihm das Wissen um seine Lage vorenthält. Das, was jemand braucht, um seinen Weg wählen zu können, ist Wissen. Was kommt dabei heraus, wenn man einen Mann, der weder Notenlesen noch Klavierspielen lernen durfte, vor ein Klavier stellt und ihm die freie Wahl über die Tasten läßt?

(*GW*, 8:328)

5. Thomson, "A Classic Hang-Up."
6. Seidel, "Vom Kaderwelsch," 1089.
7. Brecht, *Arbeitsjournal*, 1009 (20 Aug. 1953).
8. Erwin Leiser, "Brecht, Grass und der 17. Juni 1953," (*Die Weltwoche*, 11 Feb. 1966), cited by Völker, *Bertolt Brecht: Eine Biographie*, 395.
9. *GW*, 8:882–83.
10. Tatlow, *Brechts chinesische Gedichte*.
11. Horace, *Odes* 1.2 is commonly suggested as the reference, but Morley, "Brecht's *Beim Lesen des Horaz*," demonstrates the weakness of this view, and suggests *Epistles* 1.2. Morley points out the fallaciousness of early readings of this poem and insists on its negative tone of resignation.
12. Völker, *Bertolt Brecht: Eine Biographie*, 395.
13. Schuhmann, *Untersuchungen zur Lyrik Brechts*, 109–11.
14. Schwarz, *Lyrik und Zeitgeschichte*, 122.
15. Link, *Die Struktur des literarischen Symbols*.
16. Ibid., 53.
17. Ibid., 54.
18. Ibid., 55.
19. Ibid., 68–69.

Chapter 6

1. Völker, *Bertolt Brecht: Eine Biographie*, 228.
2. GW, 4:21.
3. Brecht, *Arbeitsjournal*, 1008 (4 March 1953).
4. Mayer, *Brecht in der Geschichte*, 233.
5. Ibid., 236.
6. I find myself in disagreement here with Morley ("Kontinuität und Wandel"), who does not differentiate between this poem and the others he discusses as examples of the poet Brecht's difficulties after 1948.
7. Pike, "Brecht and Stalin's Russia." See also Pike, *German Writers in Soviet Exile, 1933–1945*, esp. chap. 11, which describes the fate of the German communist intelligentsia in Russia once the purges began.

Chapter 7

1. Mayer, *Brecht in der Geschichte*, 189.
2. Hinck, *Ausgewählte Gedichte Brechts*, 153.
3. Ibid., 155.
4. Ibid., 153.
5. Mayer, *Brecht in der Geschichte*, 192. Mayer is referring to Ernst Bloch's essay "Ein Leninist der Schaubühne" on Brecht's plays.
6. Pietzcker, *Die Lyrik des jungen Brecht*, 358.
7. Ibid., 358–59.
8. Hecht, *Bertolt Brecht: Sein Leben*, 311.

Bibliography

Primary Sources

Works by Bertolt Brecht

Arbeitsjournal. Frankfurt a.M.: Suhrkamp, 1973.
Briefe. 2 vols. Edited and with commentary by Günter Glaser. Frankfurt a.M.: Suhrkamp, 1981.
Gedichte aus dem Nachlaß, 1913–56. Frankfurt a.M.: Suhrkamp, 1982. [Supplementband 2 of *Gesammelte Werke in acht Bänden*.]
Gedichte über die Liebe. Frankfurt a.M.: Suhrkamp, 1973.
Gesammelte Werke in acht Bänden. Frankfurt a.M.: Suhrkamp, 1967.
Tagebücher, 1920–1922; Autobiographische Aufzeichnungen, 1920–1954, edited by Herta Ramthun. Frankfurt a.M.: Suhrkamp, 1973. [These are separate collections. The *Tagebücher* are four handwritten diaries dating from the early 1920s; the *Aufzeichnungen* are entries in notebooks or scattered items found in the Nachlaß. References in the text and the notes distinguish between the two; page numbers refer to the volume edited by Ramthun.]

Works by Other Authors

Bronnen, Arnolt. *Vatermord*. In *Stücke*. Kronberg: Athenäum, 1977.
Goethe, Johann Wolfgang von. *Faust I*. In *Werke, Band 3*. 8th ed. Hamburg: Christian Wegner, 1967.
———. "Das Göttliche." In *Werke, Band 1*. 8th ed. Hamburg: Christian Wegner, 1966.
———. *Die Leiden des jungen Werthers*. In *Werke, Band 6*. 6th ed. Hamburg: Christian Wegner, 1965.
Hasenclever, Walter. *Der Sohn*. Leipzig: Kurt Wolff, 1917.
Hoffmann, E. T. A. *Der Sandmann*. In *Fantasie- und Nachtstücke*. Munich: Winkler Verlag, 1964.
Lasker-Schüler, Else. *Gesammelte Werke*, edited by Friedhelm Kamp. Munich: Kösel.
Sterne, Laurence. *Tristram Shandy*. Oxford: Clarendon Press, 1983.
Villon, François. *Balladen*. Translated by K. L. Ammer. Berlin: Kiepenheuer, 1930.
———. *Oeuvres*. Volume 1. Edited by Louis Thuasne. Geneva: Slatkine Reprints, 1967.
Werfel, Franz. *Gesammelte Werke: Das lyrische Werk*, edited by Adolf Klarmann. Frankfurt a.M.: Fischer, 1967.

Secondary Sources

Adorno, Theodor W. "Engagement." In *Noten zur Literatur*, 3:109–35. Frankfurt a.M.: Suhrkamp, 1965.
———. "Rede über Lyrik und Gesellschaft." In *Noten zur Literatur*, 1:73–104. Frankfurt a.M.: Suhrkamp, 1958.
Arendt, Hannah. *Men in Dark Times*. New York: Harcourt, Brace & World, 1968.
Bathrick, David. "Concerning Legends." *New German Critique* 9 (1976): 139–41.
Baumgärtner, Klaus. "Interpretation und Analyse. Brechts Gedicht *Die Literatur wird durchforscht werden*." *Sinn und Form* 12 (1960): 395–415.
Baumgart, Reinhart. "Schwacher Brecht." In *Literatur für Zeitgenossen*, 141–50. Frankfurt a.M.: Suhrkamp, 1966.
Bay, Jürgen. Review of Peter Paul Schwarz's *Brechts frühe Lyrik, 1914–1922*. *Brecht Jahrbuch* (1974): 166–69.
Becker, Jürgen. "Gute Zeiten, nicht nur für Lyrik." In *Ausgewählte Gedichte Brechts mit Interpretationen*, edited by Walter Hinck, 64–66. Frankfurt a.M.: Suhrkamp, 1978.
Benjamin, Walter. *Versuche über Brecht*. 3d ed. Frankfurt a.M.: Suhrkamp, 1971.
Benn, Gottfried. "Probleme der Lyrik." In *Gesammelte Werke in acht Bänden*, 4:1058–96. Wiesbaden: Limes, 1968.
Berlau, Ruth. "Notwendige Bemerkung zu Bertolt Brechts 'Rat.'" *Das Blatt* (Berlin) 6, nos. 2/3 (1955): 2.
Birkenhauer, Klaus. *Die eigenrhythmische Lyrik Bertolt Brechts. Theorie eines kommunikativen Sprachstils*. Tübingen: Niemeyer, 1971.
Blume, Bernhard. "Das ertrunkene Mädchen: Rimbauds *Ophélie* und die deutsche Literatur." *Germanisch-romanische Monatsschrift* 4 (1954): 108–19.
———. "Motive der frühen Lyrik Bertolt Brechts: I. der Tod im Wasser." *Monatshefte* 57 (1965): 97–112.
Bohnert, Christiane. *Brechts Lyrik im Kontext: Zyklen und Exil*. Koenigstein: Athenäum, 1982.
Booth, Wayne C. *The Rhetoric of Fiction*. Chicago: University of Chicago Press, 1962.
Bormanns, Peter. "Brecht und der Stalinismus." *Brecht Jahrbuch* (1974): 53–76.
Brandt, Thomas Otto. *Die Vieldeutigkeit Bertolt Brechts*. Heidelberg: Stiehm, 1968.
Brecht, Walter. *Unser Leben in Augsburg, damals*. Wiesbaden: Insel, 1984.
Bronnen, Arnolt. *Tage mit Bertolt Brecht*. Darmstadt: Luchterhand, 1976.
Brooke-Rose, Christine. "Self-Confrontation and the Writer." *New Literary History* 9 (1977/78), 129–36.
Brown, Thomas K. "Brecht and the 17th of June, 1953." *Monatshefte* 63 (1971): 48–55.
———. "*Die Plebeier* und Brecht: An Interview with Günter Grass." *Monatshefte* 65 (1973): 5–13.

Brüggemann, Heinz. *Literarische Technik und soziale Revolution.* Reinbek: Rowohlt, 1973.

———. "Theodor W. Adornos Kritik an der literarischen Theorie und Praxis Bertolt Brechts." *Alternative* 15 (1972): 137–49.

Bunge, Hans. *Fragen Sie mehr über Brecht. Hanns Eisler im Gespräch.* Munich: Rogner & Bernhard, 1970.

Claas, Herbert, and Haug, Wolfgang F., eds. *Brechts Tui-Kritik.* Supplementary vol. 11 of *Argument.* Karlsruhe: Argument Verlag, 1976.

Demetz, Peter, Green, Thomas, and Nelson, Lowry, eds. *The Disciplines of Criticism.* New Haven: Yale University Press, 1968.

Des Pres, Ference. "Into the Mire: The Case of Bertolt Brecht." *Yale Review* 70 (1981): 481–89.

Dilthey, Wilhelm. *Das Erlebnis und die Dichtung.* 13th ed. Göttingen: Vandenhoeck & Ruprecht, 1957.

Dittberner, Hugo. "Die Philosophie der Landschaft in Brechts *Buckower Elegien.*" *Text + Kritik,* special Bertolt Brecht edition 2 (1973): 54–65.

Ehrenpreis, Irvin. "Personae." In *Restoration and 18th Century Literature,* edited by Carroll Camden, 25–37. Chicago: University of Chicago Press, 1963.

Ekmann, Björn. *Gesellschaft und Gewissen: Die sozialen und moralischen Anschauungen Bertolt Brechts und ihre Bedeutung für seine Dichtung.* Copenhagen: Munksgaard, 1969.

Esslin, Martin. *Brecht: A Choice of Evils.* London: Eyre & Spottiswoode, 1959.

———. *Brecht: The Man and His Work.* Revised edition of the above. Garden City: Anchor, 1971.

———. Review of Jan Knopf's *Bertolt Brecht: Ein kritischer Forschungsbericht. Brecht Jahrbuch* (1976): 185–88.

Ewen, Frederic. *Bertolt Brecht: His Life, His Art and His Times.* New York: Citadel, 1967.

Fetscher, Irving. "Brecht und der Kommunismus." *Merkur* 304 (1973): 872–86.

Fish, Stanley E. *Is There a Text in This Class?* Cambridge, Mass.: Harvard University Press, 1980.

———. "Literature in the Reader: Affective Stylistics." *New Literary History* 1 (1970): 123–63.

Fleisser, Marieluise. "Erinnerungen an Brecht." In *Gesammelte Werke in drei Bänden,* 2: 297–308. Frankfurt a.M.: Suhrkamp, 1972.

Foulkes, A. Peter. "On the Wings of Fictionality." In *The Uses of Criticism,* edited by A. Peter Foulkes, 157–74. Bern: Lang, 1976.

Friedrich, Hugo. *Die Struktur der modernen Lyrik.* 2d ed. Reinbek: Rowohlt, 1968.

Frisch, Max. "Der Autor und das Theater." In *Gesammelte Werke in zeitlicher Folge,* 2d ed., 5:339–54. Frankfurt a.M.: Suhrkamp, 1976.

Frisch, Werner, and Obermeier, K. W. *Brecht in Augsburg.* Frankfurt a.M.: Suhrkamp, 1976.

Gadamer, Hans Georg. *Wahrheit und Methode: Grundzüge einer philosophischen*

Hermeneutik. 3d ed. Tübingen: Mohr, 1972.

Gouldner, Alvin W. "Prologue to a Theory of Revolutionary Intellectuals." *Telos* 26 (1976): 3–36.

──────. "The Two Marxisms." In *For Sociology*, 425–62. London: Allen Lane, 1973.

Grieser, Dietmar. "Bertolt Brecht 80 Jahre." *Zeitmagazin* 6 (3 Feb. 1978): 5–15.

Grimm, Günter, ed. *Literatur und Leser: Theorien und Modelle zur Rezeption literarischer Werke.* Stuttgart: Reclam, 1975.

Grimm, Reinhold. *Bertolt Brecht.* 3d ed. Stuttgart: Metzler, 1971.

──────. *Bertolt Brecht: Die Struktur seines Werkes.* 2d ed. Nuremberg: Carl, 1960.

──────. *Bertolt Brecht und die Weltliteratur.* Nuremberg: Carl, 1961.

──────. "The 'Brecht Industry': A Polemical Assessment." *Monatshefte* 69 (1977): 337–46.

──────. "Confession of a Poet: Poetry and Politics in Brecht's Lyrik." In *From Kafka to Dada to Brecht and Beyond*, edited by Reinhold Grimm et al. Madison: University of Wisconsin Press, 1982.

──────. "Marxistische Emblematik: Zu Bertolt Brechts *Kriegsfibel*." In *Wissenschaft als Dialog*, edited by Renate V. Heydebrand and Klaus Günther Just, 351–79. Stuttgart: Metzler, 1969.

Hamburger, Käte. *Die Logik der Dichtung.* 2d ed. Stuttgart: Klett, 1968.

Hammer, John. "Brecht and the Intellectuals." *German Life and Letters* 4 (1976): 382–88.

Hartinger, Christel. "Das lyrische Werk Bertolt Brechts, 1945–1956." Ph.D. diss., University of Leipzig, 1982.

Hauptmann, Elisabeth. "Notizen über Brechts Arbeit 1926." *Sinn und Form*, Zweites Sonderheft Bertolt Brecht, 1957: 241–43.

Hayman, Ronald. *Brecht: A Biography.* New York: Oxford University Press, 1983.

Hecht, Werner. *Bertolt Brecht: Sein Leben in Bildern und Texten.* Frankfurt a.M.: Suhrkamp, 1978.

Heinrichs, Hans-Jürgen. "Methodendiskussion mit Brecht." *Text + Kritik*, special Bertolt Brecht edition 2 (1973): 171–91.

Hermand, Jost. "Zwischen Tuismus und Tümlichkeit. Brechts Konzept eines klassischen Stils." *Brecht Jahrbuch* (1975): 9–34.

Hernadi, Paul. "The Actor's Face as the Author's Mask. On the Paradox of Brechtian Staging." *Yearbook of Comparative Criticism* 7 (1976): 125–36.

Heselhaus, Clemens. "Brechts Verfremdung der Lyrik." In *Immanente Ästhetik, ästhetische Reflexion*, edited by Wolfgang Iser, 307–26. Munich: Fink, 1966.

──────. "Die Masken des Bertolt Brecht." In *Deutsche Lyrik der Moderne von Nietzsche bis Yvan Goll*, 2d ed., 321–38. Düsseldorf: Bagel, 1962.

Hildebrand, Alexander. "Bertolt Brechts Alterslyrik." *Merkur* 20 (1966): 952–62.

Hinck, Walter. *Die deutsche Ballade von Bürger bis Brecht.* Göttingen: Vandenhoeck & Ruprecht, 1968.

---. "Die Dialektik von Werk und Wirkung. Brechts lyrische Reflexionen zu einer lesergerichteten Literatur und einer 'totalen' Wirkungspoetik." In *Festschrift für Benno von Wiese*, edited by Vincent J. Günther et al., 514–21. Berlin: Schmidt, 1973.
---, ed. *Ausgewählte Gedichte Brechts mit Interpretationen*. Frankfurt a.M.: Suhrkamp, 1978.
Hultberg, Helga. *Die ästhetischen Anschauungen Bertolt Brechts*. Copenhagen: Munksgaard, 1962.
Iser, Wolfgang. *Der Akt des Lesens: Theorie ästhetischer Wirkung*. Munich: Fink, 1976.
---. *Der implizierte Leser*. Munich: Fink, 1972.
---. "The Reading Process: A Phenomenological Approach." *New Literary History* 3 (1972): 279–99.
Jacobs, Jürgen. "Brecht und die Intellektuellen." *Neue Rundschau* 2 (1969): 241–58.
---. "Wie die Wirklichkeit selber. Zu Brechts *Lesebuch für Städtebewohner*." *Brecht Jahrbuch* (1974): 77–91.
Jauss, Hans Robert. *Literaturgeschichte als Provokation der Literaturwissenschaft*. Constance: Universitätsverlag, 1967.
Kaiser, Gerhard. *Benjamin, Adorno: Zwei Studien*. Frankfurt a.M.: Athenäum Fischer, 1974.
Kantorowicz, Alfred. *Deutsches Tagebuch*. 2 vols. Munich: Kindler, 1959/1961.
Karasek, Hellmuth. *Bertolt Brecht: Der jüngste Fall eines Theaterklassikers*. Munich: Kindler, 1978.
---. "Besson machts möglich." *Die Zeit* 14 Feb. 1969: 26.
Kersten, Paul. "Bertolt Brecht Epigramme: Anmerkungen zu einigen Kurzgedichten." *Text + Kritik*, special Bertolt Brecht edition 2 (1973): 66–73.
Killy, Walter. *Elemente der Lyrik*. Munich: Beck, 1972.
---. "Das Nichts Gegenüber: Der junge Brecht." In *Wandlungen des lyrischen Bildes*, 5th ed., 136–53. Göttingen: Vandenhoeck & Ruprecht, 1967.
Klotz, Volker. *Bertolt Brecht: Versuch über das Werk*. 4th ed. Bad Homberg: Athenäum, 1971.
Knapp, Gerhard. "Welt und Wirklichkeit: Zur späten Lyrik Bertolt Brechts." *Text + Kritik*, special Bertolt Brecht edition 2 (1973): 41–53.
Knopf, Jan. *Bertolt Brecht: Ein kritischer Forschungsbericht*. Frankfurt a.M.: Athenäum, 1974.
---. *Brecht Handbuch: Lyrik, Prosa, Schriften*. Stuttgart: Metzler, 1984.
Kohlhase, Norbert. *Dichtung und politische Morale*. Munich: Nymphenburger Verlagshandlung, 1965.
Konrad, George and Szelenyi, Ivan. *The Intellectuals on the Road to Class Power*. Brighton: Harvester, 1979.
Korsch, Karl. *Marxismus und Philosophie*. Frankfurt a.M.: Europäische Verlagsanstalt, 1966.
Kraft, Werner. "Krisen Brechts im Gedicht." *Augenblicke der Dichtung: Kritische Betrachtungen*. Munich: Kösel, 1964.
Kreuzer, Helmut. "Zur Periodisierung der 'modernen' deutschen Literatur."

In *Zur Lyrik-Diskussion*, 2d ed., edited by Reinhold Grimm, 500–529. Darmstadt: Wissenschaftliche Buchgesellschaft, 1974.

Lehmann, Hans-Thies. "Das Subjekt der *Hauspostille*. Eine neue Lektüre des Gedichts *Vom armen B. B.*" *Brecht Jahrbuch* (1980): 22–42.

Lehmann, Hans-Thies, and Lethen, Helmut, eds. *Bertolt Brechts 'Hauspostille.'* Stuttgart: Metzler, 1978.

Lerg-Kill, Ulla Klara. *Dichterwort und Parteiparole: Propagandistische Gedichte und Lieder Bertolt Brechts*. Bad Homberg: Gehlen, 1968.

Licher, Edmund. "Kommunikationstheoretische Aspekte der Analyse einiger Gedichte Bertolt Brechts." *Amsterdamer Beiträge zur neueren Germanistik* 3 (1974): 163–211.

Link, Jürgen. *Die Struktur des literarischen Symbols: Theoretische Beiträge am Beispiel der späten Lyrik Brechts*. Munich: Fink, 1975.

Lukacs, Georg. "Das Problem geistiger Führung und die 'geistigen Arbeiter.'" *Taktik und Ethik: Politische Aufsätze* 1 (1975): 53–62. Darmstadt: Luchterhand.

Lyon, James K. *Bertolt Brecht and Rudyard Kipling*. The Hague: Mouton, 1975.

———. *Bertolt Brecht in America*. Princeton: Princeton University Press, 1980.

———. *Bertolt Brecht's American Cicerone*. Bonn: Grundmann, 1978.

Lyon, James K., and Fuegi, John B. "Bertolt Brecht." Part 1 of *Deutsche Exilliteratur seit 1933*, edited by John M. Spalek and Joseph Strelka, 268–98. Bern: Francke, 1976.

McLean, Sammy K. *The Bänkelsang and the Work of Bertolt Brecht*. The Hague: Mouton, 1972.

Marsch, Edgar. *Brecht-Kommentar zum lyrischen Werk*. Munich: Winkler, 1974.

Martens, Günter. *Vitalismus und Expressionismus*. Stuttgart: Kohlhammer, 1971.

Maurer, Karl. "Formen des Lesens." *Poetica* 9 (1977): 472–98.

Mayer, Hans. *Anmerkungen zu Brecht*. 2d ed. Frankfurt a.M.: Suhrkamp, 1967.

———. *Bertolt Brecht und die Tradition*. Pfullingen: Neske, 1961.

———. "Bosheiten von literarischem Rang." *Frankfurter Allgemeine Zeitung* 17 Jan. 1976: 64.

———. *Brecht in der Geschichte*. Frankfurt a.M.: Suhrkamp, 1971.

Mennemeier, Franz Norbert. *Bertolt Brechts Lyrik: Aspekte, Tendenzen*. Düsseldorf: Schwamm-Bagel, 1982.

Milfull, John. *From Baal to Keuner: The "Second Optimism" of Bertolt Brecht*. Bern: Lang, 1974.

———. "Mühen der Gebirge, Mühen der Ebene." In *Die Mühen der Ebenen*, edited by Bernd Hüppauf, 233–48. Heidelberg: Winter, 1981.

Mittenzwei, Werner, ed. *Dialog und Kontroverse mit Georg Lukács: Der Methodenstreit deutscher sozialistischer Schriftsteller*. Leipzig: Reclam, 1975.

Morley, Michael. "Brecht's *Beim Lesen des Horaz*: An Interpretation." *Monatshefte* 63 (1971): 372–79.

———. "An Investigation and Interpretation of Two Brecht Poems." *Germanic Review* 46 (1971): 5–25.

---. "Kontinuität und Wandel in Brechts Gedichten nach 1945." In *Die Mühen der Ebenen*, edited by Bernd Hüppauf, 249–70. Heidelberg: Winter, 1981.
Müller, Joachim. "Zu einigen Spruchgedichten Brechts." *Orbis litterarum* 20 (1966): 66–81.
Müller, Klaus-Detlev. "Brechts *Me-Ti* und die Auseinandersetzung mit dem Lehrer Karl Korsch." *Brecht Jahrbuch* (1977): 9–29.
Münsterer, Hans Otto. *Bert Brecht: Erinnerungen aus den Jahren 1917–1922*. Zurich: Arche, 1963.
Muschg, Walter. "Der Lyriker Bertolt Brecht." In *Von Trakl zu Brecht: Dichter des Expressionismus*, 335–65. Munich: Piper, 1961.
Nelson, Lowrie. "The Fictive Reader and Literary Self-Reflexiveness." In *The Disciplines of Criticism*, edited by Peter Demetz et al., 173–92. New Haven: Yale University Press, 1968.
Ong, Walter J. "The Writer's Audience is Always a Fiction." *PMLA* 90 (1975): 9–21.
Pachter, Henry. "Brecht's Personal Politics." *Telos* 44 (1980): 35–48.
Parmalee, Patty Lee. *Brecht's America*. Columbus: Ohio State University Press (Miami University), 1981.
Pestalozzi, Karl. *Die Entstehung des lyrischen Ich*. Berlin: de Gruyter, 1970.
Pietzcker, Carl. "Gleichklang. Psychoanalytische Überlegungen zu Brechts später Lyrik." *Deutschunterricht* 34 (1982): 266–77.
---. *Die Lyrik des jungen Brecht: Vom anarchischen Nihilismus zum Marxismus*. Frankfurt a.M.: Suhrkamp, 1974.
---. "Von der Kindesmörderin Marie Farrar." In *Brechtdiskussion*, edited by Joachim Dyck et al., 172–206. Kronberg: Scriptor Verlag, 1974.
Pike, David. *German Writers in Soviet Exile, 1933–1945*. Chapel Hill: University of North Carolina Press, 1982.
---. "Brecht and Stalin's Russia: The Victim as Apologist (1931–1945)." *Brecht Jahrbuch* 11 (1982): 143–96.
Pinthus, Kurt, ed. *Menschheitsdämmerung*. Hamburg: Rowohlt, 1959.
Powroslo, Wolfgang. *Erkenntnis durch Literatur: Realismus in der westdeutschen Literaturtheorie der Gegenwart*. Cologne: Kiepenheuer & Witsch, 1976.
Raddatz, Fritz J., ed. *Marxismus und Literatur*. 3 vols. Reinbek: Rowohlt, 1969.
---. "Der sozialistische Egomane." *Merkur* 36 (1982): 266–77.
Ramthun, Herta. *Bertolt Brecht Archiv: Bestandsverzeichnis des literarischen Nachlasses*, vol. 2 (poetry). Berlin and Weimar: Aufbau, 1970.
Rasch, Wolfdietrich. "Bertolt Brechts marxistischer Lehrer." *Merkur* 17 (1963): 988–1003.
Riha, Karl. *Deutsche Großstadtlyrik*. Munich and Zurich: Artemis, 1983.
---. "Literarisches Kabarett und Rollengedicht." In *Die deutsche Literatur in der Weimarer Republik*, edited by Wolfgang Rothe, 382–95. Stuttgart: Reclam, 1974.
---. "Notizen zur *Legende vom toten Soldaten*. Ein Paradigma der frühen Lyrik Brechts." *Text + Kritik*, special Bertolt Brecht edition 2 (1973): 30–40.

Ruttkowski, Wolfgang. *Das literarische Chanson in Deutschland.* Bern: Francke, 1966.
Schlenstedt, Silvia. "Lyrik im Gesamtplan der Produktion. Ein Arbeitsprinzip Brechts und Probleme der *Gedichte im Exil.*" *Weimarer Beiträge* 2 (1978): 5–29.
Schöne, Albrecht. *Über politische Lyrik im 20. Jahrhundert.* Göttingen: Vandenhoeck & Ruprecht, 1965.
Schuhmann, Klaus. *Der Lyriker Bertolt Brecht, 1913–1933.* Berlin: Rütten & Loening, 1964.
———. *Untersuchungen zur Lyrik Brechts: Themen, Formen, Weiterungen.* Berlin: Aufbau, 1973.
Schumacher, Ernst. *Die dramatischen Versuche Bertolt Brechts, 1918–1933.* Berlin: Rütten & Loening, 1955.
Schumacher, Ernst, and Schumacher, Renate. *Leben Brechts.* Berlin: Henschel, 1979.
Schwarz, Peter Paul. *Brechts frühe Lyrik, 1914–1922: Nihilismus als Werkzusammenhang der frühen Lyrik Brechts.* Bonn: Bouvier, 1971.
———. *Lyrik und Zeitgeschichte. Brecht: Gedichte über das Exil und späte Lyrik.* Heidelberg: Stiehm, 1978.
Seidel, Gerhard. "Vom Kaderwelsch und vom Schmalz der Söhne McCarthys," *Sinn und Form* 32 (1980): 1087–90.
Seiler, Bernd W. *Die leidigen Tatsachen.* Stuttgart: Klett, 1983.
Seliger, Helfried W. *Das Amerikabild Bertolt Brechts.* Bonn: Bouvier, 1974.
Sherry, Peggy M. "*Vom armen B. B.* as Signature: Between Text and Speaking Subject." *Modern Language Notes* 94 (1979): 455–74.
Smith, Barbara Herrnstein. "Poetry as Fiction." In *New Directions in Literary History*, edited by Ralph Cohen, 165–87. London: Routledge and Kegan Paul, 1974.
Sokel, Walter. "Brecht und der Expressionismus." In *Die sogenannten zwanziger Jahre*, edited by Reinhold Grimm and Jost Hermand, 47–74. Bad Homburg: Gehlen, 1970.
Spinner, Kaspar H. *Zur Struktur des lyrischen Ich.* Frankfurt a.M.: Akademische Verlagsgesellschaft, 1974.
Staiger, Emil. *Goethe*, vol. 1. Zurich: Atlantis, 1956.
———. *Grundbegriffe der Poetik.* 4th ed. Zurich: Atlantis, 1959.
Steinweg, Reiner. *Das Lehrstück: Brechts Theorie einer politisch-ästhetischen Erziehung.* Stuttgart: Metzler, 1972.
———, ed. *Brechts Modell der Lehrstücke.* Frankfurt a.M.: Suhrkamp, 1976.
Sternberg, Fritz. *Der Dichter und die Ratio: Erinnerungen an Bertolt Brecht.* Göttingen: Sachse und Pohl, 1963.
Szczesny, Gerhard. *Das Leben des Galilei und der Fall Bertolt Brecht.* Frankfurt a.M.: Ullstein, 1967.
Tatlow, Anthony. *Brechts chinesische Gedichte.* Frankfurt a.M.: Suhrkamp, 1973.
Thiele, Dieter. *Bertolt Brecht: Selbstverständnis, Tui-Kritik und politische Ästhetik.* Bern: Lang, 1981.

Thomson, Philip. "A Classic Hang-Up: Brecht and Intellectuals." *Proceedings of the Australasian Universities Language and Literature Association* 20 (1980): 218–24.

———. "Sachlichkeit und Pathos: Brecht und der Expressionismus." In *Expressionismus und Kulturkrise*, edited by Bernd Hüppauf, 183–205. Heidelberg: Winter, 1983.

Trilling, Lionel. *Sincerity and Authenticity*. Cambridge, Mass.: Harvard University Press, 1972.

Völker, Klaus. *Bertolt Brecht: Eine Biographie*. Munich: Deutscher Taschenbuch Verlag, 1978.

Vollmar, Klaus. *Ästhetische Strukturen und politische Aufklärung*. Bern: Lang, 1976.

Wagenknecht, Regine. "Bertolt Brechts Hauspostille." *Text + Kritik*, special Bertolt Brecht edition 2 (1973): 20–29.

Warning, Rainer. *Rezeptionsästhetik*. Munich: Fink, 1975.

Weisstein, Ulrich. "Bertolt Brecht: Die Lehren des Exils." In *Die deutsche Exilliteratur, 1933–1945*, edited by Manfred Durzak, 373–96. Stuttgart: Reclam, 1973.

Wekwerth, Manfred. "Brief an einen westdeutschen Journalisten." *Kürbiskern*, Feb. 1968: 189.

Wellek, René. "Genre Theory, the Lyric, and 'Erlebnis.'" *Festschrift für Richard Alewyn*, edited by Herbert Singer and Benno von Wiese. Cologne: Böhlau, 1967.

Whitaker, Peter. *Brecht's Poetry: A Critical Study*. Oxford: Oxford University Press, 1985.

Willett, John. *Brecht in Context*. London: Methuen, 1984.

Willett, John, and Manheim, Ralph, eds. *Bertolt Brecht: Poems, 1913–1956*. London: Eyre Methuen, 1976.

Wilson, W. Daniel. "Readers in Texts." *PMLA* 96 (1981): 848–63.

Zimmermann, Bernhard. "Der Leser als Produzent: Zur Problematik der rezeptionsästhetischen Methode." *Lili* 4.15 (1974): 7–11.

Zimmermann, Hans-Dieter. "Die Last der Lehre: Fünf Thesen zu den späten Stücken Bertolt Brechts." *Brecht Jahrbuch* 11 (1982): 101–7.

Index

Poems by Brecht are listed according to the title or first line given in the *Register* of the *GW*, 4.

Amann, Marie Rose, 39
An die Nachgeborenen, 1, 100, 109–19, 179
An die Studenten der Arbeiter- und Bauernfakultät, 162–63
An meine Landsleute, 178–79
Apfelböck oder Die Lilie auf dem Felde, 17, 49–52, 54–56, 64
Aufbaulied, 175–77
Ausschließlich wegen der zunehmenden Unordnung, 100–103, 107, 109, 184–85
Authorial role, 60, 63–67, 69, 82–83, 84, 85, 89–95, 112, 117, 123, 155, 189. See also Image; Masks

Ballade, in der Macheath jedermann Abbitte leistet, 116
Ballade von den Seeräubern, 71–74
Bei der Lektüre eines sowjetischen Buches, 141–42
Bei der Lektüre eines spätgriechischen Dichters, 150–51
Bei der Nachricht von der Erkrankung eines mächtigen Staatsmannes, 186
Beim Lesen des Horaz, 144–45, 197 (n. 11)
Benn, Gottfried, 2, 6, 9
Böser Morgen, 1, 134–35, 136–39, 157
Brief an die Mestizen, da erbittert Klage geführt wurde, 92–93
Bronnen, Arnolt, 53–54, 89

Das Amt für Literatur, 159–60
Das Lied vom Hauch, 4
Däubler, Theodor, 56–57
Der Blumengarten, 156–57
Der Einarmige im Gehölz, 124
Der Himmel dieses Sommers, 130–31, 132
Der Radwechsel, 145–49
Der Rauch, 155, 156, 157
Der schöne Tag, wenn ich nutzlos geworden bin, 187, 190

Die Auswanderung der Dichter, 190
Die Kelle, 131–32
Die Literatur wird durchforscht werden, 173–75
Die Lösung, 126, 127
Die Musen, 153
Die neue Mundart, 121, 126–28
Die Städte sind für dich gebaut, 80–81
Die Verbesserungen des Regimes, 97–98
Die Wahrheit einigt, 140–41

Eisen, 142–43
Epistel, 92
Erinnerung an die Marie A., 1, 20, 21, 38–43
Exile, 21, 96–119, 165, 166–69, 171–72, 175
Expressionism, 50, 52–60

Frisch, Max, 13
Früher dachte ich, 90–91

Gedanken über die Dauer des Exils, 107–9
Gesang von einer Geliebten, 66–67
Geschichten vom Herrn Keuner, 2, 23
Gewohnheiten, noch immer, 124
Ginge da ein Wind, 150
Glückliche Begegnung, 164–65
Goethe, Johann Wolfgang von, 3, 4, 6, 75
Große Zeit, vertan, 132–33
Guillemin, Bernard, 1, 23

Harrer, Johann, 69
Hasenclever, Walter, 52–53, 54
Heißer Tag, 125
Hoffmann, E. T. A.: *Der Sandmann*, 33–35
Hollywood-Elegien, 151–52
Homer hatte kein Heim, 96

Ich benötige keinen Grabstein, 181–82, 187–88, 190, 191
Ich, der Überlebende, 115–16
Ich habe ihm gesagt, er soll ausziehen, 82
Ich merke, ihr besteht darauf, 84–85

209

Image, 19, 22–23, 25, 87, 90, 107, 109, 117, 138, 154–55, 157, 191–92
Inbesitznahme der großen Metro durch die Moskauer Arbeiterschaft am 27. April 1935, 166–67

Jakobs Söhne, 129, 130
Jensen, Johannes Vilhelm, 77

Kipling, Rudyard, 64

Laske-Schüler, Else, 57
Laßt eure Träume fahren, 78–79
Laute, 155–56, 157
Leavis, F. R., 11
Lebensmittel zum Zweck, 121, 128–29, 161
Lied von meiner Mutter, 65–66
Lob der Vergeßlichkeit, 185
Loewenson, Erwin, 56
Lyrisches Ich, 10–11, 44

Marxism, 44–48, 76, 96, 112, 127, 180
Marxist criticism, 12–15, 16, 47
Masks, 21, 63–65, 68, 82, 85, 89–95
Moritat, 4, 28, 29, 54
Münsterer, Hans Otto, 68

New Criticism, 7, 10, 11, 31
Nicht feststellbare Fehler der Kunstkommission, 158–59
Nicht so gemeint, 160–62, 172

Oft in der Nacht träume ich, 83–84

Panzereinheit, ich freue mich, 163–64, 169–70
Poetry as *Erlebnis*, 6, 8–10, 12, 15, 17–18

Reader-response theory, 7, 8, 20–21, 37–38; characterized (fictive) reader, 28–35, 36, 37, 39, 113, 194 (n. 7); implied reader, 30–37, 39–44, 194 (n. 7)
Rhetoric, 2, 25, 44, 83, 101–7, 114, 123, 161–62, 183–85, 187–91; as evasion, 138–39
Rimbaud, Arthur, 5, 25, 60, 61, 64, 70
Rudern, Gespräche, 139, 156, 163

Schlechte Zeit für die Jugend, 106–7
Schlechte Zeit für Lyrik, 1, 99–100, 101, 103, 104–6, 107, 109, 112
Sinclair, Upton, 75, 77
Staiger, Emil, 9, 11, 12
Sterne, Laurence: *Tristram Shandy*, 32–33

Tannen, 143–44
Trakl, Georg, 5
Tritt an! Warum kommst du so spät?, 81
Trommeln in der Nacht, 70

Über die Städte, 75
Unglücklicher Vorgang, 132–33

Verwisch die Spuren, 81–82
Vier Aufforderungen an einen Mann, 79–81
Villon, François, 4, 25, 28, 29, 60, 64, 70, 116, 117, 181
Vom armen B. B., 1, 87–90, 93, 116, 118, 196 (n. 15)
Vom ertrunkenen Mädchen, 61–64
Vom Schwimmen in Seen und Flüssen, 58–61, 63, 64
Von der Kindesmörderin Marie Farrar, 20, 21, 26–31
Vor acht Jahren, 124–25
"Vor Moskau, Mensch" (*Kriegsfibel*), 171

Wahrnehmung, 158, 178
Warum soll mein Name genannt werden?, 182–88, 190
"Was macht ihr, Brüder?" (*Kriegsfibel*), 171
Wer aber ist die Partei?, 168–69
Werfel, Franz, 57

Zukunftslied, 177–78

www.ingramcontent.com/pod-product-compliance
Lightning Source LLC
Chambersburg PA
CBHW020756160426
43192CB00006B/341